CLASSICAL MARXISM IN AN AGE OF CAPITALIST CRISIS

Will capitalism survive forever?

Capitalism has always lived in and with crisis. Wars, revolutions, economic depression and repeated recessions, the threat of nuclear annihilation and ecological disaster have all failed to break the dominance of this economic and political system.

Challenging the predominance of capitalism in a world fraught with inequalities, this book returns to classical Marxism to reaffirm its relevance. It explores the contradictions within capitalism as well as explaining why Marxism has been unable to mount a sustained challenge to capitalism. In order to explore concrete alternatives in a period of increasing capitalist globalisation and crisis, it goes on to present perspectives by which theory and practice might be reunited to building independent political and organisational structures.

A search for "something better", this volume will be an engaging read for scholars and researchers of politics, especially political theory and political economy, economics, and sociology.

William Briggs is an academic affiliated to the School of Humanities, Social Sciences, Arts and Education at Deakin University, Australia.

CLASSICAL MARXISM IN AN AGE OF CAPITALIST CRISIS

The Past is Prologue

William Briggs

Routledge
Taylor & Francis Group
LONDON AND NEW YORK

First published 2019
by Routledge
2 Park Square, Milton Park, Abingdon, Oxon OX14 4RN

and by Routledge
605 Third Avenue, New York, NY 10017

First issued in paperback 2020

Routledge is an imprint of the Taylor & Francis Group, an informa business

British Library Cataloguing in Publication Data
A catalogue record for this book is available from the British Library

Library of Congress Cataloging-in-Publication Data
A catalog record has been requested for this book

ISBN 13: 978-0-367-73146-5 (pbk)
ISBN 13: 978-1-138-34428-0 (hbk)

Typeset in Sabon
by Taylor & Francis Books

FOR ROSE, WHOSE INSISTENCE, IDEAS, SUPPORT AND A REFUSAL NOT TO BELIEVE THAT THE OUTCOME WOULD BE POSITIVE FIRST MOTIVATED ME AND ALLOWED ME TO MAINTAIN THE FOCUS REQUIRED TO COMPLETE THIS TASK. I THANK YOU.

CONTENTS

Acknowledgements viii

Introduction 1

1 Capitalist crisis and the relevance of Marxism 15

2 Learning from Marxism's historical crisis 34

3 Validating Marxist analysis 53

4 The development of the capitalist state 69

5 A qualitative change in capitalism and its implications 87

6 Responding to capitalist globalisation 110

7 The promise of Marxism 135

8 Conclusion 160

Bibliography 171
Index 195

ACKNOWLEDGEMENTS

It is sobering to stop and consider those to whom I am indebted. Certain people stand out. Without their guidance, the ideas that follow would not have seen the light of day. Academic staff at Deakin University – Andrew Vandenberg, Geoffrey Robinson, Dean Coldicott, Danielle Chubb all deserve my thanks. David Hundt warrants special notice. He has acted as a guide and mentor to me and I am hugely indebted to him.

Acknowledging those who have assisted in bringing this book to a conclusion is more than a list of names, as important as that is. It promotes reflection. The physical task of completing such a project obviously occurs within a specific time frame. The thoughts represented in the book are the product of a much longer period and are the result of an evolution of ideas and the development of a worldview that has been a lifetime in the making.

I would, therefore, like to acknowledge all of the people who have, in various ways, influenced my thinking over the years. These people's lives and actions have been informed by Marxist thinkers and activists. They read and accepted the clarity, the truth, the logic of Marxism and have, across generations, given this worldview its humanity and its optimism. Some 45 years ago I first, probably injudiciously, declared myself to be a Marxist. It was a declaration based on little more than a wish for a world that was fair, equitable, and just. The subsequent decades have reaffirmed that desire. Today I have a better understanding of what Marxism is all about. I still call myself a Marxist and possibly have some small right to so label myself. I owe Marxism and all those Marxists who helped me to understand, a debt of gratitude.

INTRODUCTION

Capitalism, throughout its often-blood-stained history, has always lived in and with crisis. Wars, revolutions, economic depression and repeated recessions, the threat of nuclear annihilation and ecological disaster have all failed to break the dominance of this economic and political system. Countless millions are forced to 'make do' while an increasingly tiny minority 'do' astonishingly well. Its survival has nothing to do with any innate power of the market, or of ability, or of any inherent strength.

Why then does capitalism survive? First, there is the relationship between the state and capital. The state exists to promote the interests of capitalism and has magnificently promoted an artificial sense of unity between the classes. Second there has been no viable theoretical and practical structure to counter the rule of capital While Marxism remains fragmented and disjointed, capitalism remains secure. Such has been the reality of the past century, but it need not, and nor can it be, a projection for the future. The future, after all, is not pre-determined. As Marx so eloquently put it, "Men make their own history, but they do not make it as they please; they do not make it under self-selected circumstances, but under circumstances existing already, given and transmitted from the past" (1986a: 96).

At the same time there is a palpable sense of despair that has infused the thinking of too many. Ionesco's bleak proclamation that "God is dead, Marx is dead and I'm not feeling too well myself" can and must be overcome. There is no solace in nihilism, and nor can there be in acquiescence, acceptance or hand-wringing. Trotsky, writing just months before his death remarked that "life is beautiful. Let the future generations cleanse it of all evil, oppression, and violence and enjoy it to the full" (Hallas 1970). The past, after all is but prologue. There must be a brighter future. There must be something better.

This book is part of that search for 'something better'. It seeks to inject a sense of optimism into debates about what can or cannot be done. It argues for Marxism as the only rational answer to the madness of the world in the 21st century and calls for a return to a classical Marxist approach, to not simply interpret the world but, importantly, to change it. The last century has seen Marxism poorly served by many who have professed themselves to be Marxists. Marxism has long dwelt in a world of crisis and dislocation, seemingly more and more removed from the world and the people it was created to serve. Wallerstein (1986) spoke of 'a thousand Marxisms'. He might have exaggerated a little, but the point is well made. Describing the range of scholarly approaches to Marxism, to the academic pursuit of Marxism, certainly has validity but it is not the primary focus of this book. The same can be said of the range of 'activist' Marxist groups and organisations. It is illuminating to look at the programs of the various trends and tendencies among the left, but again, this work is about more than that. Having said that it remains an unfortunate fact that so many ideological 'flowers' have bloomed and so many of these 'hybrid' blooms lack an essential scent. These variations on a theme of Marxism serve to confuse the reader and take that reader ever further from the elemental truths upon which Marxism was founded. The task that this work sets itself is to play a small part in resituating Marxism at the centre of opposition to capitalism and, unapologetically, argues for classical Marxism as the way toward emancipation. The arguments that follow, while polemical in style, are not simply an assault against this or that view of Marxism. At the same time, they are certainly critical of much of what constitutes contemporary Marxist theory and so, consciously promote a particular worldview.

The motivations for a book about Marxism that criticises much within Marxism needs some clarification. I argue and show that Marxism has been riven by disputation and division almost from its inception. I further demonstrate that capitalism survives and remains without serious challenge in large part because of the dislocations in Marxism, but that Marxism, as a theoretical and practical force can and must challenge the rule of capitalism. That, after all, is what Marxism is for. These arguments form the basic premise of the book.

An invitation

A remarkable event occurred in 1848. Marx and Engels published the *Manifesto of the Communist Party*. Since then it has rarely been out of print. Millions of copies have been printed in all languages spoken on the planet. It has influenced and continues to influence people around the world. It speaks in a language and style that is accessible, and its message has remained relevant across the decades. I invite you to imagine for just a moment. Someone comes upon the *Manifesto*. He or she reads it and easily grasps the message it contains. It is written with clarity and authority and above all else it makes sense. After all that is why it was written. Our reader is moved by the message and looks for other Marxist writings. Neither Marx, Engels, Lenin, Trotsky or Luxemburg pose any problems. These are some of the voices that first articulated what we can call classical Marxism. They are all equally accessible, but soon things get a little bit tricky. Our same reader now seeks contemporary Marxist literature to better understand what is going on in this century. Which current of Marxism, which school, which thread is to be followed? Is it to be Western, or libertarian, or structural or cultural, or analytical Marxism? Perhaps it might be neo-Marxism, or Marxist Humanism, or Marxist Feminism or even post-Marxist Marxism. The analysis of classical Marxists is devalued by these schools of thought. Each strand becomes more and more obtuse, less readable, and ultimately confusing. Things no longer make sense. Our hypothetical man or woman reads more and understands less, is no longer uplifted but depressed, no longer sees a future for humanity but only a miasma. He or she then reads that Marxism is no longer relevant, that the working-class movement is no longer relevant and that the ideas that sprang so clearly from the pages of the *Manifesto*, are merely the noble thoughts of a long dead philosopher and economist.

This same person might bravely shrug off such slights and search for like-minded comrades who wish to bring about the changes to society that the *Manifesto* advocates. Where should he or she turn? There are any number of political organisations and parties to choose from. Each claim to offer the truth, but in too many cases provide little by way of clarification or political education. Only the confusion remains. It is unlikely that our imagined friend will sit down and weigh up the pros and cons of each program that is on offer. There are so many.

Today we have either an abundant and dislocated theory that is largely without a practice, or a practice-of-sorts with a fragmented and diffuse theory. Marxists are all-too-familiar with the statement that theory without practice is sterile and practice without theory is blind. It has never been more obvious, and yet there has never been a greater need for a theory and practice that will challenge capitalism. Marxism, as an answer to and antithesis of capitalism, almost instinctively calls to the minds and hearts of so many. While this remains a truth, Marxists continue to read obituaries for Marxism. These obituaries are written and re-written with almost every passing decade. The problem is that Marxism won't stay dead. There is another problem, and this is at the core of this book. Attesting to Marxism's relevance is made that little more difficult when 'Marxists' continue to obscure the message and focus on issues that are more and more at a remove from the real business at hand; combatting capitalism, understanding the world and changing it. The business of this book is to give that 'reader' of the *Manifesto* another option. That option is to return to the Marxism that seeks to fuse theory and practice, to confront and to overcome capitalism and to return to the core values that underpin Marxism.

In contributing to that challenge of renewing a sense of optimism to our 'reader', two interrelated issues will be addressed. The first is a defence of Marxism's relevance in the 21st century, and especially a defence of classical Marxism, and the second is a critique of capitalism's recent developments. These issues are linked, and both revolve around a pivot of crisis.

The idea of crisis is central to the arguments that follow. Capitalism, as the enduring and dominant economic and political idea, has been framed by and has appeared to be adaptive to cycles of stabilisation and crisis from its very inception (I use the term capitalism throughout the book to describe an economic formation, political system and state structure). Crisis has been a motivating factor for capitalism's growth and has been the engine for its expansion. Its apparent resilience has proven to be troublesome for critics of capitalism and for many contemporary Marxist theorists. Marxist analysis has long sought to 'adapt' to suit new and changing conditions. In doing so it has often succumbed to a tendency to react to events rather than seek to offer decisive leadership. The 20th century did not see the collapse of capitalism, but it did herald deep and on-going problems in Marxist thought. While it has often been argued that Marxism is a failed ideology, the crisis that has engulfed capitalism in recent decades has encouraged a re-examination and critique of capitalism. Scholars, economists, political economists and political activists from Marxist and non-Marxist backgrounds have either questioned the future of capitalism or offered possible solutions to its problems.

These deeply rooted problems in capitalism have also encouraged a re-examination of Marxist theory as a means of understanding, interpreting and combatting capitalism and its development. It is my contention that a fragmented Marxist opposition and a theory marked by dislocation and discord, has played a significant role in allowing capitalism to go unchallenged. I further contend that a conscious return to core assumptions of Marxist theory and practice can lead to a successful challenge to capitalism. These core values of Marxism form the basis of a classical Marxist approach. First, however, it is necessary to clarify what is meant by classical Marxism.

Classical Marxism: ground zero

To declare oneself to be a classical Marxist invites a range of responses; scepticism from some, derision from others and the raised eyebrow of either puzzlement or misunderstanding from still more. Wallerstein's comment about the emergence of a 1,000 Marxisms in the post-World War II period is apt. There are many Marxist schools of thought, Marxist analyses of just about everything and in just about every area of physical or mental endeavour. Marxist critiques flourish, not only of capitalism but of other Marxist theories. There are a dizzying array of texts, conferences, papers and commentaries from legions of ever more shrill and discordant Marxist thinkers and writers. Perversely there is one thing that unites a great many of these writers and theorists. It is the view that classical Marxism, while representing an important place in history, is pretty much a museum-piece, with little on-going, let alone over-arching relevance in the crowded and modern world of ideas. The first task of this book, therefore, must be to define and determine just what is meant by classical Marxism.

Deutscher's (1965) perception of classical Marxism can be a useful starting point:

> Marxism is not an intellectual, aesthetic, or philosophical fashion, no matter what the fashion-mongers imagine ... Marxism is a way of thinking, a generalization growing out of an immense historical development; and as long as this historic phase in which we live has not been left far behind us, the doctrine may prove to be mistaken on points of detail or secondary points, but in its essence nothing has deprived it, and nothing looks like depriving it, of its relevance, validity, and importance for the future. But at the same time we face the problem of degeneration in Marxist thinking. We have the divorce between theory and practice, and we have a striking, and to a Marxist often humiliating, contrast between what I call classical Marxism – that is, the body of thought developed by Marx, Engels, their contemporaries, and after them by Kautsky, Plekhanov, Lenin, Trotsky, Rosa Luxemburg – and the vulgar Marxism, the pseudo-Marxism of the different varieties of European social-democrats, reformists, Stalinists, Khrushchevites, and their like.

Ideas necessarily spring from and exist in an historical context. The individuals and political perspectives criticised by Deutscher are historical. However, while individuals may be long-dead, they have been replaced by new voices that have systematically relegated the role of the working class to history, rejected the working class as a revolutionary subject, and renounced the primacy of economic issues. What remains constant, today as it was when Deutscher was writing, is that Marxism is not merely a useful tool to be used to develop an understanding of the world and of the trajectory of capitalism but significantly an organisational structure through which the working class can seek and attain its emancipation and thereby change the world. Deutscher's is at once a simple description and at the same time throws down a polemical gauntlet to many of Wallerstein's thousand Marxisms of the 20th century and beyond.

Classical Marxism, in its simplest telling, has at its centre, the economic, philosophical and political theories of Marx and Engels. Revolutionary theorists such as Plekhanov, Lenin, Trotsky, Luxemburg and others followed this tradition. There are essential elements that denote a classical Marxist approach. These include the Marxist conception of alienation, the base-superstructure concept whereby economic issues ultimately determine political responses, the class nature of society, the importance of historical materialism, and an acknowledgement that ideology is used to construct and maintain consciousness within capitalist society. The classical Marxist view of the world of theory and significantly of practice, underpins what will follow.

Cox (1981: 128) observed that theory is always for someone and for some purpose. Marxism, too, exists for a purpose. That purpose is to promote a theory and practice that will equip the working class to confront and combat capitalism. Central to this purpose is Marxism's capacity to respond to, address and provide answers to the questions that capitalism, in the 21st century, raises. If Marxism can achieve these goals then it has relevance, it has purpose and it has a future. Marxism exists to counter capitalism in an age of capitalist crisis. Something, however, seems to be amiss. Capitalism is undeniably in a state of intensifying crisis and yet remains largely unchallenged. It is not, as some observers might argue, that capitalism is inherently 'stronger' than its opponents, or that it is 'resilient', or that it is in any way a 'natural order' of things. Understanding how capitalism has survived and has maintained a position of supremacy allows for an appreciation of the weaknesses that have developed over time among those whose stated aim has been to confront and combat capitalism. Marxism's own 'crisis' has permitted capitalism to survive a deep and growing crisis of its own.

A house divided

This book began its life as a PhD thesis. I argued that Marxism, over the course of a century of ideological dislocation, missed opportunities, and disappointments, had moved further and further away from core elements of classical Marxism and that this was to the detriment of the theory and of its historical objectives of combatting capitalism and effecting revolutionary change. It was completed in 2017 – the centenary of the Russian Revolution. While this was purely coincidental, it did focus my attention on what are best described as echoes from a century ago. The all-consuming contradiction between a globalising capitalist economy and the continuing need of a strong nation-state, the rise of economic nationalism, the growth of populist movements, increasing nationalist rhetoric, are all too clearly reminiscent of an earlier century. Another disturbing echo was in the response of much of the Marxist milieu to this deepening crisis. Marxists, whether from an activist or academic tradition, shared similar responses. While the world seemed to be spiralling towards war and while nationalism became more pronounced, Marxist theorists and activists seemed less willing to engage with issues that defined the substance of Marxist theory. The centenary year of the Russian Revolution was replete with scholarly conferences with some even going so far as to reference 1917 and its significance. However, the focus of too many conferences and symposia dwelled within a terrain far removed from the objective requirements of Marxist theory. Common themes recurred in these conferences. 'Marxist' debates were conducted around issues such as gender and sexuality, 'queering' Marxism, the monogamous family, and a whole range of issues that can be loosely categorised as representative of identity politics. While these debates might be relevant, and were doubtlessly interesting discourses, it seems that for Marxists they might be less pressing than war, revolution, the working class, global economic crisis and the rise of nationalist demagogues. The centenary of the revolution was taken up in some of these conferences, but all too frequently within narrow geographical confines; for instance, in the context of Latin America. The Russian Revolution was directly considered by at least one conference with a debate on the 'Bolshevik seizure of power'. Unfortunately, this conference, by implication, chose to describe 1917 as a *putsch* and not the planned response of an ideologically equipped working class with a Marxist leadership in the form of the Bolshevik party.

Arguments that were decisive a century ago, of the centrality of the working class, of the core foci of Marxist theory and practice, are central to a defence of classical Marxism. Similarly, they have a direct impact on any analysis of capitalism in the 21st century. Two dialectically connected issues lie at the heart of this book. The first is abundantly clear. Capitalism, in the 21st century, is riven by crisis and contradiction and has lived by crisis and contradiction since it became an economic and political paradigm. The second is that Marxism, as the antithesis of capitalism, appears equally riven by crisis and contention. A Marxist response to the crises and contradictions that have marked capitalism's past, present and future is therefore presented, which, in turn, answers the question of how capitalism has managed to remain unchallenged in an era of crisis. A Marxist analysis of the problems that are evident in Marxism is also offered. The case for classical Marxism in an age of capitalist crisis is, therefore, presented and defended in order to promote a political response that situates Marxism as a combative and decisive force that can challenge capitalism and thereby change the world.

Aims and objectives

Marx's analytical approach begins with class alignments and moves ultimately to global systems. I maintain that such an analytical framework provides answers to questions that motivate this book. Why did Marxism fragment in the face of capitalist re-stabilisation and why, under conditions of deepening capitalist crisis, does Marxism appear seemingly incapable of repositioning itself as a global movement for emancipation? A Marxist analysis explains the growth of inequality, the constrained and limited position of the working class and within a capitalist economy and state, and the objective necessity to overcome the limitations that are evident in interpreting Marxist ideology.

The nation-state has long been the political foundation upon which capitalism has been based. A contradiction is evident between this nation-based political structure and a rapidly globalising economic system. The latter part of the 20th century was marked by intensification of crisis within capitalism and the subsequent growth of globalisation. The rapidity of economic globalisation, from the 1970s onward, points to a qualitative change emerging in capitalism. Critics of globalisation and of capitalism have sought to understand the processes that are underway and to intervene in order to alter the course of globalisation, despite its inevitability as capitalism develops. They often claim to promote the interests of the working class, and of all those whose lives are negatively impacted upon by globalised capital. Unfortunately, these efforts have largely been from a non-class or supra-class perspective that might call for changes but not to fundamentally alter economic structures. Marxism, from its first articulation, called for emancipation and for fundamental change to the class relations extant in capitalism. Increasingly, however, contemporary Marxist theorists have diverged from such an uncompromising position, choosing, rather to defend existing positions and to ameliorate the worst excesses of capitalism. I argue that there is a dialectical relationship between the fragmentation and perceived weaknesses within Marxism and the capacity for capitalism to maintain its paradigmatic position of strength. In other words, an ideologically weakened Marxism has allowed capitalism to function without challenge.

The changes evident in global capitalism demand new ways of advancing that call for emancipation. Marxism remains the most appropriate vehicle by which to understand and address rapidly changing economic structures. However, a re-appraisal of Marxism is required in order for it to better respond to the objective conditions and realities presented by the changes within globalised capitalist relations. This is necessary if capitalism in the 21st century is not simply to be understood but to be challenged.

Isolating problems

The relationship between capital and labour has traditionally been antagonistic. At various stages in the development of the capitalist state this relationship has been more, or less obvious, but overt class hostility was minimised by an adaptive state mechanism. The 20th century was a time of crisis within the Marxist movement, whose task it was to offer ideological leadership to counter capitalism. Marxism has long dwelled in a contested and conflictual world. The ideological conflict that engulfed Marxism and continues to do so was reflected in differences in method. Neither the 1917 Russian Revolution, World War I, nor the Depression led to capitalist collapse. Consequently, Marxist theorists began to question the Marxist historical and dialectical materialist approach, regarding it as insufficient to address new realities that arose from what appeared to be failures in theory and practice. Neo-Marxists sought, among other things, to replace the class essence of Marxist method with one that focused on social conflicts. The essential Marxist proposition of class as the predominant feature of societal and economic development and therefore a pivot around which capitalist development revolves was similarly called into question.

Marxism is best understood as being an interplay of two complementary aspects – a theory of interpretation and an activist practice. Marxist theorists sought to react and respond to problematic issues that flowed from both the Stalinisation of the Marxist movement and the stabilisation of capitalism in the post-war period. Attempts to 'rescue' Marxism, however, served to weaken the theory, initially as interpreter of and consequently limited its potential as an agent for fundamental change. Femia (2007: 96), for example, argues that '*Western*' Marxism saw its mission as chiefly a cause of saving the theory from the distortions of Stalinism. Korsch in *The Crisis of Marxism* (1931) regarded Marxism as being enmeshed in an historical and theoretical crisis. He was writing in 1931 at the height of the Stalinisation of the European Marxist movement. Neither Korsch nor any of the subsequent reformers within Marxism regarded the essence of the theory to be at issue but ultimately, as Anderson in his *Considerations on Western Marxism* (1979: 42) contends, the 'rescuers' were a product of defeat. Marxism found itself in retreat. Theoretical realignments and attempts to 'reform' Marxism saw Marxist theory progressively turn its focus from the working class and from its call for emancipation in favour of a philosophical position promoting individual human freedom. Marxist theory became less connected to political economy and more to human psychology. A core element of Marxist theory – that economics drive political responses – was disregarded. The conception of the working class as revolutionary subject was at first downplayed and later discounted. Femia remarks that "Western Marxism involved combinations of Marxism plus 'something else'. Nowadays radical thinkers seem more interested in developing the something else" (2007: 116).

By the 1970s capitalism was entering a new phase as its internal contradictions became more pronounced. The rapidity of globalisation and its effects on states and their inhabitants began to be felt more and more acutely. Social inequality rose and continues to rise ever more sharply. Alienation and disintegration of societies became more readily identifiable. Economies were restructured to suit the new requirements of capital. Reactions to this took many forms and came from many quarters – Marxist and non-Marxist alike. What became especially evident was an apparent ideological weakness and disconnect in Marxist responses to these changed conditions. This had its beginnings decades earlier when capitalism, faced with existential threats from war, revolutionary upsurges, and economic depression, did not collapse but stabilised. Marxism became fragmented and was increasingly seen to be ineffectual and impotent as an actor to effect change, while still being a valuable tool by which to understand the processes at work in political economy. Any re-positioning of Marxist theory to suit the realities of the 21st century remains difficult, but the crisis of capitalism requires that the crisis in Marxism be overcome.

Sticking with Marx

The contradiction between globalised economic realities and nationally based political authority is becoming more pronounced as the crisis of capitalism intensifies. The world is experiencing far-reaching changes and pressures. Social inequality is rising, and while there is widespread discontent, and while large numbers are being drawn into protest and dissent, there appears to be no direct challenge to capitalism. While Marxist theory offers valuable analysis, an on-going crisis of leadership has seriously limited opposition to capitalist rule.

An expanding literature indicates that the crisis affecting capitalism is becoming sharper. What is being increasingly recognised is a structural change that is occurring within capitalism and a growing incapacity for globalised capital to restore stability and equilibrium. This has re-focused attention to oppositional theories and particularly to Marxism as a rational means of explaining and understanding the challenges that globalisation and capitalist crisis present.

The development of capitalism and of globalisation is best reflected and observed in an examination of the class nature of society and the economic relations that drive capitalist development. Such an examination, in the context of classical Marxism, is based on historical materialism as an integrating and unifying theoretical tool. What needs to be recognised is that divergence, fragmentation and contestation have seriously weakened the oppositional ideology envisaged by Marx. The world has not been changed.

The strength of Marxist analysis lies in its integrated historical and materialist approach. The fact that capitalist globalisation has been occurring at such a rapid pace is both logical and explicable if viewed from such a materialistic outlook. Marx and Engels recognised that "the bourgeoisie cannot exist without constantly revolutionising the instruments of production, and therefore the relations of production, and with them the whole relations of society" (1977: 38–39). Consequently, as Solomon and Rupert assert, historical materialism "approaches the question of globalization not with puzzlement over dramatic changes in forms of accumulation, but fully expecting them" (2002: 284). Lukacs declared that:

> historical materialism eclipses all the methods that went before it, on the one hand, inasmuch as it conceives reality as a historical process, and on the other hand, inasmuch as it is in a position to understand the starting point of knowledge at any one time. Knowledge itself is understood to be just as much a product of the objective process of history (2000: 105).

This work consciously adopts a process of theory building (or the promotion and re-affirmation of a pre-existing theory) based firmly on such an analytical approach. This methodological approach offers an understanding of capitalist development, globalisation and crisis, and also of the problems and ideological weaknesses that have afflicted

Marxism. The dialectical connection between the twin crises of capitalism and of Marxism's apparent inability to challenge capitalism is central to this theory building process. Analysing how and why Marxism became so mired in discontent, does not discredit, but enriches Marxist theory. Such analysis allows us to discard that which is unnecessary in favour of integrating, wherever possible, new insights into a working theory.

The relevance of this work must be considered against a backdrop of growing globalisation and capitalist instability. The Marxist analytical approach that is offered not only allows for an appreciation and understanding of the changes affecting the world, but also identifies that which much of contemporary Marxist scholarship either understates or ignores. What is lacking is the capacity to resolve an ideological crisis that has weakened its ability to offer a serious critique of late capitalism.

It would appear, therefore, that a re-appraisal of Marxism is required. In presenting such an appraisal it is necessary to draw attention to weaknesses within contemporary Marxism. This is done with the aim of promoting debate among those opposed to capitalism, globalisation and neo-liberal theory. Such an approach will be regarded by some as provocative, but if capitalism is to be seriously challenged, there needs to be a critical analysis of 'anti-capitalist' theories and an equally critical engagement with much of contemporary Marxism.

It all comes down to relevance

It is necessary to isolate the fractures that have occurred in Marxist theory and practice. The role of Stalinism is, perhaps, the dominant factor in the crisis that has engulfed and continues to engulf Marxism. Stemming from the Stalinisation of Marxism came reactions and responses among Marxist theorists and, as has already been indicated, a shift in focus away from the working class as the dominant force in combatting capitalism.

At the same time, capitalism has not been able to overcome its inherent contradictions or its potential for crisis. From the 1970s on, this tendency to crisis has become even more acute. Globalisation of capitalist relations and production has become ever more pronounced as a qualitative change in capitalism becomes evident. In arguing that a direct relationship exists between the twin crises of capitalism and Marxism, I operate within a clearly defined framework of dialectical and historical materialism.

This book, then, consciously seeks to develop a theoretical response to these two contradictory, but linked, phenomena. In doing so it illuminates the interconnectedness of crisis in both capitalism and Marxism in the 21st century. It also re-asserts the relevance of Marxism, not only in its explanatory form, important as this is, but as a means of promoting organisational structures that will challenge the rule of capitalism and offer a realisable path to fundamental political and economic change. In adopting such a course, the book contributes to debates within contemporary Marxism, making Marxism relevant in an age of capitalist crisis and making the case for classical Marxism as the most relevant vehicle for effecting fundamental economic and political change.

Structure

The book is comprised of two distinct but interrelated parts.

The opening chapters establish a theoretical framework through which I affirm Marxism's relevance for the 21st century. Later chapters that deal more specifically with contemporary issues build on this framework.

Chapter 1 includes a broad analysis of the major schools of thought as they relate to the issues addressed in the book and introduces an overarching question of how can Marxism affirm its relevance in an age of capitalist crisis? Current Marxist thinking relating to the capitalist state and its response to capitalist crisis, the effects of globalisation, the ideological problems within Marxism is analysed. This is done as a means of establishing a framework upon which my central arguments rest.

Chapter 2 presents Marxism as the most effective mechanism by which to explain the growth and development of capitalism, globalisation and the tendency toward crisis that is an inherent feature of capitalist development. It also isolates the weakness, fragmentation and discord that exists within Marxism. These weaknesses occur because of historical and economic factors including the crisis in Marxism that emerged in the period between the wars and the economic prosperity and stability in the post-war decades.

Chapter 3 outlines how a Marxist analytical approach both explains the contradictions that plague capitalism but is equally effective in defining and seeking resolution to the crisis within Marxist theory and practice. A Marxist method of inquiry allows not only for an analysis of problems that are so evident in capitalism but also within Marxism itself. The chapter, in describing the methodological background of the study, explicitly argues in support of Marxism's claim to be a science that provides descriptions of the overarching economic system, while drawing social implications from those economic structures.

Following this largely theoretical and historical assessment, are a series of discrete but inter-related chapters outlining the inherent crisis in capitalism, the crisis in Marxism, the necessity for capitalism's tendency to globalise, and critical responses to capitalist globalisation, confirming

Marxism's relevance for the 21st century. These chapters relate to issues of theory and practice that have, in the past century, plagued Marxist debates and are directly linked to the theoretical framework provided in the opening chapters as they focus on Marxism's evolution alongside that of capitalism. An explanation of capitalism's survival, not from any innate sense of resilience but, in large part, as a result of Marxism's inability to offer an effective alternative to the rule of capital is offered.

Chapter 4 briefly analyses the development of capitalism. It illustrates the tendency of capitalism to fall into crisis and of how crisis has been managed as a means of promoting capitalist development. Chapter 5 raises the question of whether there has been a qualitative change in capitalism. In arguing that this is the case, the chapter analyses issues within capitalist development and particularly the intensification of crisis as a motivating factor behind the rapidity of globalisation in recent decades. A qualitative change in capitalist relations is indicated and is reflected in the rise of social inequality and corresponding rise in social discontent.

Chapter 6 addresses questions that arise from capitalist globalisation and the range of dissenting responses to globalisation. The chapter clarifies the issue of whether globalisation is necessarily the problem, arguing rather that globalisation is a developmental process of capitalism. It also focuses on mobilisation – both class-based and non-class mobilisation – and particularly on identity politics of gender, race, ethnicity and environment and of why capitalism has remained largely without effective challenge. In achieving this, the chapter identifies the strengths and weaknesses that exist in social movement politics and the limitations to effecting fundamental change that become evident when issues of ideological leadership become diffused.

Chapter 7 again addresses issues arising from an ideologically divided Marxism. It asks what, if any, potential there might be to forge a principled unity in order to challenge capital. At the heart of this chapter is the issue of Marxism's role in the 21st century. It argues that divisive issues of class and social identity need to be re-examined in the face of on-going and intensifying capitalist crisis. The chapter promotes the view that there exists a crisis of leadership within 'anti-capitalist' opposition movements and that a re-invigorated Marxism offers the best means for challenging capitalism.

1

CAPITALIST CRISIS AND THE RELEVANCE OF MARXISM

Marxism's oft-stated purpose is to combat capitalism, an economic system that has always existed under conditions of crisis. Crisis, however, has been a motivating factor for capitalism's growth and an engine for its expansion. Critics of Marxism have pointed to capitalism's 'resilience' and 'adaptability' as a testimony to Marxism's 'failure' as an ideology. Capitalism has not collapsed, but remains the dominant economic paradigm. Marxists sought, over time, to redefine their theory and to adapt to new circumstances. What resulted was increasing divergence, dissent, isolation, and what appeared to many to be irrelevance in the face of capitalist rule and ideology.

On-going economic crisis, accompanied by an intensification of globalisation, has prompted a re-examination of capitalism. Critiques from Marxist and non-Marxist scholars have also encouraged a re-assessment of the ability of Marxist theory to interpret capitalism and of its relevance in the 21st century.

Capitalism has entered a qualitative new stage of development and one marked by deepening crisis. The cycle of crisis and stabilisation that has framed the development of capitalism has become ever more sharp. Capitalist globalisation is an expression of a crisis that is increasingly enveloping economic and political structures and is less able to be either contained or resolved. While capitalism lives and must live with crisis, Marxism, too has been riven by crisis. It is necessary to link these two interconnected elements of crisis, and so, an analysis of the irresolvable contradictions that exist within capitalist globalisation, as well as the apparent incapacity of a fragmented and divergent Marxism to effectively challenge capitalism shall be presented. This analysis leads to a theoretical response to this weakness and in doing so, affirms the relevance of Marxism for the 21st century.

Most analyses of capitalist globalisation have one of three starting points: statism, neo-liberalism, or various schools of Marxist thought.

Crisis, as a defining feature of globalisation, occupies a limited place in statism and neo-liberalism. It is within Marxist theory that this issue is best addressed, although its resolution and the promotion of an ideological framework that would fundamentally challenge capitalism, is often either downplayed or ignored. In defending the propositions of classical Marxism, it is necessary to isolate those things that contemporary Marxism either ignores or deflects. What appears as an exercise in theory building might be more accurately described as a return to an already vibrant theory. What is important, however, is that a new and innovative approach to Marxist theory and practice be advanced that will provoke debate and reinforce the relevance of Marxism within those debates.

We need first to clarify key terms and concepts; namely the state, globalisation, the interactions between the nation-state and globalisation and of crisis as a motivating factor within capitalism. From such a beginning, a discussion of those ideological perspectives that trace their beginnings to Marxism and of the ideological disputation and divergence that has affected Marxism for much of the last century and into the 21st century can follow. Next, an overview of state development from contending perspectives and of the state's relationship with capitalism is given. I shall describe the interconnectedness of state and capital and of how the state acts to support and maintain the economic structures of capitalism. This assumes even more significance as crisis and contradiction within capitalism becomes more acute. This discussion explores crisis as an integral feature of capitalism and as a motivating factor for its rapid globalisation. Capitalist globalisation has prompted critical reactions ranging from attempts to reverse the process of globalisation, to promoting global responses. The diverse reactions to globalisation highlight the fragmented and divergent ideological perspectives that exist within Marxism. A crisis has marked Marxism's trajectory for a century and must be addressed. However, regardless of this often-debilitating crisis, it remains an irrefutable fact that Marxism, both as an analytical tool and importantly as a strategy to effect fundamental change, is not simply relevant or viable, but central to combatting capitalism.

The state and its relationship with capitalism

Perceptions of the state are largely determined by the ideological perspective of the observer. The state has been defined in any number of ways, including being an organisation offering protection in exchange for revenue (Gilpin 1981: 15). The state has been described as a specific "form of macro-political organization with a specific type of political orientation" (Jessop 1990: 34). Poggi (1990: 3–8) speaks of the state as an agency of power, and especially social power and its components of coercion, command and legitimacy, before engaging with concepts of sovereignty and autonomy and the capacity to successfully produce one's own rules as being a fundamental component of the structure of the state (Poggi 1990: 21–22). As de Jasay (1985: 15) characterises it, the state emerges through conquest and quickly becomes a rational organisation through a form of social contract. Ideological perspectives may differ, but there is a certain degree of consensus about notions of power, coercion, and a sense of legitimising control.

Just as definitions of the state vary, so do conceptions of it. Pluralist, elitist and Marxist conceptions of the state illustrate how ideological interpretations and world views differ. Hirst (1993) outlines the essential characteristics of the *pluralist* conception of the state. It is a view that sees liberty as the most important political value within society while state sovereignty is an 'ideal' through which society is regulated. Dahl's (1967: 325) desired state is one where no single organised political group or interest group exercises control but negotiation and dialogue between all potentially conflictual parties is the norm.

In contrast, *elite theory*, as described by Michels (1962) argues that the state inevitably becomes controlled by a small and powerful group of actors. For elite theorists (Evans 2006: 39) there are a set of essential features that characterise societies – rulers are a socially cohesive group and remain territorially based. The rulers remain apart from those they rule and the members of the elite are chosen, by virtue of economic, political, and ideological factors. In this vision, Mills (1963: 167–169) depicts the executive branch of government, major capitalist interests and representatives of the military establishment jointly exercising power.

Marxist interpretations, and this is what is significant for this discussion, maintain that the state is ultimately about power and class interests. However, there is no 'one-size-fits-all' view of the state among the variants of Marxist thought. Hay (1999: 153–155) identifies four separate 'Marxist' interpretations of the state – the state as the repressive arm of the bourgeoisie, the state as an instrument of the ruling class, the state as the ideal collective capitalist and the state as a factor of social cohesion.

Carnoy (1984: 50) maintains that the core representation of Marxist theory rests in the concept of the state as the 'repressive arm of the bourgeoisie'. Such a view is immediately apparent in the writing of classical Marxists and especially in Lenin's (1977a: 243–244) oft-repeated reference to "special bodies of armed men" and in Engels' (1986: 566) description of the various arms of the repressive state. The second interpretation, the 'instrumentalist' theory (Sweezy 1949: 243) sees the state as an instrument in the hands of the ruling class that guarantees the stability of the class structure of society. In a similar vein, Milliband (1969: 23) describes the use of the state as an instrument for the domination of society.

The third interpretation, the state as the 'ideal capitalist', adopting Engels' (1959) description of the modern state as a 'capitalist machine' and a 'personification of national capital' has lent weight to the idea of the state as the 'ideal capitalist' (Offe 1974: 40). The final interpretation, the state as a 'factor for social cohesion' is promoted by Poulantzas (1975: 24–25) and Gramsci (1971: 244), among others, and draws on the description of the state as "seemingly standing above society" (Engels 1986: 576) as a means of maintaining a sense of order and stability.

The state, however, as Marx and Engels (1964: 36) made clear, evolves in a contingent manner depending upon social, political and economic necessities. Some might argue that much of the 'theoretical' work concerning the state by various interpretations of Marx are simply differing shades of the same colour. However, it must be remembered that the state advantages class interests and, depending upon historical and economic conditions, can present in any of the above formulations.

The role of the state in capitalist development has long been a focus in Marxist literature and polemic. Harman (1991) offers a useful critique of the relationship between state and capital, or more precisely the role of the state in assisting the development of capitalism. This relationship between state and capital became transparent and acutely important during the period of the Global Financial Crisis (GFC) and in its immediate aftermath. It is a theme that Choi, Berger, and Kim (2010: 834) take up when they highlight state responses to the potential collapse of significant banks in the US. At the core of such analysis is the understanding that the relationship between state and capital works to secure the present and future for capitalism.

Capitalism retains a position of security regardless of the depth of problems and crisis within the economic structure itself. This capacity for capitalism to maintain itself is due, in large part, to the ideological expertise of the state. Capitalism relies on exploitation, but this becomes less obvious as the relationship between labour and capital becomes deliberately obscured. Engels (2000), in his letter to Mehring, offered the view that ideological processes can and often are used to effectively mask what is the real class nature of society. What Marx and Engels described as 'false consciousness' was adapted by Gramsci to become 'cultural hegemony'. Cox (1993: 51) describes this as a situation arising from the ruling class seeming to offer concessions in a bargain for both acquiescence and ultimately acceptance of state power. Lebowitz (2004) reflects that if the 'left' does not actively seek to both explain capitalism and to advocate for change then it is part of the reason that capitalism survives. This is especially the case when considered against the framework of intensifying capitalist crisis.

Capitalism and crisis

Marx and Engels in *The Manifesto of the Communist Party* (1977: 35–49) made the point that crisis was an essential and inescapable aspect of capitalism. Harvey (2010a: 171) isolates seven 'activity spheres' within the evolutionary process of global capitalism as it continues to search for profit. These include technologies, social relations, administrative arrangements, production and labour processes, relations to nature, reproduction of daily life and mental conceptions of the world. Harvey comments that:

> Capital cannot circulate or accumulate without touching upon each and all of these activity spheres in some way. When capital encounters barriers or limits within a sphere or between spheres, then ways have to be found to circumvent or transcend the difficulty. If the difficulties are serious, then here too we find a source of crises (2010a: 172).

The period from the 1970s has witnessed a rapid globalisation of capitalist relations. This becomes the province of *globalisation theory*. According to Held et al. (1999) there are three contending schools of thought in globalisation theory, which they describe as *sceptical, transformational* and *hyper-globalist*. Each of these three schools can be observed and are reflected in the works of authors broadly operating within a Marxist framework. While accepting the interconnectedness and unity that links capitalism and globalisation each arrive at different conclusions, but such has been the trajectory of Marxist scholarship for decades.

The first of these are the highly *sceptical* propositions of Hirst and Thompson (1999). They argue that the move towards economic globalisation is not in any real sense unprecedented. The level of economic integration in the world is, in their view, no higher than it was in 1914, the political structures of governance of the international economy were in place for the greater part of the 20th century, and, while accepting that economic integration continues, capitalist globalisation is almost an artificial construct. It is a perspective that gained considerable support but one that actively seeks to minimise the extent and impact of capitalist integration and its effect on perceptions of nation-state autonomy.

Wood (2004) presented a more *transformationalist* view when she argued that the nation-state remains a vital element in world capitalist organisational structures and as a key actor within capitalist globalisation.

Hers was a perspective that acknowledged the objective reality of the nation-state as administrator for capitalism, but which maintains a national perspective for struggle against globalised capitalism.

Diametrically opposed to these views are *hyper-globalists* such as Robinson (2004) who argue vigorously that capitalism has entered a new, fourth epoch. He maintains that these epochs include that of primitive accumulation, competitive capitalism and monopoly capitalism. We are, according to this view, witnessing the beginnings of globalisation and with it the birth of a transnational ruling class and consequently the end of the nation-state system. This view, while correctly assessing qualitative changes in capitalism, fails to acknowledge the political reality of the nation-state. This wide and discordant range in the way Marxist thinkers have recently addressed the relationship between globalisation and capitalism offers another illustration of my premise that a deeply fractured Marxism cannot effectively oppose the dominance of capitalist ideology.

Globalisation is an expression of capitalist development. Its drive to seek resolution to more destructive elements of its own contradictions becomes an engine for dispossession and inequality. Marx's observation in *Capital Volume 1* (1986b: 604) that wealth can only be accumulated at one end of the spectrum if misery is similarly accumulated at the other is echoed in the work of Dallmayr (2002: 144). Martins (2011: 12) likens the inequality that runs parallel to the globalisation of capital with that which accompanied the industrial revolution.

Globalisation is integral to the development of capitalism. It inevitably alters both the way nation-states operate and affects interactions between states. Strange (1997a: 4–6) expressed a sense of unease with what she regarded as the breadth in scope of the very term globalisation. She argued that state power is waning and that this is a response to the enveloping power of the growing world economy. Such an interpretation of globalisation is explored by Hardt and Negri (2000). They maintain that the shift that has occurred in capitalist relations stemming from the development of globalisation is constructing a source of supranational political and economic power. These analyses accurately reflect a general movement within capitalist development which is in accord with a classical Marxist view. However, while this tendency exists, it would be incorrect to regard such development as seamless. Capitalism is globalising and will continue to do so. At the same time, a contradiction exists between globalised capitalism and the nation-state as political administrator. National capital is still a significant force, as attested to by a renewal of economic nationalism. Capitalism, whether in global or national form, is fundamentally bound by this contradiction.

Much attention has been paid to crisis as an integral and motivating factor within capitalist development. While crisis and its analysis has assumed greater intensity in the most recent period, Clarke maintains that the "distinctive feature of the capitalist system is not the market economy, but a system of production in which production of things is subordinated to the production, appropriation and accumulation of surplus value". Crisis "arises when capitalists face a fall in their realised profit" (1994: 284).

Crisis is a term that inevitably carries a degree of concern if not fearfulness. Definitions often refer to it as denoting either a turning point for better or worse in a medical sense, a dangerous situation requiring serious attention, or an unstable situation that carries a very real possibility of an undesirable result. Gamble argues that the feeling at the end of the Depression of the 1930s was that:

> crisis gradually paved the way for a new regime, a new growth model and a new world order, which eventually resolved the crisis, and it was not long before the claims, that capitalism no longer had to worry about the spectre of crisis coming back, began again. There continued to be many small crises, but none of them seemed to pose dangers for the system as a whole, and were successfully confined to national or to regional level (2009: 42–43).

There is an expanding and often contradictory literature that seeks to analyse, describe and isolate factors underlying the current and irresolvable dilemmas facing capitalism. Responses vary. Reich (2015) argues that there is no such thing as a free market and that capitalism is the primary driver of inequality. While critical of how capitalism might be managed, he is, at the same time, seeking ways by which it can be 'saved', because it is still regarded as the best possible option for the globe. At the opposite end of the spectrum is the work of Robinson (2014). His appraisal of the situation is that we are witnessing a systematic crisis in capitalism. Wealth is being voraciously redistributed away from the poor, social inequality is rising at a dangerous rate, and a crisis of legitimacy could potentially lead to a global police state.

Theorists engage, often eclectically, with various aspects of the crisis of capitalism. There is a sense of fear, or possibly hand-wringing, in these analyses. Sharpe (2010), for instance, catalogues the steps toward economic crisis in the USA with a view to reversing the trend. Posner (2009) addresses the symptoms that affected global capitalism's malaise, especially that of US capitalism in the early 2000s before arguing that the banks should be re-regulated as a means of resolving the problem. Bresser-Pereiro (2010) focuses on the financialisation of capital and perplexingly suggests that a democratic capitalism will emerge. Another response to the GFC of 2008 is to massively promote socially useful spending and democratise the ownership of production (Foster and Magdoff 2009). The kindliest spin that can be put on such 'demands' in a time of intense economic discord and austerity is that they are well-meant but utopian. It is in such an eclectic mix of responses that many of the weaknesses existing in contemporary theory, broadly critical of 21st-century capitalism, are exposed. There is consensus that there are major problems in the structure of capitalist relations but finding the means to resolve these problems and to offer a viable alternative is quite another issue.

In examining the contradictions of capitalism and globalisation some authors consciously vindicate Marxist analysis. Amin (2011), Jellissen and Gottheil (2009), Kliman (2011), Harman (2010), all focus on the tendency for profit to fall as a dominating feature of capitalist crisis and for the drive to globalisation. This feature, the theory of the falling rate of profit, is something of a weather-vane in relation to interpreting both capitalism and Marxism. The decades following World War II and the relative stability within capitalism saw the theory become discredited in the eyes of many, but conditions of heightened and prolonged crisis have re-focused attention on this central element in understanding capitalism.

Marxist theory identifies a range of specific features that underpin the general crisis of capitalism. These are: the tendency of the rate of profit to fall, the concentration of capital, the growth of the working class, a tendency toward under-consumption (or conversely, over-production) and the development and influence of finance capitalism.

The sad reality is that these features are often addressed in isolation from each other, when they are so palpably connected. Maito (2014) argues that there has been a general global reduction in the overall rate of profit. There are few more telling statistics than those offered by recent Oxfam reports (2014, 2016) showing the concentration of capital into increasingly fewer hands. The issue of a growing working class assumes an intensely global character. The global working class at the end of the 20th century was estimated to amount to two billion people with the same number again occupied in closely related areas (Harman 1999: 615). Today 60 per cent of the working class are to be found outside the industrialised world (Harman 2010: 337). Silver's (2006) work, describing the link between capital flows and the growth of the working class into developing nations, becomes particularly relevant.

Lapavitsas (2009: 142–146) focuses on finance capitalism, as another contributing factor in describing possible crisis points in capitalism. He describes the significance of financialisation in tracing the trajectory of the current crisis of capitalism. A feature of contemporary capitalist globalisation has been the influence that dominant states have been able to exert (Amin 2011). Peet outlines the significance of finance capitalism in the 21st century, arguing that:

> The main difference between Hilferding's finance capital and today's global finance capitalism is a greater abstraction of capital from its original productive base, the faster speed at which money moves across wider spaces into more places, the level, intensity and frequency of crises that take financial rather than productive forms, and the spread of speculation and gambling into every sphere of life (2009: 245).

What is increasingly evident is that the rapidity of capitalist globalisation is a response to a growing and insoluble crisis within capitalism. Crisis itself is an integral component of capitalism but from the period of the 1970s onward this crisis and capital's response has led to qualitative changes in capitalist relations, nationally and internationally.

The period from the 1970s (and especially after the 2008 GFC) heralded a new stage in that crisis and one that is increasingly difficult for capitalism to resolve. However, many contemporary analysts remain tightly focused on individual aspects of crisis. There is a widespread disinclination to engage with the dialectical unity of those component parts. This is a problem that exists within Marxism itself and eloquently describes the crisis that exists and has existed for the better part of a century in Marxism. This, in turn, has had a significant effect on responses and reactions to capitalism and globalisation.

Responding to capitalist globalisation

Reaction and opposition to capitalist globalisation has become both a theoretical and practical exercise in recent decades. Reflected in this phenomenon is a growing body of thought that has, as its broad focus, opposition to capitalism but often more specifically opposition to globalisation. The two articulations of 'opposition' are often divided, although the one is inevitably an expression of the other. While this assumes a variety of forms, the starting point generally is that globalisation must elicit a response and that the response needs to be from a critical perspective. This might appear to be rather amorphous, but so, too, have been the responses to the globalisation of capitalism. Among a range of these responses is the proposition that the working class can best react to a globalised capitalism through a globalised or transnational union movement. Another response is to advance either social movement politics, or identity politics, as a means of fostering resistance to globalisation. Similar propositions can be found in the project to reinvigorate social democracy through the third way movement. Perspectives that effectively call for reversing globalisation have also had their moment in the sun.

Bello (2004, 2013) for instance, argues forcefully that globalisation is in disarray and that 'deglobalisation' is becoming a very real option. It is a view that promotes as an ideal, the revitalisation of national economies. Other writers, including Rodrik (1997), describe what they perceive to be a backlash against the more destructive consequences of globalisation. Burgoon (2013) contends that the rise in social inequality that accompanies globalisation can move political parties to effective anti-globalist action. The anti-globalisation movement as described by Eschle (2005) is marked by agreement on the need to oppose neoliberalism, but such agreement has elicited diverse and often dislocated responses. Such a dislocated movement appears at odds with Lloyd's (2001) perspective that the anti-globalisation movement challenges social democracy. So much theory has been constructed but, it would seem, to so little avail.

Globalisation is a process and a continuation of capitalist relations that have been developing since capitalism emerged as the dominant economic formation. The process of capitalist globalisation is an irreversible one. While many activists might wish to reverse this process, they risk being characterised, as Marx and Engels (1977: 63–64) characterised petty-bourgeois socialism's desire to hold back the historical processes, as being at best, utopian.

A feature, commonly observed in the work of many ostensibly Marxist writers regarding the working class and its response to globalisation, is to present a pessimistic balance sheet of the negative effects that capitalist globalisation has had on the organisations of the working class. This is quickly followed by an optimistic presentation of working-class responses. Beynon (2003) reflects on the setbacks to the workers' movement, as a consequence of capitalist globalisation, but concludes his analysis by expressing the view that in the 21st century the union movement 'might' be able to respond effectively to such challenges. Stevis and Boswell (2008) echo this sentiment while seeing the future as a mixture of regional and national union movements becoming an important part of the institutions of global governance. Gordon and Turner (2000) describe a situation whereby trade unions can promote the interests of labour in a global sphere. Waterman (1998) reviews the literature and still finds optimism for the future and of a revival of interest in labour issues in the face of capitalist globalisation. Munck urges that now "is perhaps the time when an incipient global labour movement rediscovers some of its original characteristics of combination, a common moral economy and an instinctive internationalism" (2010: 232). Levesque, Fairbrother, and Hennebert (2013) write of workers' growing insecurity stemming from neoliberal and globalised capitalist relations and of how this is making union organisation a more desirable prospect. They describe union responses as often being defensive in nature but also speak of situations where defensive tactics give way to offensive struggles by workers and their unions. Offensive struggles are becoming more frequent, but often despite the actions of trade union leaderships.

Waterman (1993) and Moody (1997) seek to broaden the reach of traditional trade union political activities into wider, often non-class or supra-class actions. Fairbrother, in discussing social movement unionism, argues that "trade unionism is and will remain a core dimension of the challenge to the state and capital ... It has the potential to be core to alternative social movements" (2008: 219).

Social movement and identity politics is a theoretical construct that has won considerable support within the broad anti-capitalist and anti-globalisation movement. Its advocates seemingly become intoxicated by their own rhetoric. They have variously argued that protest movement politics have the capacity to bring changes to institutions (Moore 1999), that protest politics can effect changes in democratic perceptions (della Porta 1999) and that the peace movements in the USA and Europe resulted in the end of the Cold War (Meyer 1999). In this regard Castells' definition of social movements as being "purposive collective actions whose outcome, in victory as in defeat, transforms the values and institutions of society" (2004: 3) is worth noting as something of an anthem for utopianism in the face of the reality of capitalist class relationships. Aronowitz (1992) goes so far as to argue that class-based politics have acted to the exclusion of ethnicity, racial and gender issues. Post-Marxist scholars (Laclau and Mouffe 2001) adapt identity politics to present the case for a movement that entirely separates itself from class-based political strategies. Social movement and identity politics are similarly promoted by Castells (2004: 145–148) as he draws on the 'anti-globalisation' protests against the World Trade Organization (WTO) meeting in Seattle to describe the broad nature of the protests and of how labour unions were prominent. Social movement scholars have brought much to debates concerning globalisation and the idea of resistance, but in doing so have acted to relegate class issues and the primacy of the working class as an agent for change, to a position of insignificance.

Davidson (2000: 116–117) effectively declares the traditional working class to have little relevance. He has also been compelled to acknowledge that the effectiveness of social movement politics, while having the capacity to engage disparate groups and to involve significant numbers, has been less effective in forging long-lasting coalitions. Thanim (2011: 104–110) describes how identity politics has an immediate appeal and offers apparent possibilities for oppressed minority groups. From such heights he denounces Marxist criticism of identity politics as undermining "any joint large-scale resistance against the capitalist political economy and its logic of exploitation" (2011: 108).

Debates about capitalist globalisation and critical responses to it focus on whether the processes of globalisation are politically driven or the result of economic forces. It is an argument that clearly differentiates classical Marxism from the multiplicity of 'Marxisms' that have evolved in the past century. Castells (2004: 145) maintains that globalisation is and has been essentially a political decision while still accepting the term capitalist globalisation. Classical Marxism, on the contrary, argues that globalisation is a process of expansionary capitalism – an economically driven process rather than a political one.

Castells is by no means alone when he lays specific emphasis on political responses and reactions as a means of confronting globalisation. An example of this tendency can be immediately seen in the work of influential theorists who promote a 'third way' that might sit between the 'old left' and the 'new right'. While Driver and Martell (2000) acknowledge that the terminology of left and right remains important they also assert that there might well be space for other 'variants' between the two traditional ideological poles. Former British Prime Minister, Blair, famously championed the cause of third way politics as he sought to re-position British social democracy. Giddens, (1998) however, remains the principal ideological force behind what is an attempt to revitalise social democracy in the face of rising neoliberalist theory and the decline of the welfare state. He argues that social democracy essentially developed as a social movement, only to be outflanked by new social movements and a devalued sense of government that has grown with the burgeoning of neoliberalism. He regards social democracy, through the context of the third way, as the best option for the future. Hamilton (2001), however, raises obvious criticisms of such a theory when he describes its failure to critically analyse modern capitalism.

The relationship between Marxism and social democracy has, since the collapse of the Second International and the beginning of World War I, been marked by contention. Social democracy, and its call to ameliorate the worst excesses of capitalism, nevertheless, remain at odds with Marxism's goal of removing and replacing capitalism.

Issues of social democracy and its future, set against the backdrop of capitalist globalisation, remain central elements for debate. This is especially so when considered in the context of the working class, whose future has been inextricably linked with the political structures of social democracy. What remains, however, is that social democracy itself is inherently a product of the nation-state and it is this relationship that is potentially threatened by globalised economic processes.

The inevitable rise of capitalist globalisation has seen responses that ostensibly provide the working class with the means to defend itself. These include transnational unionism, re-interpreting social democracy and in promoting social movement and identity politics as broad supra-class and non-class expressions of resistance. There is a strong current within contemporary Marxist literature that examines the capacity of resistance to globalisation with some going so far as to promote the idea that globalisation might be reversed. Responses to globalisation and capitalism ultimately reflect a divergence of ideological perspective. Such dislocation does little to promote a practice that will challenge capitalism. Marxism can only be regarded as relevant if it offers coherent theory and practice. There has been a dislocation between these two elements that has been increasingly evident throughout the past century – a dislocation characterised as a crisis in Marxism.

The crisis in Marxism

The trajectory of Marxist theory and its path to 'crisis' begins with classical Marxism, based as it is on historical materialism as a way of understanding and interpreting the world. Classical Marxism, as espoused by Marx, Engels, Lenin, Luxemburg, and Trotsky, among others, maintained that there would be an inevitable clash of classes whose interests were impossible to reconcile, and this class antagonism would result in a new economic and social order. A fundamental concept of classical Marxism was that socialism would inevitably be constructed as a world system and not confined within national borders (Marx 1974, Trotsky 2010). The Russian Revolution followed. The development of a world revolution was, however, not to be, and after Lenin's death Marxist theory was conscripted into the service of Stalinism and subsequently caricatured by Stalinism.

The Stalinisation of Marxism gave rise to a wave of theoretical responses in the period between the two world wars. The *Frankfurt School* arose as the fore-runner of *Western Marxism*, and the over-arching label of *Neo-Marxism*. The work of the Frankfurt School has been outlined and described by many scholars (Jay 1996, Bernstein 1994,

Tarr 2011). Its theorists included Lukacs (1976), whose political life was set against the Stalinisation of Marxism. Bloch (2015), represented a trend in critical thought that promoted utopian perspectives. While consciously advocating his views within the Marxist tradition, Bloch's utopianism stood starkly in contradiction to Marx and Engels' criticisms of utopian socialism. Marcuse (1972a), in attempting a synthesis of Marxist philosophy with the work of Freud and his promotion of national liberation movements (1972b), saw him situated as a theoretician of the '*New Left*' of the 1960s.

Developments in Marxist theory and practice assumed new forms in the years following World War II. This 'Golden Age' of capitalist stability and prosperity (Glynn et al. 1990) presented new and troubling challenges for Marxist theorists. The theory had been predicated on the idea of capitalist collapse. The apparent resilience of capitalism and its capacity to overcome what seemed to be moments of existential crisis were, for many, an indication of a flaw in Marxist theory. The old verities of economic determinants, of the importance of class and of the revolutionary potential of the working class were more and more called into question. The theoretical responses were in many respects an echo of theoretical disputations that had led to the split in Marxism in the lead up to World War I. A significant and damaging aspect was a further distance between theory and practice which has long plagued Marxism.

Marcuse's (1972c) *One Dimensional Man* is a pivotal work in some respects. It focuses on a decline in the capacity and potential for revolutionary change that was deemed to be evident in capitalist society and that 'individuals' were being drawn into a system of production and consumption. It had an appeal and especially in a period when the immediate aspirations of the working class were ostensibly being met by welfare statist governments and a profitable and seemingly benign capitalism. The relative affluence of the working class in capitalist states in this period propelled many within the neo-Marxist movement to further distance themselves from the core premises of Marx and the class nature of society. This New Left ideological perspective, responding to the changing conditions within capitalist society, rests heavily on what it considers to be the significance that culture plays as a transformative tool. It was also deeply influenced by third world radicalism and anti-colonial struggles. This adaptation to an anti-colonial, anti-imperialist perspective had little to do with elemental Marxist values but was regarded as a means of re-affirming a sense of relevance and to build constituencies among a radicalising youth culture that was growing in Europe.

This shift in focus from Europe to third world and anti-colonial movements found a responsive audience. Farred (2000) describes how these issues rallied and radicalised student activism in the West. What was seen as a failure on the part of the 'old left' with its focus on class and particularly working-class models of struggle led to the embrace of new forms of struggle and new arenas for activism. Piven (1995) sums up the feeling within contemporary Marxist thinkers that it was identity politics that provided the most fertile ground to oppose capitalism. Deutscher (1973: 68–72), on the other hand, pointed out that no society has effected change while relying on groups of minorities and maintained that a stable class, rather than more transitory non-class alignments, is the only effective basis for a movement for social change. Smith (2008) is similarly critical of such non-class and supra-class approaches maintaining that identity politics is unable to encompass the emancipatory needs of the oppressed.

The growing divergence in Marxist thought from its original focus on class and working-class emancipation, indicates that achieving common ground is becoming ever more difficult, if not unlikely. *Post-Marxism* emerged in the late 1960s but the work of Therborn as well as Laclau and Mouffe in later decades gave prominence to this latest adaptation of Marxist theory. The post-Marxists relegate issues of class and class struggle further into the background. Therborn (2008), in arguing the case for post-Marxist theory, returns to issues that have become central to Marxist debates – the issue of the Russian Revolution and the effect of the collapse of the Soviet Union. This becomes important in any appraisal of Marxism and in asserting its continued relevance. This relevance, in the final analysis, can only be gauged by its capacity to unite a coherent theory with a practice that can confront and combat capitalism. The crisis in Marxism begins with the Soviet Union but would not seem to be about to end with its demise. The conditions that informed Marxist theory a century ago remain unchanged. How Marxists respond to those conditions and the crisis of capitalism remains the essential question. Therborn (2012) discusses what he sees as the passing of the 'working-class century' and argues that a new era with new relationships mixing class, nation and ideology will become the focus of challenge to capitalism. Laclau and Mouffe are quite definitive in their conceptions of the future of Marxist thought:

> Only if we renounce any epistemological prerogative based upon the ontological privileged position of a 'universal class', will it be possible to discuss the present day degree of validity of the Marxist categories ... It is no longer possible to maintain the conception of subjectivity and classes elaborated by Marxism, nor its vision of the historical course of capitalist development (2001: 2–4).

Laclau and Mouffe's renunciation of class and of Marxism's vision of the historical development of capitalism, is the product of a decades-long divergence in Marxist thought. It represents a sense of demoralisation and defeatism. Marxism's central arguments are, in Laclau and Mouffe's opinion, irrelevant. Capitalism's crisis, however, has become sharper. The relevance of Marxism for the 21st century has frequently been called into question. This is due largely to the divergent and fragmented nature of Marxism during the past century. Wallerstein (1986) described the emergence of a 'thousand Marxisms' and particularly in the post-World War II period. Marxist theory and analysis, however, remains pertinent and relevant. Such a proposition is based, in part, on the growing crisis in capitalism. None of the internal contradictions of capitalism have been resolved. Core features of Marxist theory, including the primacy of economic issues and the class nature of society, allow for renewal of a theory that is connected to practice. Marxism developed through an interchange of ideas and through often intense polemics. It remains important today to engage with contending Marxist perspectives in order to trace the trajectory of Marxist thought and to affirm Marxism's on-going relevance.

Boucher argues:

> The emancipatory social movements of the future will draw their inspiration from Marx, and Marxism, among others. This is because Marxism is a politics of mass struggle and popular mobilization in the name of a social alternative to the profit system, and this is likely to remain a feature of political life in the future (2012: 2).

Boucher's remark encapsulates much that is positive regarding the relevance of Marxism while (possibly unconsciously) exposing problems within contemporary Marxism. Boucher's work, like that of Bidet and Kouvelakis (2008), among others, is valuable in outlining variants of Marxist thought and illuminating some of the disputes and philosophical discord that has been so problematic for Marxism. At the same time, Boucher takes special care not to become 'partisan' and it is here that some of the problems lie. Marxism first developed as a means of challenging capitalism and changing the world. Contemporary Marxist theory has come to focus less on Marxism as an activist ideology and more as an intellectual movement divorced from its activist roots. Despite, or possibly as a result of a century of contention within Marxist theory, capitalism, while riven by irresolvable contradictions remains unchallenged. The ideological discord and confusion in Marxism has allowed for capitalism's on-going survival.

The cycle of crisis and stabilisation that is central to capitalist development is reflected in a general decline in Marxism's influence. The growth of 'official' Soviet Marxism from the 1920s also played a prominent role. Korsch (1931) in coining the phrase 'the crisis of Marxism' declared Marxism to be in an historical and theoretical crisis. While he correctly identified the problems within Marxism in the 1920s and 1930s, he failed to offer a consistent approach to counter this 'crisis'. Declarations of the demise of Marxism have frequently been articulated. The 20th century heard a range of pessimistic and optimistic voices. Lowenthal (1964) was by no means the first or last to write of the terminal crisis of Marxism. Lowenthal's arguments, based as they were on the divisions and disputation between 'communist' regimes, ultimately highlighted the theoretical weakness in Stalinism rather than any inherent weakness in Marxism. Burawoy (1990) was among those in latter decades to defend the basic premise upon which Marxism rests. He regards the collapse of the Soviet Union as a liberating moment for Marxism. In more recent times the relevance of Marxism has been reasserted (Bidet and Kouvelakis 2008: xiv). Bidet and Kouvelakis regard Marxism as inherently adaptive while recognising that elemental issues of class, exploitation and political domination remain central to Marxism and of its relevance. The problems in re-invigorating Marxist practice, however, are real and the dislocation in theory has effectively mirrored the growing crisis of capitalism.

The range of responses to capitalist development advanced by Marxist theorists over the past century reflect the highly contested state that has long existed in Marxism. An often-heated contestation has significantly shaped the many paths that Marxist theory has traversed. Each adaptation to the challenges that capitalism and global political and economic realities present have served to remove the theory from a practice that aims not simply to understand but to change the world. Marxist theory became increasingly isolated and removed from class-based economics and politics even as conditions of capitalist crisis visibly deepened.

A coyness in contemporary Marxism

To suggest that there might be anything resembling momentum for a serious convergence of ideas within the increasingly contested arena that is Marxism would be naïve. At the same time, Marxist theory offers a framework that enables a serious study and understanding of capitalist development. The core elements of Marxist theory also provide a bridge between theory and practice. It is in the practice that Marxism has appeared weakest in the most recent past. Contemporary Marxist theorists and historians who have traced this heritage and its trajectory do many things well. They offer an often-rich understanding of elements of state development and of the relationship between state and capital. Their analyses of developments within Marxist thought is equally thorough. The crisis of capitalism has been widely reported and analysed from differing ideological perspectives. There exists a broad range of theoretical responses to the rapidity of globalisation and how to respond. There remain, however, serious omissions, limitations and a sense of coyness in this expanding literature.

The areas outlined above are invariably discussed in isolation from each other, although there are inevitable links and connections between them. This is especially so when considering the crisis in Marxism. At various times, and not infrequently, voices have proclaimed the malaise, death and resurrection of Marxism but these same voices all but ignore the issue that there exists a direct and dialectical link between capitalism's capacity to survive in the face of growing and irresolvable contradictions and crises and Marxism's seeming inability to present an effective theoretical and practical opposition to capitalism. Capitalism survives because it has no credible opposition. It is an area that so many Marxist theorists and scholars either overlook, downplay or ignore. These limitations need to be exposed, but importantly a platform upon which new theoretical research needs to be built.

In providing such a theoretical platform, I consciously adopt a structure that is firmly based in classical Marxism. It is an analysis rooted both in an historical materialist perspective and the concept that economics drive political outcomes. Fragmentation and divergence has been the hallmark of Marxist theory for the past century. This format describes and discusses a range of factors that have influenced the crisis in Marxism and provides an analysis that isolates the individual components that have led to the crisis in theory.

These components are then synthesised as a means of explaining how Marxist theory has been regarded as irrelevant. Theorists have pointed to the experience of Stalinism as a means of 'proving' the irrelevance of Marxism. Some claim that Stalinism was the direct continuation of Marxism (Kotkin 2014). Marxist scholars and analysts from the late 1920s and 1930s sought to 'save' the theory. Femia (2007) describes this as variously a rescue mission against Stalinism, or from an intellectual movement away from western Europe, or as a response to lost opportunities after the Russian Revolution. Anderson (1974) argues that ultimately these 'rescuers' reflected a sense of defeatism. In any event, these moves distanced successive theorists, not simply from the sterile terrain of Stalinism, but from the essential component of class. The stabilisation of capitalism after World War II saw Marxism move further from the working class as a force for change. Each of these isolated occurrences must be regarded in their entirety and in their historical context.

Such an analytical process isolates contributions to theory that are both positive and negative. This is done not simply as a vehicle to polemicise, although I am highly critical of much within contemporary Marxism. I also explore the prospect of a fusion, if such a potential exists, of perceived positive elements and a recommitment to the core values of Marxism. This, if possible, might allow for a strengthening of Marxist theory as it seeks to confront the crisis of globalised capitalism.

Such a hope, after more than a century of ideological shifts and division, might appear to be unrealistic. If this is the case, then so be it. Marxism's 'development' has been one of departure from core assumptions that framed the theory. Reconstructing and re-presenting a theory that can challenge capitalism and change the world, however, will affirm Marxism's claim to relevance. That journey of reconstruction begins with appreciating and understanding the underpinnings of Marxism's 'decline' in the 20th century in order to reaffirm its claim to relevance in the 21st century.

2

LEARNING FROM MARXISM'S HISTORICAL CRISIS

Capitalism is subject to irreconcilable crisis and contradiction. Marxism, too, it has been shown, is riven by crisis and contention. Marxism, nevertheless, despite the depth of this contention, remains, not merely relevant, but central to combatting and replacing capitalism. The previous chapter described the essential foundations of the theory and of Marxism's road to 'crisis'. Earlier, I described this work as being an exercise in theory building, or possibly more appropriately, a contribution to reaffirming a theory that can change the world. What follows is a first step towards making a case for the relevance of Marxism in the 21st century. It does so by acknowledging the problems that have plagued the development of Marxist theory and exposing the dilemma that this has posed for Marxism.

It is important to draw on a classical interpretation of Marxist theory which is an essentially optimistic view of the world and of its economic and political future. Such an exploration points to Marxism's critique of capitalism as an expanding, globalising system. It focuses on the historically combative nature of Marxism and of its goal to challenge and displace capitalism. An historical lens allows for an appreciation of how ideological dislocation developed in Marxist thought throughout the 20th century and how such discontent drew into question the relevance of Marxism as a means of opposing capitalism.

We must also reflect on the development of Marxist crisis that derives from early attempts to 'improve' or 'revise' Marxist theory. Much of the later disputation and conflict within Marxism are echoes of these early polemics – the question of whether a reformist or revolutionary path ought to be followed. Consequently, I briefly visit the rapidly developing theoretical shifts that occurred between the wars when Marxism appeared to be in serious retreat.

Such an exploration inevitably leads to a consideration of the post-war period – the 'golden age' of capitalism and the responses that were elicited in a Marxism that had increasingly shifted its attention away from core

Marxist values – of the primacy of the working class and fundamental issues of class and economy.

An optimistic view of the world

As has already been described, the materialist conception of history is the foundation upon which Marxism is built. As such it is ultimately an optimistic worldview, arguing that the movement of history is predicated upon a dialectical clash of opposing forces. These opposing forces are represented by the existence of classes and the class nature of society. The interests of these opposing forces cannot be reconciled without fundamental changes to the political and economic structures of society. Marx argued that these antagonisms must inevitably translate into class struggle that, in turn, would result in a new economic and social order.

In his *Contribution to the Critique of Political Economy*, Marx (1918: 11–12) contended that social existence determines consciousness and that through social production people enter into sets of relationships that are independent of their own will. In so arguing, Marx described the processes by which class relations and society operate. These class antagonisms are, in Marx's view, transitory. He maintained that economic formations and society advanced in accordance with the materialist conception of history. The capitalist mode of production and its inherent contradictions and antagonisms are an integral part of this process, because, "the productive forces developing in the womb of bourgeois society create the material conditions for the solution of that antagonism" (Marx 1918: 13).

Marx summarised his contribution to the development of political ideas in three succinct points. These were, that social classes were simply stages in historical development, that the class struggle necessarily leads to the 'dictatorship of the proletariat' and that this, too is a transitional stage towards the creation of a communist society that would promote the free development of the individual (Carver 1991: 10). Marxist philosophy and economic theory emphasise the interaction between social classes, changes in material conditions, how society is organised, and of the primacy of economic factors over political ones as engines for change.

Boucher, describing Marxist theory, states that:

> on the basis of scientific analyses of the contradictions of capitalism's political economy, Marx predicted that the system was headed for deep crisis and long-term stagnation. He maintained that capitalism would be overthrown by the exploited class of that system, the working class … in a socialist revolution that would lay the foundation for a radically new form of society …

> the social scientific side of Marxism is concerned with the revision and correction of these hypotheses and predictions, in light of economic developments, political history and sociological data (2012: 4–5).

Marx viewed the world from a highly partisan perspective. It was a position framed by an understanding of the class nature of society and of the inequality that such divisions breed (Marx and Engels 1977: 48). Capitalism, for Marx, was an engine of growth that both revolutionised productive forces and which simultaneously drove millions into poverty. It was Marx's vision that the machinery of capitalism would be taken and used for the needs of humanity and not for private wealth. Socialism, therefore, builds on this economic base and provides a better, more sustainable future for humanity.

Marx and Engels understood capitalism to be a globalising force. Renton (2005: 9–10) draws a connection between their work and modern globalisation theorists, recognising that states and regions were being affected by developments in the global economy. Marx and Engels wrote of the disorder and crisis that capitalism engenders and of the contradictions that lead to economic crisis. Capitalism and the bourgeoisie, in seeking to manage these critical moments, react and respond by engaging in:

> on the one hand enforced destruction of a mass of productive forces; on the other, by the conquest of new markets, and by the more thorough exploitation of the old ones. That is to say, by paving the way for more extensive and more destructive crises, and by diminishing the means whereby crises are prevented (1977: 42).

Central to the approach of classical Marxism was the belief that socialism would be constructed as a world system and not be confined within national borders. Such a foundational premise was based on the knowledge that capitalism was already moving beyond the limitations of nation states. Capitalism was impelled towards globalisation precisely because of its very 'nature' and because of its internal contradictions. Marx and Engels famously stated that "the need of a constantly expanding market for its products chases the bourgeoisie over the whole surface of the globe. It must nestle everywhere, settle everywhere, establish connexions everywhere" (1977: 39).

Marxist theory was predicated on the eruption of class struggle, the breakdown of capitalist economics and the replacement of capitalism with socialism. An international movement was built upon these foundations and there was an expectation that Marx and Engels' theories would, in a relatively short time, come to fruition. It was a theory that was intimately connected with practice and, in this context, was fraught with potential difficulties. It was, after all, an ideological perspective that existed in the real world and in real time. Capitalism's continued existence seemed to question the validity of elements of Marxism. The developing and on-going polemics and disputes among Marxists was hardly surprising. This is especially obvious as those same adherents of Marxist ideas lived and worked in an atmosphere infused with bourgeois ideology that was exacerbated by disappointment and missed opportunities.

The seeds of crisis: reform or revolution

Capitalism's survival and re-stabilisation has been and remains for many Marxists – theorists and practitioners alike – disturbing and disheartening. The Russian Revolution failed to signal a world revolution. Revolutionary moments had come and had been defeated. Marxism was in retreat. The working-class movement in Europe was more and more dominated by nationalist sentiment. Social democratic political parties maintained the support of the majority of the working class. For many there appeared to be something fundamentally wrong in Marxism's optimistic view of the future. While created to expose the crisis in capitalism and to offer the necessary leadership to overthrow capitalism, Marxism itself was increasingly exposed to crisis. Despite its confident estimation that capitalism was producing its own grave-diggers (Marx and Engels 1977: 48) capitalism maintained its position of dominance and Marxism appeared unwilling or unable to present any real challenge. Nothing much would appear to have changed in the decades since.

The polemics that enlivened Marxism from its earliest days until the outbreak of World War I represented, in part, the strivings of Marxists to engage with theory in order to better promote revolutionary struggle. It was also a struggle to combat ideas that were diverting the theory from its proclaimed goal of effecting revolutionary change. This reflected a divergence within Marxist thinking that centred on questions of reformist or revolutionary paths to emancipation, and arose from Marxism's growth, and particularly in Germany. This stemmed in part from Germany's relatively late development of a capitalist economy, the subsequent rise of an industrialised working class and to the rapid growth of social democracy as a political expression of Marxism. A prolonged argument ensued, as to whether revolution was the means of defeating capitalism and building socialism, or whether the path could be traversed by a series of reforms. The debate pitted the merits of revolutionary or evolutionary socialism against one another. In the 1920s Luxemburg (1988) defined it as 'reform or revolution'.

Bernstein published what Renton aptly describes as "the nearest thing available to a *Communist Manifesto* of reformism" (2002: 76). First published in 1907, Bernstein's *Evolutionary Socialism* (1975), engaged with both Marxist strategy and philosophy as well as criticising the essential internationalism that had underpinned Marxism. He argued that the working people were increasingly becoming 'citizens' of individual nation-states with allegiances more closely aligned to the nation than to class. Bernstein's principal objective was to correct what he deemed to be problems with Marxist theory and philosophy. He sought to 'revise' Marxism. The concept of revisionism has become a pejorative term in the lexicon of Marxism. Lenin railed against the development of revisionist theories stating that

> there is a well-known saying that if geometrical axioms affected human interests, attempts would certainly be made to refute them … no wonder, therefore, that the Marxian doctrine, has had to fight for every step forward in the course of its life (1977d: 49).

The criticisms that came from many Marxist theorists focused particularly on a phrase that Bernstein used to situate his philosophical position. "To me that which is generally called the ultimate aim of socialism is nothing, but the movement is everything" (1975: 202).

Bernstein's work also divided Marxist thought around the question of whether or not Marxism is a science. At the turn of the 20th century Bernstein promoted the idea that socialism could not be regarded as scientific. It was a debate that has continued and echoes across the last century. Science, in Bernstein's estimation, was based on experience, while socialism's focus was on a future social system which, by definition, could not have an experiential basis. It is a view that was rigorously contested by Plekhanov (1976: 33) who, in the first years of the 20th century, asserted that it was eminently realistic to suppose that a scientific study of the present allows an opportunity to 'foresee', with some degree of accuracy, what is likely to occur in the future. This, he maintained, was not the province of prophecy, or of arbitrary declarations, but on the basis of experience and the accumulation of knowledge.

However, it was the economic analyses of Bernstein that proved to be the most controversial. The argument centred on the question of whether capitalism was a self-regulating system or prone to economic breakdown. Luxemburg (1988: 10–11) remained one of the more vocal critics of Bernstein. She referred specifically to Bernstein's premise that capitalism was unlikely to move into a general decline due to its capacity to adapt to changing conditions. This presented a major departure from Marxist orthodoxy and would, over time, come to differentiate Marxist from social-democratic theories of social change. Bernstein sought to:

> demonstrate the possibility of the 'self-regulation' of capitalism. Cartels, credit, the improved system of communications, the rise of the working class, insofar as they act to eliminate or at least mitigate the internal contradictions of the capitalist economy, hindering their development and aggravation, ensure for the system the possibility of unlimited survival (Colletti 1974: 54).

It was a contention that Luxemburg rigorously rejected. She argued that Bernstein was presenting an idealist perspective whereby the, "objective necessity of socialism, as the result of the material development of society, falls to the ground" (1988: 13). Capitalism's real or perceived capacity for self-regulation, and for reform to render revolutionary paths to socialism obsolete, became an axis around which Marxist and social-democrat polemics would rage.

This divergence in theoretical trajectory also underpins on-going disputes within Marxism. Capitalism appears to be remarkably resilient and adaptable, or at least that is the perception that is given to us. It was and is clearly beset by cycles of crisis and stability and yet its status as economic and socio-political paradigm has remained unassailed. This has been an on-going source of challenge for Marxists.

One feature of capitalist cycles of crisis and development that has featured in Marxist thought was presented in the work of the Soviet economist Kondratieff (1984) and his articulation of the 'long wave' theory of capitalist cyclical development in the 1920s. Kondratieff argued that the 'normal' business cycles of capitalism are driven by the dynamics of capitalist production and that there were no fundamental differences between these and the 'major' or extraordinary cycles. It was a theory that did not differentiate between long and short periods of cyclic upheaval. Capitalism, can, from such a perspective, be seen as a self-perpetuating, self-regulating system. The 'long wave' theory came to occupy a dominant position in economic theory.

Many Marxist economists and notably Mandel (1978) sought to bring Krondatieff's theory and classical Marxism into a position of accord and in particular, an accord between Trotsky and Krondatieff (Day 1976). Trotsky (1986: 276–277), however, had argued that the major, or extraordinary, turning points in capitalist development are ultimately unpredictable in character. These significant moments defied, and denied, the automatic sense of periodicity that was the basis of Krondatieff's theory. Marxism's attempts to maintain relevance in the face of a still dominant capitalist ideology and economy inevitably led to divergence of views. Some Marxists maintained that they were renewing, revising and adapting Marxism to suit new and ever-changing realities. Other voices have decried such ideological departures as 'opportunist' or 'revisionist'.

The decades leading to the collapse of the Second International and World War I, were also a time of development of Marxist theory itself. Gamble (1999a: 3–4) argues that from the beginning there was never a single 'monolithic' Marxism but, rather, a rich and diverse political movement. While this may well be the case, the essence of Marxism, encapsulated in the classical tradition, was that irreconcilable contradictions exist between labour and capital. The significance of Marx's contribution was his view that the working class must organise itself as an independent force if it was to achieve emancipation and, therefore, the resolution of that same contradiction. The essential combative component of Marxism; the search to develop theory and strategy as a means of advancing the interests of the working class, has, over time, diminished. The crisis in Marxism that developed almost from the publication of the *Communist Manifesto*, has revolved around that very question. As the 20th century unfolded, the crisis in both capitalism and in Marxism deepened. The period between the two world wars exposed this crisis as Marxists reactively strove to maintain a sense of relevance.

A deepening crisis: the period between the wars

The years following World War I brought, not the end of capitalism, but rather, a continuation of crisis for Marxism. The Second International had collapsed and an irretrievable rift between social-democracy and Marxism dominated theoretical discourse. The Russian Revolution and the beginning of the Third International gave an impetus for Marxism, but the attendant optimism quickly dissipated. Marxist theory and practice, it was argued, needed to be re-evaluated due to the defeat of the revolutionary upsurge in Europe, the rise of Stalinism and with it the stultification of Marxist thought, the promotion of the theory of socialism in one country, and the subsuming of the international Marxist movement into the service of Stalinist policies.

Jay (1996: 3–4) describes one consequence of the Russian Revolution that would come to play a significant role in the development of Western Marxism. The Revolution moved the political centre of gravity eastward. He argues that the Marxist intelligentsia, and particularly in Germany, saw three possible responses. These were either to support Moscow's leadership and that of the Third International, back the non-revolutionary socialist movement in Germany, or pursue a complete 're-examination' of Marxist theory in order to prepare for future actions. It was the latter path that the fore-runners of Western Marxism chose to follow. Jay argues that:

> The split that divided the working class movement in Weimar between a bolshevized Communist Party (KPD) and a non-revolutionary Socialist Party (SPD) was a sorry spectacle to those who still maintained the purity of Marxist theory. Some attempted a rapprochement with one faction or another. But as demonstrated by the story of Georg Lukács, who was forced to repudiate his most imaginative book, *History and Class Consciousness*, shortly after its appearance in 1923, this often meant sacrificing intellectual integrity on the altar of party solidarity (1996: 4).

The dilemma that these Marxists faced was further complicated by the disintegration of the Marxist movement in Europe that came with the failure of revolutionary moments immediately after the Russian Revolution and World War I. The apparent victory of nationalism over internationalism that the Second International's collapse signalled is reflected in the development of Western Marxism. Anderson (1979: 94) asserts that Western Marxism was ultimately more 'Western' than Marxist. Anderson argues that historical materialism, as the base upon which Marxist theory is built, is only fully valid and able to exercise its full powers if "it is free from parochialism, of any kind. It has yet to recover them" (1979: 94).

The reality of defeat and stagnation as well as the growing acquiescence of the European working class was demoralising, and especially for Marxist theorists who were beginning the march away from revolutionary practice. Understandably, Marxists such as Korsch (1931) sought to wage a struggle against what they saw as a degeneration of Marxist theory and practice. It was Korsch who first introduced the idea of there being a crisis in Marxism. Korsch was critical of the German Communist Party's perceived ideological weakness that played a significant role in the failure of the German revolution. His position drifted over time from an alliance with Trotsky's 'Left Opposition' as a means of reviving Marxism's fortunes, to his later theses arguing that:

> today, all attempts to re-establish the Marxist doctrine as a whole in its original function as a theory of the working classes social revolution are reactionary utopias … Marx is today only

> one among the numerous precursors, founders and developers of the socialist movement of the working class. No less important are the so-called Utopian Socialists from Thomas More to the present (1950).

Such a trajectory, during the turbulent years between the wars, was not uncommon. Anderson (1979: 24) refers to a mutation of ideas that came to be known as Western Marxism in which an 'altered universe' within Marxist theory became more and more apparent. Anderson (1979: 28) points to the concerted move to shift the centre of Marxist thought away from Eastern and Central Europe and back to Germany, France and Italy. He argues that the ramifications of this shift have been considerable. In particular, a separation of theory from practice became apparent, as the working class in Europe had become more closely identified with the politics and economics of social democracy.

What transpired was the beginning of a movement that sought, consciously, to separate itself from the dialectical materialism that was the hallmark of Marxist theory. The Frankfurt School sought to reconfigure Marxist theory to suit the new realities of the post-war period. The defeats of the European working class and its growing accommodation to social-democracy led to a shift in focus away from the working class as the axis around which change would turn. Wiggerhaus argues that the leaders of the Frankfurt School did not "put any hopes in the working class … Adorno expressly denied that the working class had any progressive role to play" (1994: 123). Another feature of Western Marxism was the removal of the classical Marxist construction that argues that the superstructure of society, political and institutional, rests upon an economic base and it is this economic base that is primary. By inverting this relationship, Western Marxism changed the emphasis and trajectory of Marxism.

In the 1930s, Horkheimer (1982) further clarified the ideology of Western Marxism in his development of the concept of *Critical Theory*. Critical Theory, for Horkheimer, was a term that could be used to replace Marxism. He contended that Critical Theory was, in essence, a movement to abolish social injustice. It was within this theoretical framework that Bloch (2015), writing twenty years later, developed his neo-utopian vision within Marxism. Bloch's call for a return to utopian perceptions was, of course, a major departure from Marxist theory. Lenin commented on Marxism's perspective stating that Marx "studied the *birth* of a new society *out of* the old, and the forms of the transition from the latter to the former" (1977c: 272, emphasis in the original). The utopian construct, by contrast, maintained that the "true genesis is not at the beginning, but at the end" (Bloch 2015).

Hudson (1982: 33) outlines Bloch's contention that the emphasis on science, so elemental to Marxism, was a limiting feature, as was the emphasis that Marx placed on the primacy of economic factors. Popper in the 1950s famously and strenuously argued that Marxism is not science. To his credit he did accept that Marxism identifies trends and tendencies that occur in social change and that these trends can neither be questioned or denied. However, Popper argued that 'trends' are not 'laws', in language that strongly echoed Bernstein's. Laws after all are timeless. Popper further stated that a trend, even if consistent "for hundreds or thousands of years may change within a decade, or even more rapidly than that" (2002: 106). More recent criticisms of scientific socialism are found in the tendency towards neo-utopianism. Panitich and Gindin (2000) call for 'imaginative' thought in the face of the collapse of communism and the failures of third way social democracy. They describe a movement that begins with pre-Marxist utopian ideas and seek to re-introduce such a philosophy that is in direct contrast to Marxism's appeal to scientific analysis.

Critical Theory and the Frankfurt School dominated the thinking of radical and New Left activism after World War II. Bronner (2011) outlines how Critical Theory has 'enriched' an understanding of family, sexuality and repression, teaching practice, genocide, entertainment, and literary analysis. He also states that it has added to an understanding of power imbalances, the state and global activity. This 'enrichment' in Anderson's view was in fact a reflection of a broader political defeat that had resulted in:

> A remarkable range of reflections on different aspects of the culture of modern capitalism. But these were never integrated into a consistent theory of its economic development, typically remaining at a somewhat detached and specialised angle to the broader movement of society (1998: 72).

Anderson (1979: 25) argues that Critical Theory, as an expression of Western Marxism, displaced the traditions upon which Marxism had been constructed. The focus of Marxism, as outlined in Critical Theory, shifted away from the working class and class consciousness and "in the direction of philosophy and literature rather than empirical and historical research" (Little 2007: 238). Adorno and Horkheimer actively sought to replace the concept of class conflict for a theory based upon the idea of universal domination and the conflict between man and nature. "The term 'class' vanishes from the terminology of Critical Theory" (Lubasz 1984: 80). What is particularly evident is that the crisis in Marxism that

Korsch first identified diverted and distorted Marxist theory. What was, at first, a reaction to disappointments and set-backs were the first steps in a move away from classical Marxist theory and practice. The *raison d'etre* of Marxism had been and remains to both explain capitalism and to consciously act to replace it. Marxism was formed as a revolutionary movement. Lenin observed that "without revolutionary theory, there can be no revolutionary movement" (1977c: 109). The years after World War I saw a flowering of theory but it was a theory that was becoming divorced from practice. Nationalism, defeats, and missed opportunities, all demanded that 'old' ideas needed to be re-examined. Developing a theory for a 'new' period, however, led to the effective abandonment of core elements upon which Marxism had been built. Marxist theory, from the perspective of classical Marxism was in disarray. However, the period between the wars was marked by an intensity of questioning and debate as to the way forward. Capitalism had survived. Further strains would soon press upon Marxism with the end of World War II, capitalism's renewed strength and the dawn of a new era of capitalist prosperity.

The 'golden age' of capitalism and beyond

The end of World War II coincided with capitalism's 'golden age'. It was a period marked by economic stability and growth, an apparently contented, or at least acquiescent working class, and a burgeoning welfare state. Cold War politics and the experience of Stalinist regimes in Eastern Europe saw Marxism further relegated, in the eyes of many, to a position of obscurity. Thoughts of a Marxist renewal, as a force that might lead a movement that would fundamentally change the economic order, appeared to be fantasy. A 'golden age' for capitalism was for many Marxists the beginning of a 'dark age'. Marxism in this period again proved to be reacting to events rather than attempting to influence events. Marxism became more defensive and remote from its core values of developing a theory to promote practice and from its objectives of emancipation.

Two events in the mid-1950s shaped the development of Marxism in Europe. The Soviet Union's crushing of the Hungarian Revolution of 1956 coincided with the development of the New Left. Blackledge (2006) argues that the New Left reformulated a democratic vision of socialism. Such a proposition is difficult to sustain, given that the New Left movement had no agreed political or theoretical agenda. Thompson aimed to provide the intellectual basis for the New Left. He sought to differentiate himself from the Marxism that had been so badly served by Stalinism. In his vision of a humanistic socialism, Thompson (1957) criticised Marx's base/superstructure model, arguing that it was a theoretical construct used by Stalin. Thompson was, it is hoped unconsciously, drawing an almost genealogical line between Marx and Stalin.

Marcuse elaborated what was to become the basic premise of New Left ideology. He argued that rather than focusing on the industrialised working class, Marxists should seek to rally the broadly 'dispossessed'; minority groups, unemployed, and those who were yet to be integrated into the capitalist state. Capitalist development, in the post-war period, posed a dilemma for Marxism that such analysis seemed to easily, if simplistically, resolve. The relative affluence of the working class in capitalist states led many within the Marxist movement to further distance themselves from the essential premises of Marxism. The New Left further 'adapted' Marxist theory and came to focus more consciously on the 'transformative' role of culture. The development of the New Left also coincided with the anti-colonialist movements and third-world radicalism. Change, it was argued, was to come, not from a class-conscious workers' movement, but from spontaneous actions of minority groups. What emerged was the growth of identity and social movement politics.

As the old verities were being called into question, philosophical endeavours led to what has been labelled 'postmodernism'. Its largely sceptical approach to the world and ideas had an impact on political thought and on Marxism in the latter part of the century. Callinicos (1990) is one who regards postmodernism as a reflection of political frustration that stems from the disappointments of the radicalisation of the later 1960s. Central to the arguments of the postmodernists (Foucault, Derrida, Lyotard and others) is a reaction against arguments of science and reason that grew from the Enlightenment. Jenkins, in describing postmodernism, claims that "there never has been, and there never will be, any such thing as a past which is expressive of some sort of essence" (2005: 7–8). Postmodernism is the antithesis of Marxism in this respect. Lyotard's (1984) construction that the concept of the 'grand narrative' had lost its function and its goal was further 'clarified' by Gorz (1997) when he proclaimed that seeking to find a basis of Marx's theory of the proletariat was essentially a waste of time. Marxism, however, maintains that history is a law-governed process and largely governed by economic factors. It is also marked by the 'grand narrative' and particularly in relation to the working class and its role. The debate surrounding postmodernism is significant because post-Marxism's theoretical premise is so closely aligned with postmodernist theory.

Central to post-Marxist ideology is the dismissal of the 'old' politics of classical Marxism. In keeping with the intellectual scope of postmodernism, as well as the movement away from class-related political analysis, it is an appeal to the revolutionary potential of identity politics and broad, non-class social movements. Critchley (1997) argues, however, that socialist renewal is certainly possible by using Marx's analysis without discarding class forms of struggle. Critchley regards the development of post-Marxism in terms of a paralysis of the will that is required to change the world. Sim argues that post-Marxism is "as much a symptom of a problem as a solution to the left's ills; the problem being that radical politics has become very dispersed in the last few decades" (2011: 20).

While radical politics became 'dispersed' in the post-war period, the quest to understand capitalist political economy within a Marxist framework continued. In this sense, *Regulation theory* assumes a significant position. Regulation theory examines the interrelation between the economy and socio-political issues. It maintains that the economy is self-regulating and is part of an integrated system incorporating social and political elements. In so doing, the theory advances the position that capitalism and its development is propelled by the social structure of society. It actively seeks to overcome what neo-Marxists held to be a central problem in classical Marxism; the base-superstructure view of societal development.

Regulation theorists such as Boyer (2002), Aglietta (1998) and Jessop (2001a) maintain that it is possible to overcome what they describe as the more 'mechanistic' explanations of capitalist development. Central to Regulation theory's thesis is that an explanation of capitalism's tendency to crisis and stabilisation lies in capitalism's requirement of a degree of regulation. Capitalism operates, according to the theory, through cyclical, self-regulating crises. These crises further exacerbate the contradictions within the system. The 'mode' of development, as described by the theory, reproduces itself through these cyclical crises and leads, over time, to a structural crisis. This in turn creates an unregulated system which must be resolved and a new regulated capitalist mode is constructed. Husson cites Lipietz's commentary that "one is a regulationist as soon as one asks why there are relatively stable structures when, given that they are contradictory, logically they should disintegrate" (2008: 178). Very little, it appears, is new or novel in the armoury of the 'adaptors' of Marx. Such observations as those promoted by the Regulationist's echo earlier debates within Marxism and especially between Bernstein and Luxemburg regarding the capacity for capitalism to adapt or to break down.

Aglietta (1998) argues that capitalist accumulation in the post-war period is markedly different from that during the Great Depression and that in different periods of accumulation different forms of regulation of capitalism emerge. These were broken into three distinct periods or 'modes': 19th-century competitive capitalism, early 20th-century intensive accumulation and post-war monopoly modes of regulation (Brenner and Glick 1991). In the 21st century, capitalism has entered a period of intractable crisis and instability. How Regulation theory has responded becomes particularly relevant.

Hirst and Zeitlin maintain that the Regulationists, in rejecting classical Marxist analysis of capitalist breakdown, are seeking a 'middle' way between revolutionary socialism and reformist social democracy. "Regulation theory remains concerned with capitalism as a global system and it seeks policies for the international economy that will promote stability and growth" (1992: 93). Husson (2008: 187–188) contends that Regulation theory has, in recent years, moved further from its Marxist roots, and it now argues, amongst other things, for new forms of wage earning through worker share-holdings and a range of profit-sharing compromises with employers.

The 20th century dawned amid capitalist crisis and unresolved contradictions. It was a century that saw wide divergences and developments in Marxist theory but with capitalism still secure. Marxism remains divided. Marxism was formed with the objective of fundamentally changing society. Its focus was the class nature of that society. Many 'Marxisms' evolved in the last century. Each of these divergent trends have built and extended theoretical positions, but with each new representation, the importance of class and working-class struggle has diminished. How can Marxism be considered relevant when it is in such disarray? Can there be a resolution to the crisis within Marxist thought that has disrupted Marxist practice for so long?

Can there be resolution?

Chodos (2007: 190–193) offers an astonishing argument that the movement for socialism, in the 21st century must avoid the linking of economic and political relationships. He maintains that a key 'flaw' in Marxist analysis is its insistence that socialism represents the assumption of power by the working class. It is painfully clear that the question of the working class remains problematic for many contemporary Marxist thinkers. For many the working class became, not a force for change, but an obstacle in the path to change. Gorz (1997) articulated this antipathy for the working class. He elaborated a theory of labour and the working class that increasingly regarded the working class as either impotent in the face of the structures of capitalism, or as representative of a privileged minority. He regarded the working class as a shrinking force that was incapable of playing a conscious role against capitalism. He argued that the unemployed and underemployed in society possessed the capacity to become the basis upon which an emancipatory project might develop. Such a pessimistic construction, a total abandonment of Marxism while still seeking to occupy a space within

Marxist thought, can only limit a renewal of Marxism, either as interpreter, or as agency for changing the world. Marxism expresses the consciousness of the proletariat and its central task is to illuminate that which is hidden by bourgeois reality (Lukacs 1970). The issue of the working class and its role in the transformation of society has been and remains at the centre of Marxist theory and practice. It has also been at the centre of dislocation within Marxism.

Debates as to Marxism's utility continue. Callinicos (1991) optimistically declares Marxism to be a powerful, historically oriented social theory. Singer (1999) argues that radical movements will not disappear while there is exploitation. He is referring specifically to the broad, anti-globalisation protest movements and argues, one assumes with a straight face, for a 'realistic' utopian future. For some, Marxism's combative future is beyond question. Disappointment, disillusionment and demoralisation, colours the thinking of others. The radical, non-class appeal to a spontaneous movement, sits between the two camps. What remains central, however, is that all schools of thought are consciously or unconsciously drawn into the overarching question of the role of the working class. For the optimists, the working class remains central. For the pessimists, the perceived weakness of working-class consciousness becomes a critical issue. For the radical social movement activists, the working class is simply 'another' element. Shandro discusses the issue of spontaneity in terms of an accommodation "to bourgeois hegemony ... not through a failure of proletarian commitment to the struggle for socialism ... but through failure to mount a political project of proletarian hegemony" (2007: 17).

Recent debates within Marxism have focused less on economics and more on philosophical questions. Marx began his professional life as a philosopher and moved resolutely to the field of economics. Western Marxism consciously developed its theory and ideological base on the philosophy of Marxism rather than its economic propositions. It has been a process that has seen Marxism's focus shift inexorably away from the working class and has diffused the classical Marxist position that economics and economic struggle between classes is the dominant and motivating force. To arbitrarily separate the component parts of economics and philosophy can only weaken Marxist theory. Similarly, theory and practice act as an integrated whole. To separate one from the other leads to a theory that is baseless. Gramsci described it as the "result of a dialectical process in which the spontaneous movement of the revolutionary masses and the organizing and directing will of the centre converge" (Forgacs 2000: 129). Colletti (1969) enlivened debates within Western Marxism that promoted the philosophy of Marx ahead of economics. Just a few years later he stated that

> the only way in which Marxism can be revived is if no more books like *Marxism and Hegel* are published, and instead books like Hilferding's *Finance Capital* and Luxemburg's *Accumulation of Capital* – or even Lenin's *Imperialism* ... are once again written (1977: 350).

In seeking to renew its claim to relevance, Marxism more and more diverged from its fundamental premise of class and class struggle as a means of combatting capitalism. If Marxism is to make a serious claim to relevance, then the unity of theory and practice needs to be more obviously integrated. It is thus appropriate to re-visit some of the theoretical observations of Marxism and particularly in relation to issues of class and class consciousness.

Class, as a defining element in capitalist society, has long been a central component of Marxist analysis. Anderson (1974: 49) explains Marx's concept of class-in-itself as opposed to the state of class-for-itself which denotes a conscious and independent movement to pursue its own interests. Such a position is difficult to attain but the failure to reach such a position has serious consequences for the working class. The essence of class consciousness, and its possibly elusive character, is further articulated by Anderson (1974: 60–61). Two components – a radicalised intelligentsia that can offer an ideological leadership and a motivated working class – provide a framework within which consistent class consciousness might develop. Such a view is based on Marx's (1956: 195–197) conception of the development of class relations whereby the working class seek to consciously promote, and struggle, for its own interests. The working class, no matter how militant it may be, remains limited in its potential if it has to act within the constraints of the capitalist state from which it seeks emancipation.

An essential component of class consciousness is not simply a militant approach to perceived enemies, but a leadership either from within the working class or acting with the working class to advance its perceived interests. Lenin's (1977c: 113–114) comments – that mass strike behaviour without effective and conscious leadership is but an embryonic form of class consciousness – remains pertinent. Such energy must be channelled or it is energy too easily spent. Trotsky, describing the necessity of political leadership, remarked that "without a guiding organisation the energy of the masses would dissipate like steam not enclosed in a piston box" (Trotsky 1965: 17).

Political leadership, and the role of the working class, remain central to Marxism's claim to relevance. This understanding is fundamentally linked to the question of Marxism's purpose. Marxism emerged to describe and offer a critique of capitalism. This has remained its strength. Integrated with this, however, is the *purpose* of Marxism: to organise and offer leadership to the working class in its quest for emancipation. The role of the working class and the combative nature of Marxism, however, became less central to Marxist thinking in the 20th century. The working class remains numerically strong and globally visible (Harman 2010: 331). McCarney (1990: 192) sums up much of the left's problems with the role and perception of the working class when he differentiates between 'third world' workers and those in advanced capitalist countries. In capitalist countries, the working class has been criticised for failing to act as a revolutionary force.

Marxism in the 20th century sought to develop a theory that would answer the questions posed by contemporary life. These questions were framed against the realities of stable capitalist relationships and the perceived acquiescence of a more secure and affluent working class after World War II. Contemporary Marxist theorists also sought, and often successfully, to analyse the developing capitalist crisis, while at the same time overlooking the effect this is having on the working class. There are other, fundamental propositions that have also been less well considered. These relate to the ultimate purpose of Marxism, of the need to re-engage with class issues, and of how Marxists respond to the question of leadership as a means of advancing an emancipatory program. It is a question of re-integrating theory and practice. Whether there can be anything like a *rapprochement* between the divergent manifestations of Marxist thought is unclear. North, paraphrasing Marx, argues that "we live and fight in the world of 'objective conditions', which is both the source of our present-day troubles and their ultimate solution. Whatever shall emerge in the future shall be the product of conditions that exist today" (North 2015: 132). Such a proposition serves to reinforce Marxism's on-going claims to relevance.

Marxism, as an economic, philosophic, and social worldview, has a history that has been plagued by disputation and division. Today there are many 'Marxisms' and yet all stem from the one intellectual and theoretical base: the analysis of Marx and Engels, who presented a deep critique of capitalism and of its evolution. The purpose of this critique was not simply to analyse and to appreciate the development of capitalism, but to provide a theoretical base that would be used to combat capitalism and to replace it. Burawoy and Wright claim that Marxism is "a comprehensive worldview for understanding the social world. It provides the theoretical weapons needed to attack the mystifications of capitalism and the vision needed to mobilise the masses for struggle" (2006: 462). Marxism, however, despite providing these 'weapons' has not been able to mobilise the 'masses for struggle'.

Marxism remains relevant only if it answers fundamental questions that confront the working class. These questions are inextricably linked to the potential and capacity for the working class and its allies to develop an independent consciousness that both responds to and combats capitalism and the state. As Marx famously declared, "philosophers have only interpreted the world, in various ways; the point is to change it" (Marx and Engels 1964: 647). The world, or more specifically the economic and political structures of capitalism, has not been changed.

Marxist theory, at the beginning of the 20th century, was focused on the nature of capitalism and how to respond to imperialism as a globalising force. Prominent among the debates were questions of revolution or reform – of whether capitalism was to be understood by breakdown theory or whether it was a self-regulating system. In the 21st century the nature of capitalism as a globalising force is again being debated and the regulatory 'nature' of capitalism is once again being discussed and disputed.

The theoretical shifts in Marxism have a common thread. In seeking to maintain relevance in a changing world, contemporary Marxism has become a reactive force. There was a perception among many Marxists that the 'revolutionary potential' of the working class had dissipated. The class nature of society had been a cornerstone of Marxist theory. This shift in emphasis evolved over decades. Marxist theory sought to adapt to new perceptions and new challenges. Western Marxism, in the period between the wars, reacted to a political and geographical shift eastward that followed the Stalinisation of Marxist theory. It was also responding to the gathering strength of social democracy and a working class that exhibited a weakened sense of consciousness. Capitalist stabilisation after World War II and a more acquiescent working class led many Marxists to pursue new, alternative paths in a quest for relevance. New Left activists and postmodernist, post-Marxist theorists argued new ways of engaging in struggle were required.

Marxism, despite theoretical disputation and divergence, remains a valuable vehicle for analysing and understanding of capitalism and capitalist globalisation. This, of itself, does not make Marxism relevant in an era of capitalist crisis. Marxism was created to provide analysis and critique of capitalism. Inseparable to this was its role of offering guidance and leadership in the course of combatting capitalism and of fundamentally changing economic and societal structures. How Marxism responds to the latter historical component will frame its future, its relevance and the future of capitalism. Gamble asks: what sort of future does Marxism have? "It might linger on like mediaeval scholasticism … with no observable connection to anything in the real world" (Gamble: 1999a: 4). He hopes that this is not the future because "there is an intellectual core to Marxism which is worth preserving and which is capable of further development" (1999a: 4). Another question remains but is often unasked. Can Marxism not only answer the questions that modern capitalism poses, but also act as a catalyst for fundamental change?

The future of Marxism and its capacity to answer these questions is ultimately tied to Marxism's analytical approach. The following chapter offers an overview of the key elements of this approach and how it can be used, not merely to understand the crisis that plagues capitalism but also how Marxism became mired in discord and crisis.

3

VALIDATING MARXIST ANALYSIS

Marxist thought has influenced a range of disciplines as diverse as art history, cultural studies, philosophy and the social sciences (Little 2007: 230). The recurrent themes of alienation, labour theory, class conflict, modes and relations of production, have become the focus for different approaches to Marxist analysis. Little points out that "there are many areas where Marxist methods have been employed, and there are many strands within Marx's thought that have given rise to these various approaches" (2007: 230). This plethora of Marxist interpretations of just about everything is both a blessing and a curse. The 'currency' is certainly cheapened when the tag 'Marxist' can be so liberally attributed to any field of research, but we can leave this aside in our quest to validate Marx's analytical and methodological approach to the world and to capitalism. At the same time, if we are to defend classical Marxism it is important to stress that which is pertinent and to discard that which is not.

Maguire (2010), while outlining a range of contemporary perspectives within Marxism, argues that whether a school of thought is regarded as neo-Marxist or post-Marxist is of little consequence. What is important, for Maguire, is how Marxism deals with what he describes as practical problems (2010: 155). Whether by intent or by accident, what emerges in such a construction is a tendency towards relativism. For more than a century Marxism has attempted to deal with 'practical' problems as they have arisen. Bernstein's (1975) attempts to 'revise' Marxist theory was an initial point of departure that ultimately led to Laclau and Mouffe's claim that "it is no longer possible to maintain the conception of subjectivity and classes elaborated by Marxism, nor its vision of the historical course of capitalist development" (2001: 2–4). The simple fact is that there has been and remains a crisis within Marxist theory and that this has played a role in the ability of capitalism to withstand its own crises. Lukacs' defence of 'orthodox' Marxism and his conviction that "all attempts to surpass or 'improve' it has led and must lead to over-simplification, triviality and eclecticism" (1976: 1), is well worth remembering. Marx's method of analysis was a response to society as it existed. His approach involved a "willingness to make those assumptions he felt were necessary in order to make sense of things that he, unwaveringly and unchangingly, felt had to be accounted for" (Rosen 1996: 7). Marxism, necessarily seeks first to understand capitalism and then to challenge it.

It is important to briefly outline how Marxist analysis operates. A Marxist analytical process draws together the component parts that constitute capitalist relations – a synthesis – beginning with the role that labour plays in the process that is capitalism and concluding with the development of capitalist globalisation. Historical materialism sits at the core of a Marxist analysis. I unequivocally defend this as a scientific approach to analysing and understanding the world. I argue that Marxism can be regarded as 'scientific' despite claims from critics to the contrary and that Marxism is of continuing and deepening relevance because it provides empirically based descriptions of the overarching economic system, and it draws social implications from those economic structures. Marx also offered historical understandings of the processes by which these structures came into existence.

Capitalism's capacity to withstand extreme moments of crisis, however, resulted in a crisis in Marxism. While Korsch (1931) first coined the phrase in the period after the Stalinisation of Marxism, the roots of crisis go much deeper. Marxism famously split at the time of World War I, around the issue of nationalism. It left a deep cleavage between Western European social democracy, that fed into later disputes. The problems in Marxism are consequently analysed, and by so doing, the argument that the disputation and divergence within Marxism has inadvertently assisted capitalism's ability to remain the economic paradigm is supported. In seeking to re-define Marxist theory, latter-day Marxism has been unable to offer a viable theoretical and practical leadership to combat the persistence of capitalist ideology.

What follows then, is a brief exposition of what constitutes Marxist analysis. This includes a short introduction to the materialist conception of history and the use of dialectics as a means of explaining social and economic developments as an integrated unity. It is shown that this materialist and dialectical approach can be used to explain the development of capitalism and of its tendency toward crisis. It is further shown that the crisis in Marxism can equally be described from a materialist construction.

Elements of Marxist analysis

How can Marxism affirm its claim to relevance in an age of capitalist crisis? Marxism, for all its difficulties, and however poorly used, remains the best vehicle to offer a framework to understand and analyse issues of the state, globalisation, relations between state and capital and the place and role of the working class. A unified theory encapsulating economic, political and social factors, I argue, is essential for understanding and resolving the contradiction between the growth of global capitalism as an economic focus, and the nation-state as a vehicle for political organisation. Marxism provides such an approach.

Little (2007) encapsulates the essence of Marxist analysis as a process which must:

1 examine material institutions;
2 look at class, power, exploitation, domination;
3 not be blinded to effects that violate the materialist dicta;
4 be mindful of 'contradictions' that work themselves through historical contingencies;
5 look for underlying causes and structures (2007: 242).

In discussing Marx's method, Little focuses on its distinctive characteristics. He traces a number of assumptions or pre-suppositions that denote a Marxist methodology. These begin with assumptions about societies and historical processes:

> the social world is a causal order, that social structures have properties and causal characteristics, that individuals constitute social structures through their actions and choices, that 'social formations' fall under the categories of 'modes of production,' that modes of production consist of sets of forces and relations of production, and that classes exist (2007: 235).

Little's description of Marx's method closely accords with Marx's own. Marx (1974) argued that what was essential was to make observations that move from the simple to the complex and that show the inter-relationship of all component parts:

> simple conceptions such as labour, division of labour, demand, exchange value, and conclude with state, international exchange and world market ... The concrete is concrete because it is a combination of many determinations, i.e. a unity of diverse elements. In our thought it therefore appears as a process of synthesis, as a result, and not as a starting point, although it is the real starting point and, therefore, also the starting point of observation and conception (1974: 100–101).

Little identifies nine separate themes that are evident in *Capital Volume 1*:

1 A description of the property system of capitalism.
2 A description of the purpose of production within capitalism.
3 A developed treatment of the labour theory of value.
4 An abstract model of the capitalist mode of production.
5 A description of the workings of the competitive market.
6 An analysis of the economic and social implications of these features.
7 A sociological account of how property relations of capitalism are reproduced.
8 An historical account of how these property relations were established in pre-capitalist society.
9 A description of the life and conditions of the working class (1986: 18).

The connectivity of these themes remains an essential element of Marxist analysis and method – Marxism synthesises the components of capitalist relations, beginning with the role of labour and concluding with the development of globalisation.

"The relations of production of every society form a whole" (Marx 1956: 123). The connectedness of these relations is pivotal for Marxism. Marx's method is simply defined as "materialistic, because it proceeds from existence to consciousness, not the other way around. Marx's method is dialectic, because it regards nature and society as they evolve, and evolution itself as the constant struggle of conflicting forces" (Trotsky 2006: 4). The strength of Marxism lies in such a formulation, marked by an understanding of the interconnectedness of often contradictory elements.

Contradiction was central to Marx's understanding of capitalist development. It is a concept that denotes many of the differences between materialist and non-Marxist interpretations and methodologies:

> The apologetic phrases used to deny crises are important in so far as they always prove the opposite of what they are meant to prove. In order to deny crises, they assert unity where there is conflict and contradiction. They are therefore important in so far as one can say they prove that there would be no crises if the contradictions which they have erased in their imagination, did not exist in fact. But in reality crises exist because these contradictions exist. Every reason which they put forward against crisis is an exorcised contradiction, and, therefore, a real contradiction, which can cause crises. The desire to convince oneself of the non-existence of contradictions, is at the same time the expression of a pious wish

> that the contradictions, which are really present, *should not* exist (Marx 1968: 518, emphasis in the original).

Marxist theory specifies the features of what is characterised as *the crisis of capitalism*. These are: the tendency for the rate of profit to fall, the concentration of capital, the growth of the working class, a tendency toward under-consumption (or more significantly over-production) and the development and influence of finance capitalism. Analysis of these features and of their inter-relationships, allows for a rational response to the contradictions in capitalist globalisation. At the very centre of these analytical tools is historical materialism. Consequently, Solomon and Rupert's assertion that historical materialism "approaches the question of globalization not with puzzlement over dramatic changes in forms of accumulation, but fully expecting them" (2002: 284) is worth repeating.

Marxist philosophy and theory emphasises the interaction between social classes, changes in material conditions, how society is organised, and of the primacy of economic factors over political ones as engines for change. Marx interpreted how society, class relations and economic questions manifest themselves:

> In the social production which men carry on they enter into definite relations, that are indispensable and independent of their will; these relations of production correspond to a definite stage of development of their material powers of production … It is not the consciousness of men that determines their existence, but, on the contrary, their social existence determines their consciousness (1918: 11–12).

Marxism unites the elements of historical materialism, economic theory and the class nature of society. Such a synthesis serves as an analytical tool to explain and interpret capitalist relations. It can similarly be used to explain and interpret Marxism and the dissension that has so long accompanied it. This materialist approach provides the basis of what Marxists declared to be a scientific analytical outlook.

Historical materialism and the scientific approach

Lenin (1977b) described Marx's contributions to the study of historical materialism, his economic theories and the issues surrounding classes in society. These interrelated components form the basis of Marxist theory and its claim to the status of science. Primary among these is the concept of historical materialism. Intimately related to this is the fundamental premise that class and class conflict remain central to understanding societal developments and that economic issues drive political and societal responses. A materialist construction understands historical processes as being impelled by antagonistic relationships between classes, explains how social structures are shaped by economic factors, and sees class struggle as being framed by the labour process (Boucher 2012: 5).

Historical materialism has been traditionally presented as vindicating the claim that Marxism constitutes a scientific method of analysis. Whitefield, in the *Oxford Concise Dictionary of Politics* (1996) outlines the concept whereby "social structures derive from economic structures, and that these structures are changed through class struggles ... that human history develops as the result of contradictions, mainly among social cases".

In outlining the essential propositions that designate historical materialism and its claim to be a scientifically valid means of interpreting the world, Engels argued that:

> The materialist conception of history starts from the proposition that the production of the means to support human life and, next to production, the exchange of things produced, is the basis of all social structure; that in every society that has appeared in history, the manner in which wealth is distributed and society divided into classes or orders is dependent upon what is produced, how it is produced, and how the products are exchanged. From this point of view, the final causes of all social changes and political revolutions are to be sought, not in men's brains, not in men's better insights into eternal truth and justice, but in changes in the modes of production and exchange (1966: 50).

It was a construction that framed Marxist theory and one which has evoked wide disputation. Popper stridently criticised what he termed historicism as being:

> an approach to the social sciences which assumes that *historical prediction* is their principal aim, and which assumes that this aim is attainable by discovering the 'rhythms' or the 'patterns,' the 'laws' or the 'trends' that underlie the evolution of history (1985: 290 emphasis in the original).

Historical materialism, however, seeks to explain social transformation by identifying the dialectical interactions between productive forces and the essentially social relationship that exists in that production. The often-misleading term 'predictability' has come to represent a form of 'prophecy' rather than a conscious act of political perspective that can interpret events in a multi-faceted manner in order to make justifiable propositions. It is an analytical tool that both embraces the wide sweep of historical developments while examining the unity of the component parts that constitute the whole.

Central to an appreciation of the Marxist method of analysis, and an acceptance of its relevance, is the vexed question of whether Marxism can be designated a science or, as pseudo-science. The determination of Marxism as scientific came from Engels in what was essentially a critique of 'utopian socialism'. Nature, as Engels asserted:

> is the proof of dialectics, and it must be said for modern science that it has furnished this proof with very rich materials increasing daily, and thus has shown that, in the last resort, Nature works dialectically and not metaphysically; that she does not move in the eternal oneness of a perpetually recurring circle, but goes through a real historical evolution (1966: 45).

Grant and Woods (2002: 45) offer a simple and yet lucid example of such a dialectical process, whereby opposites interact, with a resultant qualitative change occurring. They describe the change from water to steam by the interaction with heat. Such an example, both simple and obvious, serves to illustrate the basis of dialectics. Engels (1976) described dialectics as the unity and conflict of opposites and that by their interaction, quantitative changes develop into qualitative changes.

Marx was steadfast in his belief that science was far more than merely a collation of facts but by necessity involved the development and propagation of theories. These theories are related to causal agents that act upon the world: entities, relations and processes. It is in the process of these theories acting upon the world that Marxism unites philosophical inquiry with economic analysis. The materialist conception of history stresses the overarching importance of economics as a driver of political and societal development. This does not preclude Marxist theory from an immersion in philosophical enquiry. To arbitrarily separate the two seriously limits the theoretical underpinnings of Marxism itself. Engels (1976: 42) stressed that investigative science and theory inevitably come together and that theory and philosophical endeavours are intertwined. In a similar vein Weisbord (1937) argued that scientific socialism originated as a method of analysis, as well as a body of conclusions, later becoming a combination of theory and practice. It becomes all but impossible to separate economic and political issues from that of philosophical considerations. In other words, ideas, like economics, exist and co-exist in historical time and space.

This co-existence of philosophy and economics in Marxist theory is best articulated when considered in relation to the core elements of class and class-based society. The class nature of society, the issue of class consciousness and the combative essence that imbued Marxism from its inception remain core elements of Marxist theory and of the method that Marx developed. They also remain among the most contested issues in Marxist debates.

As capitalist crisis deepens, Marxism assumes even more importance as a means of analysis. What remains significant, and Marxists, despite all manner of differences would agree, is that "two great discoveries, the materialistic conception of history and the revelation of the secret of capitalistic production through surplus value, we owe to Marx" (Engels 1966: 49–50). These 'discoveries' identified Marxism as scientific but remain mired in dispute and controversy. "The next thing, was to work out all its details and relations" (1966: 50).

A materialist reading of the 'weakness' of Marxism

The 'discoveries' that Engels spoke of, and Marx's analytical approach, are well suited to analyse capitalist development. Those same analytical tools are equally valuable in discerning and understanding the problems in Marxism. In discussing the character of Marxist analysis, Dobb (2001) draws attention to Marx's view of

> the essential character of a system of society in the pattern of its relationships, moreover in the tension or conflict inherent in them, rather than in a simple summation of its discrete elements or an analysis of its various aspects in separate departments (2001: 40).

This view of relationships between elements of a system of society can equally apply as a view of relationships between elements of an ideology. The divergent trends within Marxism represent such a pattern of relationships. They may be analysed as an integrated whole or from the perspective of their constituent parts. The differences within Marxism often stem from capitalism's capacity for re-stabilisation which many Marxists regarded as signalling structural problems in Marxism. The sterility in theory that the rise of Stalinism promoted, the failure of post-1917 revolutionary movements, the capacity of capitalism to survive economic depression and war, the post-war resurgence of capitalism and the relative growth in prosperity of the working class, the growth of the middle class, all became factors that questioned the relevance of Marxism. Scholars have often tended to explore these factors in isolation, but in doing so ignored core components of Marxism and the analytical basis upon which that theory rests.

Marxist theory has been weakened and distracted in the past 100 years by a range of factors. Anderson (1983: 15) identifies three interconnected issues that arose in the mid-1920s that significantly affected the development of Marxist thought. These were the consolidation of Stalinism in the USSR, a retreat from revolutionary challenge by the working class in the most advanced capitalist states, and a crisis in leadership that resulted in the defeat of working-class radicalisation occurring in developing European economies. Anderson isolates these three elements as a means of highlighting the geographical as well as intellectual territory that 'Western Marxism' came to inhabit. Scholars have identified these factors either as cause of the crisis in Marxism, or alternatively as a springboard for a renewal of Marxist theory, but simply tracing a set of connecting points along an historical timeline is to do a disservice to Marxist analysis. The timeline can be traced back to any given point. Each of these individual issues point towards the present and from that present to the future. They are all, in turn, connected to one root problem. In short, Marxist thought emerged in a period that was dominated by bourgeois ideology.

Marxism, as a political, economic and philosophical expression, developed quickly in the latter half of the 19th century and into the early decades of the 20th century. Its growth was especially significant in Germany, where a strong intellectual presence was linked to mass influence among the working class. Despite this, the roots of a Marxist worldview remained relatively shallow. Trotsky, in 1905, all but predicted the later capitulation of German Social Democracy (Trotsky 1971a: 210). Marxist thought, in this period, was dominated by internal polemics and disputation. It was an essential and inevitable part of its development. The 'old' bourgeois ideology came into conflict with its opposite in the form of Marxist ideology. To 'proclaim' a change is, however, very different from effecting lasting change.

Marxism was confronted with ideological dilemmas from its beginnings. The construction of a theory capable of withstanding the all-encompassing presence of bourgeois thought proved to be a formidable task. Marxism was created with internationalism as fundamental to its worldview. The rise of nationalism immediately before World War I was a telling moment for Marxism. Engels (cited in Lenin 1918), argued that any future European war would be global in nature. By implication, how the working class would respond would be pivotal. When war did loom, and Engels' propositions were being proven, most Marxist parties and theoreticians retreated into a position of nationalism and support for 'their' nation states, and by implication, 'their' bourgeoisies, and 'their' capitalism. The Zimmerwald Conference in 1915 formalised a break with the Second International. By the end of the war the Russian Revolution had revived Marxism's fortunes. What followed, however, was the ensuing and well documented list of defeats and lost opportunities. These included the collapse of the Second International, the rise of Stalinism, capitalism's survival in the face of depression and war, fascism, the post-war period of stabilisation and relative prosperity.

Each of those interconnected dilemmas played its part in Marxist theory's shift away from core elements of class and economics. The role of the working class has, as a result, been progressively relegated to a position of insignificance in much of contemporary Marxist theory. The historic conception of the working class as a revolutionary subject appeared to be out of place as capitalism stabilised after war and economic depression. There was a presumption, based on what proved to be a limited period of prosperity, that these essential Marxist perceptions were no longer valid. Marx and Engels, however, were clear in their assessment that the working class, and its leadership, must react and respond to capitalism in its entirety and not as a set of separate component parts or elements.

> It is not a question of what this or that proletarian, or even the whole proletariat, at the moment *regards* as its aim. It is a question of *what the proletariat is*, and what in accordance with this *being (Sein)*, it will historically be compelled to do (Marx and Engels 1975a: 44 emphasis in original).

The perception that is common in much contemporary Marxist literature, that the working class is no longer a revolutionary subject, or class, is reinforced by what appears to be an acquiescence on its part and by a lack of consistent leadership. Marxists live and work in the 'real' world which is dominated by capitalist economics, philosophy and politics. In this sense, it is by no means a 'level playing field'. Marx and Engels (1964: 60) famously wrote of class and of how the ideas of a ruling class in any society are intrinsically ruling ideas. Plekhanov (1976) described the essential principle of historical materialism as a means of explaining history. He argued that the thinking of people is conditioned by their being. This meant that, in the sense of an historical process, the development of ideas is essentially a product of developing economic relations. The development of Marxism reflects such a degree of conditioning.

Engels (2000) offered the view that ideological processes are often used to effectively mask the real class nature of society. This came to be known as 'false-consciousness'. Lukacs (1976: 51–55) further developed this argument as a way of explaining how the working class and the political organisations formed to promote its interests can be convinced that these interests are virtually synonymous with those of the ruling class. Such a situation, whereby the working class becomes not only economically dependent upon the capitalist state, but identifies, ideologically, with the ruling class is problematic for Marxism and its aim of emancipation of the working class and for the development of class-consciousness. It has also proven to be an issue of concern for Marxist theorists as they face what has appeared, to many, to be an impregnable ideological opponent.

This disillusionment has contributed to the ongoing crisis within Marxism. It was difficult to maintain an intellectual framework that could withstand bourgeois ideology. Trotsky wrote of this dilemma in describing how many, "when thrown against great events ... are easily lost and relapse again into petty-bourgeois ways of thinking" (1971b: 59). Korsch analysed the developing problems in Marxist theory. He described his approach as:

> the application of the materialist conception of history to the materialist conception of history itself ... It concerns the successive *phases of development* through which Marxism has passed from its original conception up to the situation today, where it is split into different historical versions. It also involves the *relationship* of these different phases to each other and their significance for the general historical development of theory in the modern working-class movement (1970: 93 emphasis in original).

He explained that the process required a re-examination of Marxist philosophy, as a means of recapturing the essence of Marxist theory, and linked such a theoretical task to one of practice:

> The scientific theory of Marxism must become again what it was for the authors of the *Communist Manifesto* – not as a simple *return* but as a *dialectical development*: a theory of social revolution that comprises all areas of society as a totality. Therefore we must solve in a dialectically materialist fashion not only 'the question of the relationship of the State to social revolution and of social revolution to the State' (Lenin), but also the 'question of the relationship of ideology to social revolution and of social revolution to ideology (Korsch 1970: 63 emphasis in original).

The twin elements of Marxist method – the historical perspective and dialectically driven forward development – that Korsch elucidated are perhaps even more relevant today. Marxist theory can only profit from retrospection that can facilitate forward movement. The Marxists of the early Frankfurt School, as described by McCarney (1990: 166), were conscious of both where they had come from and where they wished to go. While this may well be an historical truth, a contemporary truth is that there are but few examples of later Marxist analysis with anything resembling this vision.

A rift between theory and practice has long been evident and has long plagued Marxism. Marx argued that "it is not enough that thought should seek to actualize itself; actuality must also strive towards thought" (1977: 138). Lukacs paraphrased this, stating that only when "consciousness stands in such a relation to reality can theory and practice be united" (1976: 2).

Marxist theorists need "a return to the classical sources, with the intention of carrying through their unfinished programme. The task is in part one of Marxist philosophy, a matter of completing the foundations of the materialist historical dialectic" (McCarney1990: 186–187). McCarney does not imagine that this is an easy task (1990: 193–194). What, almost inevitably surfaces when contemplating the discord within Marxism, are debates around theory and practice, about method and about the label of 'scientific socialism' that has been used to both support and denigrate Marxism. The unfinished program that McCarney speaks of can only be achieved by a re-uniting of the dialectical unity between theory with practice. Marxism's task is to combat capitalism and so seek to change the world. Recognising and analysing capitalist crisis is one important step along that path.

A materialist reading of capitalist crisis

It has become almost axiomatic to speak of the 'crisis of capitalism'. Marx (1986b: 266) identified three primary elements of capitalism: the concentration of the means of production into relatively few hands, the social nature of labour and the development of a world market. These elements necessarily act in contradiction to one another and in the 21st century, globalisation, as an expression of the 'world market', is especially relevant. Crisis, for Marx, was an inescapable component of capitalism. Harvey argues that "crises are moments of transformation in which capital typically reinvents itself … but crises are also moments of danger when the reproduction of capital is threatened by underlying contradictions" (2015: 4).

Marxism, with its materialist view of economics and history, is uniquely positioned to analyse this concept of contradiction. Contradiction can, of course, simply indicate a set of contrasting ideas or statements. Crocker presents a definition within a Marxist framework where

> A and B are contradictory if and only if (1) A and B are both processes (2) A and B have natural paths of development (3) The natural path of development of A and the natural path of development of B cannot be jointly realized (1980: 560).

Marx argued that "what constitutes dialectical movement is the co-existence of two contradictory sides, their conflict and their fusion into a new category" (1956: 126). Marx's primary use of the term was connected to his analysis of the historical process of capitalism, the private ownership of productive forces and the social character of production. In this sense contradiction is necessarily antagonistic.

For Rees (1998: 1–3) a set of contradictory factors coexist in society and are easily identified. These range from the growth of poverty amid expanding wealth, the rise in life expectancy resulting from medical and scientific advances alongside high infant mortality rates and since the Cold War, a near constant state of civil war in various parts of the world. It echoes Marx's comments on contradiction:

> In our days, everything seems pregnant with its contrary: Machinery, gifted with the wonderful power of shortening and fructifying human labour, we behold starving and overworking it; the newfangled sources of wealth, by some strange weird spell, are turned into sources of want; the victories of art seem bought by the loss of character (Marx and Engels 1969: 500).

Those remarks, delivered in 1856, reflected an objective reality. They were based on observations of how capitalist society was developing and how it had to develop. Those same objective realities still exist today. It is in the observation and the linking of these contradictions that historical materialism is granted its capacity to generate propositions, or 'predict' outcomes, with anything like a degree of accuracy.

Historical processes inform Marxist analysis. It considers, on the one hand, the sweep of history and on the other, the integral component parts that constitute society at any point in time. For some this is an indication of a degree of determinism with economics as base, relentlessly driving a social and political superstructure. However, as Tosh (2010: 226) argues, the reality is closer to a perspective that sees the economic structure setting limits rather than simply determining outcomes. As Engels stated:

> According to the materialist conception of history, the *ultimately* determining element in history is the production and reproduction of real life. Other than this neither Marx nor I have ever asserted. Hence if somebody twists this into saying that the economic element is the *only* determining one, he transforms that proposition into a meaningless, abstract, senseless phrase (1999 emphasis in the original).

This interaction with 'real life' is fundamental to appreciating Marxist analysis and particularly as it pertains to contemporary economic realities. To fully come to grips with this 'reality' is to explore the abstractions that are evident and to propose possible outcomes. The Marxist method shows that

> even the most abstract categories, despite their validity – precisely because of their abstractness – for all epochs, are nevertheless, in the specific character of this abstraction, themselves likewise a product of historic relations, and possess their full validity only for and within these relations (Marx 1974: 105).

To fully understand the world, one needs first to understand just how production and reproduction of material life is organised. This, in turn allows for an appreciation, not simply of capitalist production processes since its inception, but of its inevitable progression towards a globalised present and the crisis with which it is riven. Central to an understanding of the world is an appreciation that crisis in capitalism is inevitable. Capitalism, as Trotsky (1953: 61–62) observed, lives by crises and booms. He likened the cycle to the inward and outward breath of a human being. His remarks were made in the 1920s. They are still relevant although the period between crisis points or between 'breaths' is increasingly becoming shorter as the crisis deepens. That there exists a crisis in capitalism is no secret. Economists, scholars and analysts – Marxist and non-Marxist alike – concur. In late 2015 former US Treasury Secretary Summers wrote of "the specter of a global vicious cycle in which slow growth in industrial countries hurts emerging markets, thereby slowing Western growth further. Industrialized economies that are barely running above stall speed can ill afford a negative global shock" (Summers 2015). The International Monetary fund (IMF) (2016a) continued to downgrade its global growth forecast acknowledging that global growth could be derailed if key factors including China's economic downturn were not resolved. The crisis afflicting capitalism is increasingly deep.

The rapidity of capitalist globalisation, as a reaction to intensifying contradictions and an increasing inability to resolve these contradictions, has led many to question the future of capitalism and to re-examine Marxism. Rupert and Smith (2002: 1) ask whether historical materialism remains significant in the age of globalisation. They argue that a materialist perspective is needed to "analyse the sites of political and social struggle where transformative practices and processes can be observed" (Rupert and Smith 2002: 12). Such analysis is necessary to explain the inevitability of capitalist globalisation and of its trajectory. This has direct implications, both for a constrained working class in developed capitalist centres, and for a dramatically expanding global working class that capitalism, through globalisation, is creating. It is in such an observation that a theory and practice can be constructed for the 21st century.

Capitalism has been an expanding, globalising force for all of its history. The rapidity of capitalist globalisation in recent decades has been a conscious determination by capitalist ruling classes and states, to circumvent a growing crisis within capitalism. Understanding the causes and connectivity of issues leading to crisis becomes ever more significant, but confusion is often apparent, as expressed by influential *Financial Times* columnist Martin Wolf:

> It is impossible at such a turning point to know where we are going ... What will happen now depends on choices unmade and shocks unknown. Yet the combination of a financial collapse with a huge recession, if not something worse, will surely change the world. The legitimacy of the market will weaken. The credibility of the US will be damaged. The authority of China will rise. Globalisation itself may founder. This is a time of upheaval (2009).

Marxism has a proven capacity to comprehend and analyse capitalism and its inherent crises. Despite the intensity of its crises, however, capitalism remains unthreatened. The dissonance within Marxist thought has played a role in the persistence of capitalism.

Marxism has been mired in both disputation and accommodation to capitalist ideology. The litany of defeats and disappointments that Marxism faced have been shown to have stemmed from the ideological power that the capitalist state has been able to maintain and exert.

Marxism, however, is not only relevant but is necessary to an understanding of the world. The approach of Marx and Engels allows for a reasoned analysis of developments affecting both capitalism and Marxism in the 21st century. However, a fundamental question remains. This question, of whether Marxism can act as a catalyst for change is ultimately tied to capitalism's capacity to withstand challenge. Is capitalism inherently strong and resilient or has it withstood often momentous crises because there has been no consistent and substantive challenge?

4

THE DEVELOPMENT OF THE CAPITALIST STATE

Capitalism has faced moments of crisis and even existential threats. Wars and revolutions, economic depression, cold war politics, and the threat of impending ecological disaster have failed to dislodge capitalism from its position of dominance. Such a balance sheet has led many to believe that capitalism is innately resilient, that it is a system that will eternally endure. Capitalism, however, has been able to maintain its pre-eminent position for two interconnected reasons. First, the state exists to promote and advantage the broad interests of capitalism. Through its encompassing ideology it has promoted an artificial sense of unity between classes. Second, a viable theoretic and practical framework to counter capitalism's rule has been lacking. So long as it remains fragmented and divided, Marxism will continue to fall short of its emancipatory objective of replacing the capitalist mode of production.

We need to focus, for a moment, on how capitalism acquired the dominant position that it enjoys. This requires a consideration of the development of capitalism, its motivations, the inevitability of its expansion and subsequent tendency toward globalisation. This, in turn requires an examination of what appears to be a conundrum for Marxism. I argue that the 20th century presented capitalism with a series of extraordinary threats: revolution and global war, economic depression, the threat of nuclear conflagration, and potentially devastating ecological disaster. Any of these threats, alongside the 'day-to-day' contradictions of private ownership and socially-based production, ought to have proven calamitous for capitalism, and yet the economic system survived.

Two conflicting theories have long divided Marxist theory. These antagonistic perspectives are central to appreciating the case for classical Marxism. Capitalism, we must remember, exists under conditions of contradiction and crisis. These contending arguments, that capitalism is a self-regulatory system as advanced by Bernstein as opposed to the theory of capitalist breakdown, famously argued by Luxemburg will be explained. Following this brief analysis, I draw attention to capitalism's apparent 'resilience' in the face of crisis and observe that rather than being resilient, capitalism's survival has been assisted by a lack of substantial challenge. This argument is further developed and clarified when the issue of ideology as a mechanism of political, social and economic control is discussed. The working class, under such conditions, has become integrated into the state and its organisations effectively co-opted by the institutions of the state.

The underlying contradictions within capitalism have not been and cannot be resolved so long as capitalism exists. Consequently, it is necessary to draw attention to the interaction of these contradictions. In particular, the intensification of capitalist globalisation can be linked to irresolvable contradictions stemming, in part, from a tendency for profit rates to fall, which, in turn drives capitalist expansion.

Capitalism has benefited from a lack of organised and effective opposition. This is due, to a large extent, from dislocations, both theoretical and programmatic within Marxism as well as the force and strength of the state and its capacity to maintain a sense of ideological unity across classes. Capitalism survives, not from any innate superiority, but from a lack of viable opposition and an on-going crisis of leadership.

Constructing the capitalist paradigm

The rise of the modern state mirrors the development of capitalism. While assessments of the relative autonomy of the state vary, the salient point remains that the state advantages the interests of capitalism. At the same time contradictions between state and capital remain, with the most fundamental being the contradiction between the global nature of capitalist economics, and the political role that the nation-state system plays.

Marxism regards the state as a formation based in and on class rule. Marx and Engels (1977: 38) declared that the state becomes an executive committee for managing the bourgeoisie's affairs. Lenin's (1977a: 243–244) characterisation of the state as a coercive assemblage of armed men, while equally blunt, still sits, not altogether uncomfortably, alongside Engels' contention that this power "arisen out of society but placing itself above it, and increasingly alienating itself from it, is the state" (Engels 1986: 576). Engels (1986: 577–578) also argued that the state, as an historical institution, has acted to control society. In this context, the capitalist state, as the modern representative state, becomes instrumental in the process of exploitation of the working class by capital. From such an interpretation, it becomes clear that for Marxists the state has a specific purpose and form. As Trotsky (1974: 144) described it, the state is not simply an idea, but a material apparatus.

Lenin expanded on this idea of the state being a material apparatus intimately connected to capitalist growth:

> For the complete victory of commodity production, the bourgeoisie must capture the home market, and there must be politically united territories whose population speak a single language ... Therefore, the tendency of every national movement is towards the formation of *national states*, under which these requirements of modern capitalism are best satisfied. The most profound economic factors drive towards this goal, and, therefore, for the whole of Western Europe, nay, for the entire civilised world, the national state is typical and normal for the capitalist period (2000: 396 emphasis in the original).

This was written at a time when capitalism was expanding but still dwelt largely within national boundaries. The modern state has been shaped, and effectively formed, by historical and economic processes that have reflected the development and needs of capitalism. The material success of this arrangement has been profound.

The neo-classical political economist, Gilpin (2000: 3), describes capitalism as the most successful wealth-creating economic system the world has ever seen. He studies the challenges that capitalism faces in the 21st century, especially as it assumes an ever more encompassing global character. He calls for the United States to resume its leadership role within global capitalism (Gilpin 2000: 357). Central to this analysis is an elemental contradiction facing capitalism. It is the contradiction between the relentless tendency toward globalisation and of the necessity of maintaining a sense of hegemony within the nation-state system. What is assumed to be an underlying truth in Gilpin's analysis is that capitalism is the dominant economic, and by inference dominant political factor, and while challenges are inevitable, there is no alternative to capitalism.

Capitalism has certainly been an effective wealth-creating economic system, or rather a wealth extracting system. This has come at an increasing cost to those whose task it is to actually perform the labour that creates the wealth. As a socio-political structure it has also been instrumental in revolutionising interactions between cultures and states, while simultaneously developing clear delineations of class. Marx (1977: 38) characterised capitalism as a progressive formation. While such a characterisation can be defended, and particularly from an historical perspective, it is difficult to attach a progressive label to late capitalism. Dunn points out that Marx "saw capitalism as a complex and contradictory social system. It created enormous material advances, yet because it did so for private profit, it did not necessarily produce any general social improvements" (2009: 76). Dunn is echoing Marx's assessment of the process of capitalist development. "Accumulation of wealth at one pole is, therefore, at the same time accumulation of misery, agony of toil, slavery, ignorance, brutality, mental degradation, at the opposite pole" (Marx 1986b: 604).

Robinson (2004: 4–5) argues that the evolution of capitalism can be divided into four distinct periods. These are the post-feudal mercantilist era, the period of the industrial revolution (often described as the classical period of capitalism), the rise of monopoly capitalism, and the fourth (as yet in its infancy) being the transnational phase which sees the development of a transnational ruling class. While this final stage remains contested, the path that capitalism has travelled indicates both the success of this mode of production as well as its ultimate limitations.

Capitalism has, from the beginning, been enmeshed in irresolvable contradictions. These contradictions have at once promoted capitalism's forward motion while, over time, deepened the contradictions inherent in the system. Among these contradictions are: the private ownership of the means of production and the social nature of the production process; the drive to maximise profit by expanding the productive processes and surplus value, which necessitates limiting real wages growth; the imperative to increase labour productivity contributing to the tendency for profit rates to fall; and the drive to a globalised economy while relying on the nation-state system to administer capitalist relations. At the same time, and as a response to the expansionary nature of capitalism, its progressive role, as described by Marx in the 19th century, has dissipated. Its underlying motivation of survival has remained unchanged.

Capitalism's striving to overcome its internal contradictions has meant that it has remained expansionary and outward-looking. Marx wrote of the political economy in a setting of a growing capitalism that was still essentially national in character. Significantly, he saw that capital, if it was not only to survive but to grow, was compelled to break from the confines of this national boundary and expand into a global economy (Marx and Engels 1977: 39). Bina and Davis (2015: 196–197) argue that the labour process, on a global scale, has undergone a revolutionary overhaul. The motivation for this has been the drive to extract the highest possible degree of surplus value. Globalisation, in such a context, is a "phenomenon that is contingent upon reducing the value of labour power through revolutions in technology" (2015: 197). Such a motivation inevitably means that the purchaser of labour power strives to achieve the lowest possible price for that labour. The domination and subjugation of labour to capital becomes ever more intense.

Capitalism, over time, assumed a position of dominance. This was achieved with the assistance of a state structure that empowered capitalist relations and overlaid an ideological framework that made dissent increasingly difficult. Miller describes Marx's conception of the power of ideology within society, stating that "the economically dominant class requires the existence of false beliefs for its dominance and has resources for perpetuating beliefs that are in its interests" (1991: 74). An economic and political structure that is riven by divergent and antagonistic class interests cannot expect to survive by force alone. What Marx and Engels labelled 'false consciousness' has been remarkably successful. The 20th century, for capitalism, was both the best and worst of times. There were moments of crisis that were, in effect, existential moments for capitalism. The century ended, however, with capitalism still largely secure. The crises that capitalism experienced failed to result in the end of capitalism, not because of any inherent strength of capitalism but in large part because of two inter-related elements. One was the role of the capitalist state itself and the power of an encompassing ideology that saw class conflict minimised. The other was a conflicted and theoretically fragmented Marxist opposition. The inherent crisis and the contradictions that capitalism brought with it into the 20th century remained unresolved as the 21st century dawned.

Existential threats to capitalism and a troubled 20th century

Crisis, as both threat and motivating influence, remains central to capitalist development. The cycle of crisis and stabilisation assume what appears to be an almost 'natural' rhythm. At the same time, there have been exceptional moments, including some that denote deeper, potentially catastrophic threats; moments that appeared to presage a spiral from which capitalism ought not escape. It is capitalism's apparent tenacity, its seeming resilience in response to these extraordinary moments, that has led many to falsely conclude that capitalism is a natural order and that any alternative is fantasy. The extraordinary elements of crisis that occurred in the 20th century – world war, the Russian Revolution and subsequent revolutionary upheavals in Europe, the Great Depression, the threat emanating from the Cold War, and finally the real and very present danger of environmental disaster – have sorely tested capitalism. Each of these elements are linked and have their genesis in problems inherent within capitalism. A number of features can be observed that have aided and abetted capitalism's 'miraculous' survival. Among these are missed opportunities, a lack of leadership, the role that Stalinism played in the history of the 20th century, and in the ideological problems that became acutely evident within Marxism.

Much has been written about the causes and the inevitability, or otherwise, of World War I. A Marxist perspective ascribes an important role to the development of capitalism to the point that it could no longer be contained within national boundaries:

> The national state, the present political form, is too narrow for the exploitation of these productive forces. The natural tendency of our economic system, therefore, is to seek to break through the state boundaries. The whole globe, the land and the sea, the surface as well as the interior have become one economic workshop, the different parts of which are inseparably connected with each other (Trotsky 1973: 20)

It was unrealistic, given such a framework of capitalist expansion, to believe that war could be avoided. It provided, for capitalism, enormous challenges as well as risks that individual capitalist states felt worth taking. A pre-condition for a successful prosecution of this war rested on the ability of capitalist states to engender a sense of national unity. This was achieved with remarkable success. The war acted to not only sever any sense of unity between working-class movements in Europe but within Marxist theory itself.

Despite the split in Marxism that the war and the 'logic' of nationalism engendered, revolutions did break out. The success of the Russian Revolution was the next extraordinary moment that capitalism was to encounter. Marxist theory maintained that for socialism to defeat capitalism, revolutions must spread. Socialism in one country could never be a realistic option (Marx and Engels 1977: 56; Engels 1999; Trotsky 1970: 72–73). Revolutions erupted after 1917, with the declaration of the Munich Soviet Republic in 1918, the Hungarian Revolution in 1919, and the establishment of the Persian Socialist Republic in 1920. All were crushed and the continued existence of the Soviet state was endangered. The end of the war brought revolution, but also a unity among the combatant states, pledged as they were, to secure the *status quo* of capitalist rule. Marxist theory was quickly turned on its head with the coming to power of Stalin and his deeply anti-Marxist theory of 'socialism in one country'. By dint of state force and a weakened opposition, capitalism survived the spate of post-war revolutions.

It was a relatively short respite for capitalism. Little more than a decade after the 1917 revolution came the Great Depression. This was more than a cyclical moment in capitalism. Gamble (2009: 52) describes Marx's depiction of capitalist crisis and of how the economic system would inevitably lead to a systemic crisis because of its inherent instability. How those exceptional moments of crisis were to be resolved would depend on political actions and the responses of the class forces involved. Capitalism and state structures responded, albeit in a dislocated fashion. Even today it is common for economists to remain perplexed. The Bank for International Settlements' *Annual Report* (2007) admits that no one saw the Great Depression of the 1930s coming and nor did anyone predict the Asian Economic Crisis of the 1990s.

The seemingly inevitable slide into crisis that capitalism exhibited during those pre-war years again failed to bring about any fundamental change. A few years earlier there had been war and revolution. Capitalism was again displaying structural weakness and yet once more capitalism survived. Fascism emerged in Europe and war once more loomed. World War II, from a Marxist viewpoint, was a reflection of unresolved conflicts between individual capitalist states. The war, variously described as a struggle for democracy, or imperialist in character, resulted in a strengthening of capitalism on a global scale and with it the dawning of a 'golden age' of capitalism. Global war did not spell the end of capitalism, despite the continued and strengthened presence of the USSR. What the end of the war did herald, was the beginning of a war of ideology: the Cold War.

The US emerged from World War II as the indisputable capitalist hegemon. The Cold War was a response by US capitalism to a range of ideological dilemmas that it faced, both domestically and internationally. The Cold War was, in this sense, a pre-emptive rather than reactive response to impending crisis. Hardt and Negri (2000: 176) argue that the US, in response to rising class antagonisms, invoked a feeling of hostility toward communism to best suit its domestic agenda. Anti-communism became national policy and working-class movements in the US became targets of this policy. The Cold War's formative moments, however, were not in the aftermath of World War II, but in the period immediately following the Russian Revolution which the Western powers sought, by armed intervention, to crush. The post-World War II period saw the rise of anti-colonial nationalist movements that were seen as potential threats to capitalist equilibrium. Anti-communist rhetoric was effectively used as an ideological counter to such movements.

The USSR remained as a constant reminder to capitalism of the threat of what might be. The Cold War was used to discredit the USSR and, by implication, Marxism. The eventual collapse of the Soviet Union and the formal restoration of capitalist relations removed the USSR and its influence. A poorly judged and misplaced enthusiasm drove some (e.g. Fukuyama 1992) to declare that socio-economic formation had reached its zenith with capitalism and liberal democracy. The Cold War ended. The Soviet Union was dissolved but capitalist contradictions remain unresolved.

Soon a new crisis, of capitalism's creation, emerged. Capitalism and its inherent contradictions inevitably lead to crisis. Such a statement assumes greater significance when placed alongside the crisis of climate change and ecological destruction that potentially confronts the planet. Magdoff speaks of this "second fundamental form of contemporary crisis that is also derived from the relentless pursuit of profits – namely, the rapid growth of ecological degradation" (2002). How capitalism responds to such elemental problems becomes especially significant. Those who support the notion of capitalism's ability to resolve problems point to a range of possibilities, including a move towards 'ethical capitalism' (Lovins and Cohen 2011), to more circumspect analyses (Newell and Paterson 2010) that recognise the potential for economic dislocation while still considering that capitalism will survive. The current and unfolding environmental crisis is a fundamental one, for capitalism and for the entire planet. Whether capitalism can survive such a crisis remains to be seen. What is clear is that the contradictions of capitalism remain unresolved and that extraordinary moments of crisis remain.

Cycles of crisis

Marxists and supporters of the capitalist mode of production agree on few things. Despite this, there is a broad acceptance that capitalism tends toward crisis. Clarke (1994) describes optimistic attitudes among bourgeois economists who assert that the cycle of boom and crash has been relegated to an historical past. He then points out that when economic booms come to an end, the same economists isolate specific causes behind the slump. They stress the individualistic nature of each moment of crisis without dwelling on the fact that these crises have been recurring for centuries. Clarke also notes that:

> the Marxist theory of crisis is distinguished from bourgeois theories in the first instance in being concerned with the necessity of crisis, in order to establish that the permanent stabilization of capitalism and amelioration of the class struggle ... is impossible (1990: 442).

When moments of crisis emerge the state and its financial institutions intervene:

> Capitalist economies everywhere display a recurring pattern of oscillation. Periods of relatively limited state interventions in markets and private property repeatedly encounter crises that they manage more or less well. Eventually, however, a crisis arrives that exceeds their management capacities. Then, transition occurs to a period with relatively more state economic interventions ... Then a reverse transition generates a period of relatively less state economic intervention (Wolff 2010: 133).

Capital and state both interrelate and interact in order to survive the cycles of crisis and actively engage in the promotion of capitalist relations, nationally and globally. The cycles of capitalist economic life remain problematic for both national governments and capital. To have to adjust to economic downturns and to endure periodic recessions increases pressure on state and capital alike. Gamble describes the preferred position for capitalism and national governments as one which engenders optimism. He argues that prolonged periods of economic boom and stability, however, leads to a situation whereby "calculations of risk change. By degrees everyone comes to believe that the boom will last forever, and that, finally, the secret of everlasting growth has been discovered" (2009: 37). Gamble also notes that downturns can, in extreme situations, promote political as well as economic dislocation.

Marxist perspectives of capitalism coalesce around the issue of crisis and of its inevitability. At the same time, Marxist theory is divided on the concept of capitalist breakdown (Grossman 1992; Luxemburg 1963). Central to polemical disputes within Marxism conducted a century ago was the proposition that capitalism was able to provide remedies for its cyclical ills (Bernstein 1975). Luxemburg (1963) argued strongly against such a thesis. She maintained that any perceived 'success' of capitalism in alleviating its tendency toward crisis was simply a postponement of an eventual breakdown of capitalism. A century later capitalism remains intact, although the cycle of crisis and stabilisation is still evident. Patnaik (2016: 1) contends that the end of the 'golden age of capitalism' in the 1970s heralds a period of crisis for capitalism that is not merely a continuation of its previous history, but carries far more risk to the economic system than has previously been noted.

Crises, in Harvey's words, "are essential to the reproduction of capitalism" (2015: ix). MacPherson (1989: 25) asserts that crisis suggests the threat of imminent breakdown of either capitalism or democracy. While these two critiques are contradictory, they serve to reveal something of the nature of capitalism. Crisis at once propels capitalism forward while simultaneously exposing the system to existential dangers. The two arguments, especially in an age of intensifying globalisation, promote the view that capitalism has begun to enter a qualitatively new stage of development.

Murray (2012: 198–199) outlines the argument for qualitative change in capitalism. She describes processes of global circuits of accumulation that have transcended the reach of individual nation states. Similarly, Robinson (2010) argues that a global, transnational ruling class is forming. Such a formation is the inevitable result of capitalism's inability to resolve its internal contradictions.

These depictions of late capitalism are reflections on the rise of finance capitalism (Krippner 2011). The change in capitalism's trajectory that is evidenced by the intensification of globalisation and the shift in accumulation processes is similarly addressed by Veltmeyer (2013: 107–109). He acknowledges these changes and that capitalism is emerging into a new phase which will exacerbate the contradictions that remain unresolved. At the same time, he clings to the belief that a feature of capitalism is its essential resilience, and that this alleged resilient nature that capitalism enjoys will effectively safeguard its future.

Capitalism, as a globalising force, has exhibited all of the characteristics of crisis that are depicted in Marxist theory. This has particular implications for capitalism and for its future. The constituent elements of capitalist crisis, as noted above, include the tendency of the rate of profit to fall, the concentration of capital, the growth of the working class, a tendency toward under-consumption (or as some would argue, over-production) and the development and influence of finance capitalism. These elements have long existed. The periodic crises of capitalism, the booms and slumps that have accompanied capitalist development have come and gone and have been an integral part of capitalism for centuries.

Spector (2013: 21–22) argues that the movement to capitalist globalisation that became so obvious since the 1970s allowed for a short-term alleviation of some of the more pressing contradictions in capitalism. As capitalist relations are replicated in developing economies, the contradictions of capitalism begin to be played out on a global scale. The contradictions that Spector describes consequently become more intense. The frequency of critical moments for capitalism has increased. The periods of stabilisation have shortened. The Global Financial Crisis of 2008 exposed the limitations of economists and pro-capitalist theorists to advance a satisfactory explanation of the tendency to crisis. McNally cites Merrill Lynch's chief economist in Moscow who states that "our world is broken – and I don't know what is going to replace it" (2011: 14).

Capitalism has endured the 'normal' cycles of crisis and stability. It appears to have defied Marxist theory of breakdown and collapse. The extraordinary periods of upheaval have shaken the system but still it stands. For many this is a testimony to an intrinsic quality of resilience, adaptability and tenacity that capitalism embodies. Such was the optimistic characterisation offered by Keynes (1932) at the height of the Great Depression. For many, the possibility that capitalism might not prove to be eternal, is anathema. This is a position that Wolf (2009) encapsulates when he asserts that there is no credible alternative to the market. A polar divide exists between these appraisals and those of Marxism.

Capitalism – resilient or simply unchallenged?

Despite its disruptive history many still regard capitalism as the best imaginable system and largely accept it and portray it as an almost immutable force. Forbes and Ames (2009) are particularly forceful in their declarations that capitalism will not merely survive but will 'save us'. They assert that capitalism is a moral system, that it promotes democracy and democratic values, is creative and that its most remarkable achievement lies in its ability to turn scarcity into abundance. Kaletsky (2010) is another who confidently points to capitalism's capacity to reinvent and reinvigorate itself, especially by using the experience of crisis. Capitalism is also said to be successful because it is self-correcting (Easterly 2008: 129). It is worth remembering that in the period since the beginning of the Great Depression there have been 17 significant recessions and crises that have affected global capitalism. The International Monetary Fund (IMF) reports that from 1970 to 2011 there were 147 banking crises, 217 currency crises and 67 sovereign debt crises (Claessens and Kose 2013: 27). While there is an understandable degree of overlap in these figures, they seem to show that capitalism's self-correcting capacities have, at best, been largely ineffective.

Despite this, capitalism, according to its advocates, is marked by adaptation and resilience. They assert that capitalism continually finds new ways to adapt after each and every crisis that it has faced; and through individual ingenuity and sound corporate management has proven Marx to be wrong. Such is the reasoning of Emmott (2009), former editor of the *Economist*. Emmott's arguments are echoed by British economist, Ormerod who claims that "the distinguishing feature of capitalism is not its instability, but its resilience. Markets are not perfect, but unemployment is usually low. Crises happen, but the system bounces back" (2015). From such confident proclamations, capitalism would appear to have triumphed and for all time. What unconsciously emerges from such analyses is that capitalism is a mysterious entity with an independent existence, in much the same way that the 'market' assumes a special aura of inviolability and independence. Capitalism, however, does not operate in an economic or political vacuum. Increasingly the state has acted to both promote capital's interests and to stabilise capitalism in moments of crisis. As Braudel remarks, "capitalism only triumphs when it becomes identified with the state, when it is the state" (1977: 64). The 'resilience' of capitalism is very much connected with the state and its interventions.

Held (2008: 111) paraphrases Marx when he states that capitalism's success has depended on the rapid growth of the productive forces of society. While this initially represented capitalism's progressive character, it was contradicted by the exploitative system of productive relations. Herein lies the contradiction that Marx maintained would ultimately bring capitalism to the point of destruction. Advocates of capitalist relations, as well as some Marxists, point to what is regarded as the obvious fact that history has yet to prove Marx correct. Using Australia as a case study, Hillier (2010: 74) describes state interventions that acted to stabilise the economy in the face of the GFC. He also points to the globalised nature of capitalist relations that enabled Australian capitalism to maintain equilibrium through its reliance on the strength of Asian markets. In the immediate aftermath of the crisis, Australian capitalism and the state appeared to be faring well. Resilience again appeared to be the *motif* for capitalism.

The necessity of state structures to provide stability for capitalism becomes yet another focus of contradiction. Wood (2002: 31–32) argued that capitalism, which is naturally anarchic, must inevitably rely on political organisations. At times, these appear as regulatory organisations to safeguard capitalism or in the form of interventionist bodies whose task it is to stabilise capitalist processes. The state, "no matter what its form, is essentially a capitalist machine, the state of the capitalists" (Engels 1966: 63). The role of the state as intermediary for capitalism is especially important. State intervention coincided with the post-World War II era of prosperity, but the crisis of the 1970s demanded a dismantling of such interventionist policies.

Much has been made of capitalism's recovery from the GFC. Patnaik (2016: 1–2) outlines how the media has played a pivotal role in promoting the idea of rapid recovery. The WTO (2016), and the IMF (2016b) however, both report that world trade grew at less than 3 per cent for five consecutive years. This was shown to be the slowest rate since the 1980s, indicating that rather than recovering from the GFC, the global economy is effectively in a period of stagnation. A feature of the current stage of capitalist crisis is the rise in inequality that can be observed, less obviously between states or regions, but rather, between classes (Patnaik 2016: 10–11). Again, the paradoxical nature of capitalist–state relations becomes apparent. The contradiction of a globalised, borderless capitalist economy and a system of nation-states is evident. The state, however, still plays a significant role in the ability of capitalism to successfully function and in maintaining a degree of stability.

Capitalism maintains its dominance, despite a growing tendency toward crisis and inherent instability. The state certainly plays a substantial role in this. The contradiction between the private nature of capitalism and the social nature of the production process remains. There is also a constant need for capitalism to acquire greater returns on its investments as a counter to a tendency for the rate of profit to fall. The irreconcilable contradictions of capitalism would indicate that the system itself must proceed to a point of breakdown as portrayed in Marxist theory. What Marxists refer to as the 'objective conditions' for such a breakdown already exist. What is more difficult to assemble are the 'subjective conditions'. The state and its agencies play a crucial role in maintaining a situation whereby these subjective factors either fail to materialise or remain in a weakened form. Capitalism maintains its dominance, not through any inherent strengths it might possess. On the contrary capitalism and its tendency toward crisis displays weakness. It is in the lack of effective challenge that capitalism has managed to survive.

The question of why such a challenge has not developed in the face of on-going and intensifying capitalist crisis remains. The economic base upon which capitalist society rests is framed by class antagonisms and yet the working class and its allies have remained largely acquiescent. The answer can be found in the manner in which the state has acted, over time, to ameliorate and diffuse overt expressions of class antagonisms. The state, it must be stressed, operates for and in the interests of the ruling class. It is, as Engels pointed out when commenting on apparent ruling class accommodation to the needs of the working class, for an objective reason. "The fact that all these concessions to justice and philanthropy were nothing else but means to accelerate the concentration of capital into the hands of the few" (Engels 1984: 27). This, in turn, directly relates to the degree that organisations which have traditionally represented the working class, in both a political as well as an economic sense, have become incorporated into the structures of the state. For a class-based society to function in relative harmony, there must be a degree of acceptance that the *status quo* represents the best interests of all. Force and overt coercion cannot be a permanent, or overt feature of society. At the same time, the ruling class is permanently engaged in struggle, which in turn invites a reaction (Burnham

2002: 116–117). The tendency toward 'struggle' is less explosive, however, if the capacity for class consciousness is dimmed. "For a class to be ripe for hegemony means that its interests and consciousness enable it to organise the whole of society in accordance with those interests" (Lukacs 1976: 52). While Lukacs was commenting on the potential for the working class to actively promote its own interests, it is an apt description of how the ruling class has managed class relations.

The use of ideology to maintain social stability

The class nature of society and the crucial role that the state plays in this class-based society is widely acknowledged. Capitalism and the state enjoy a mutually advantageous relationship. There is also a close connection between class society with ideology being used to foster a semblance of harmony within society. Marx and Engels (1964: 78–79) argued that once the bourgeoisie assumed the ascendancy, it became imperative for the state to preserve the existing balance and state of affairs, by force, if necessary. At the same time, the link between the bourgeoisie and state is "more internal and essential than the contingent use of control ... the state, as such, is intrinsically a bourgeois form of social relationship" (Sayer 1985: 241). This relationship has advantaged capitalism while limiting the use of force to maintain that *status quo*.

Capitalist society is framed by class relations and class interests that are ultimately opposed to one another. In order to preserve a sense of harmony and accord, the state must therefore limit any obvious manifestations of class antagonism. The use of ideology as a means of legitimising the economic structures upon which society rests assumes on-going importance. This task is made easier if the views of the working class can be aligned, or be made to appear to be aligned with those of the ruling class. An effective integration of the working class and of its organisations occurs. This integration into the structure of the state, serves to both reduce overt expressions of class antagonism and to promote capitalist development. As capitalism globalises, the role of securing the acquiescence of the working class acquires an even greater significance. Workers are less able, under such conditions, to develop an independent political perspective. As capitalism developed, the tendency toward limitation of class struggle became ever more pronounced (Moore Jr 1978: 472–475). This is a theme that is revisited by Selwyn (2013: 50) who regards the integration of labour into the capitalist state as a two-fold process, with labour's role and power being diminished due to the very real threat and prospect of the dispersal of production. In this sense, he is referring to the globalisation of capitalist relations. It is a process that has long been in evidence.

In Marxist theory, ideology is essentially an expression of the worldview of the dominant class in society. Eagleton offers a definition of ideology as "processes whereby interests of a certain kind become masked, rationalized, naturalized, universalized, legitimized in the name of certain forms of political power" (Eagleton 1991: 202). While the term is closely associated with the ideas of the ruling group in society, it also describes the views of specific groups or classes pursuing political perspectives quite opposed to those of the ruling class. Eagleton (1991: 44) observes that the terms 'class consciousness' and 'socialist ideology' become synonymous in describing anti-capitalist theory and practice. However, there is an intrinsic link, in such a construction, between the notion of ideology as the legitimisation of political power and the diminution of class consciousness. Marx described how the development of capitalism acted to promote such a state of affairs:

> The advance of capitalist production develops a working-class, which by education, tradition, habit, looks upon the conditions of that mode of production as self-evident laws of Nature. The organisation of the capitalist process of production, once fully developed, breaks down all resistance (1986b: 689).

Lebowitz (2004: 21–23) describes how capitalism maintains its position of ideological power by masking the exploitative nature of the economic system itself. The idea of labour power and the extraction of surplus value are never explicitly divulged. Capitalism, therefore, is not visibly exploitative which leads to a degree of 'mystification' of capital itself. Society, according to Lebowitz's argument, does not appear to depend on capital but rather gives the impression of autonomy. Workers are not simply dependent on capital, but on particular sections of capital. As these sections are often in competition with each other then so too are individual groups of workers in competition with other workers. This serves to intensify an already dependent relationship on capital which, in turn, reduces still further the potential for the development of class-consciousness.

This situation, whereby class antagonisms are masked, has been labelled false consciousness (Engels 2000) and cultural hegemony (Gramsci 1971: 257–264). Ramos Jr., describes the essence of Gramsci's perspective:

> In a given hegemonic system, therefore, a hegemonic class holds state power through its economic supremacy and through its ability to have, among other things, successfully articulated or expressed in a coherent, unified fashion the most essential elements in the ideological discourses of the subordinate classes in civil society (1982).

In other words, state power is maintained by a combination of economic power and control of the broad machinery of state: the institutions of control. The effectiveness of state control and of its ability to evoke a feeling, not merely of acceptance, but of willing acceptance on the part of the working class has been extraordinarily successful.

Capitalism's ability to limit overt expressions of class antagonism have been enhanced by its success in integrating the organisations of the working class into the organisations of the state. This integration has long been a reality (see for instance Enderwick 2006; Leisink 1999; Stevis and Boswell 2008). Trade unions became legitimate and, in a similar way, political expressions of working-class ideology became an accepted and acceptable component of the life of the capitalist state. Social-democratic and Stalinist parties became legitimised within the capitalist nation-state – legitimised, increasingly integrated into that state structure and actively promoting the values and mores of the state, even if this meant acting against the interests of the class they were formed to represent.

A consequence of this integration has been a diminution of working-class independence. This state of affairs – the inability of the 'legitimate' organisations of the working class to act independently – is by no means a recent development in state and class relations. "Capitalism is less and less willing to reconcile itself to the independence of trade unions. It demands of the reformist bureaucracy ... that they become transformed into its political police before the eyes of the working class" (Trotsky 1972: 11). Such a formulation accords with the observations of Mann where he argues that "to the extent that trade unions pursue economic and job control issues separately and the latter defensively, and to the extent that they do not pursue wider issues of work control, they operate to weaken workers' class consciousness" (1973: 25). While the experience of trade union organisations is a primary manifestation of integration and incorporation of working-class organisations into the structures of the state, political organisations are similarly integrated.

The capitalist state has managed, through careful and calculated use of the ideological armoury at its disposal, to maintain a semblance of harmony and class unity. It has been an objective necessity for the stability of an inherently unstable mechanism to function. Such a situation poses enormous difficulties for those seeking an independent movement for emancipation. Smith (2014: 322–323) describes the crisis of leadership that exists and how the degree of working-class consciousness remains entrenched within a framework of reformist and state-sponsored mechanisms. At the same time, the contradictions that plague capitalist development remain unresolved.

The inability to resolve inherent contradictions

Marx, while acknowledging the role of capitalism in revolutionising production, also identified what are ultimately irresolvable contradictions. These contradictions begin with the fundamental issue of contradiction between the forces of production remaining in private hands and the social relations of productive forces.

Flowing directly from such a proposition is Marx's assessment of capitalism's tendency toward overproduction. Marx argued that "capital contains a *particular* restriction of production – which contradicts its general tendency to drive beyond every barrier to production – in order to have uncovered the foundation of *overproduction*, the fundamental contradiction of developed capital" (1974: 415, emphasis in the original). The contradiction is in capital's requirement to produce more, thereby extracting a greater degree of surplus value, while actively seeking to limit wage outcomes which inevitably suppresses potential consumption (Lebowitz 2008: 148–149). This, in turn, fuels the source of contradictions and crisis points for capitalist relations in the form of the potential and tendency for profit rates to fall.

Any acknowledgement of irresolvable contradictions that exist within capitalism inevitably involves an appreciation of Marx's theory of the tendency of the rate of profit to fall. Marx was by no means the first to consider this tendency. Both Smith and Ricardo had written extensively on the question. Marx's proposition was that capitalists seek to increase competitiveness by increasing productivity. The means of production – machinery etc. – grows more rapidly than the labour force and so profitability rises. However, the degree of investment required to meet the cost of the added means of production also grows. Profit, Marx argued (1986c: 211–231), derives from the accumulation of surplus value which can only come from labour. If less labour is used as a means of reducing costs, then there is a downward pressure on profit. Capitalists must seek to redress the problem of falling profits through a range of measures: intensifying the degree of exploitation of workers through longer hours, reducing wages and increasing the use of technology. A limited reprieve is possible before the cycle repeats. Central to Marx's argument is the idea that the rate of profit will fall if the rate of surplus value rises in an inverse ratio to the growth in the organic composition of capital. The organic composition of capital in this sense is the ratio of expenditure on materials associated with production or 'constant' capital to wages or 'variable' capital.

While Marx wrote about the tendency for the rate of profit to fall, he did not state that it would be a seamless process. Among the influences that Marx identified as acting against the tendency for profits to fall, is in the area described by Marx as 'foreign trade' and which assumes even greater significance when capitalist globalisation is considered. Capitalism is compelled, both in its search for markets and in its struggle against the potential for a fall in profits, to globalise. Jellissen and Gottheil (2009) argue that it is the tendency for the rate of profit to fall that has acted as a trigger mechanism for globalisation. Their argument is that innovative capitalists, in seeking to eliminate the possibly negative consequences of a fall in profits, have little alternative but to globalise. Embedded in this strategy, of realising greater profits while simultaneously developing an industrial base, lies another important contradiction – on the one hand destroying the economic and social bases of the less developed states whilst, on the other hand, replicating the economic bases of the more developed. They share, with Marx, the perspective that this is ultimately a positive outcome and, for Marx, an inevitable one. "The country that is more developed industrially only shows, to the less developed, the image of its own future" (Marx 1986b: 19).

Globalisation leaves capitalism with a final irresolvable contradiction. For capitalism to maintain a sense of stability and continuity it is compelled to expand. At the same time, the nation-state remains the basis for political organisation. While capitalism has by nature always been a globalising force, the economic crisis of the 1970s denoted a dramatic change in these processes, with capitalist relations assuming an increasingly rapid globalising character which has widened and exposed the contradiction between an increasingly borderless economic system and political institutions still limited by geography. Capitalism's quest to maintain profitability in the face of crisis and the ever-present spectre of a falling rate of profit necessarily results in casualties.

For decades, labour's share of income has lost ground to capital (ILO 2008). Inequality is also growing steadily with wealth differentials between rich and poor at their highest in more than 30 years. (OECD 2014). In 2015 as many as 75 per cent of all workers across the globe fell into the informal category – as temporary or short-term employees (ILO 2015). Capitalism has reached across the world and there is widespread discontent with globalisation.

The contradictions of capitalism are interwoven with each posing a growing threat to capitalism's very survival and yet the political and economic structures remain unchallenged. The successful use of ideological weapons has promoted a sense of unity between people and classes where there is none, and that this has been pivotal for the maintenance of a sense of stability within capitalism. The future of capitalism and of its trajectory is significant. Capitalism's tendency toward crisis, and the inevitability of capitalist globalisation as an attempt to remediate that tendency, indicates a qualitative change in capitalist relations. Marxism must, of necessity, address this change in capitalist relations.

5

A QUALITATIVE CHANGE IN CAPITALISM AND ITS IMPLICATIONS

The motivation for capitalist development has not changed. Its function and 'nature' remain constant. Capitalism, it must be remembered, is in no sense a universal, immutable social or economic system, but is a stage in the historical evolution of society and economic relations. Consequently, capitalism is in a continual state of motion. Capitalism, in seeking to overcome its inherent and intensifying contradictions, and faced with the threat of economic breakdown, rapidly globalised. The 21st century has seen the contradiction between globalised capitalism and national governments sharpen in intensity. These developments are indications that capitalism has entered a qualitatively new stage in its history.

I shall validate this claim through four inter-related steps. We first need to focus on the intensification of crisis as a motivating factor behind globalisation. This tendency toward crisis has become more visible and more intense and is evidenced by the dramatic increase in the power of finance capital (the financialisation of capitalism), the changes in the productive use of capital, and the growing integration of the global economy.

Second, it is important to explain how we might measure such qualitative change in capitalism. The quantifiable growth of Foreign Direct Investments (FDI), whereby greater economic activity is transacted between Transnational Corporations (TNCs) and less between states, the observable integration of global capitalist relations between TNCs, and the speed by which capital flows are recorded, are all indicators that qualitative changes are evident. The theory of qualitative change may at first appear to be contradicted by the continued strength of the nation-state and of a return to policies of economic nationalism that are increasingly evident in the developed capitalist economies. However, it must not be overlooked that the dialectical interaction between an increasingly transnational capitalism and the nation-state structure remains the most fundamental contradiction facing capitalism, Marxism, and the working class in the 21st century. An institutional framework remains fundamentally important for the continued existence of capitalism. Capitalist states play two distinct roles – as administrators and innovators. It is as administrator that capitalist nation-states have a significant role as capitalism seeks to adjust and adapt to the contradictions that impel change.

The third step in understanding the qualitative changes under way, is to explore the implications of capitalist globalisation for the nation-state. While it is clear that the role of the nation-state has been challenged, it continues to inhabit a powerful place, both in economic and political terms and in its capacity to maintain a false sense of 'national unity' among the working class. If capitalism has entered a qualitatively new stage, reactions and responses from those most affected will reflect these changes. Capitalist globalisation has intensified social inequality and social discontent. Historically, capitalism has developed against just such a backdrop. The intensification of these phenomena, and the response by individual states, are further indications of change. Reactions to globalisation and an increased sense of discontent are being increasingly expressed through both left- and right-wing populism. States, as 'administrators' and as 'innovators' have sought to contain and channel this discontent.

The fourth and intensely important step is to explore the implications of capitalist globalisation for the working class. The rise in nationalist sentiment and the return of economic nationalism reflects the unresolved contradictions between globalisation and the nation-state. There are implicit dangers posed by a resurgence of nationalism, both to capitalism and to the working class. These contradictions are evident in the co-existence of global capitalism and nation-state structures.

Diagnosing the qualitative change in capitalism is, however, not enough. We need also to explore possible means of finally resolving the crisis in capitalism and, in so doing, overcome capitalism's rule. Neither capitalist free trade nor protectionism can provide answers to the problems facing the working class. What is lacking is an independent leadership. The most pressing contradiction of capitalism is between a globalising economy and a continued reliance on a strong nation-state system. This has manifested itself in a rise in nationalism, with the working class remaining locked into a nationalist perspective. This further limits its capacity to act independently and as a global force to combat capitalism.

The motivations behind capitalist globalisation

In its simplest telling, capitalism's driving force is its need to expand. To do otherwise is to court disaster. Marx and Engels (1977: 39) famously observed that for capital, not simply to survive, but to thrive, it was compelled to expand beyond the borders of the nation-state. They further noted that:

> the bourgeoisie has through its exploitation of the world market given a cosmopolitan character to production and consumption in every country. To the great chagrin of Reactionists, it has drawn from under the feet of industry the national ground on which it stood (1977: 39).

Trotsky similarly described the growing tendency toward globalisation in terms of "the future development of world economy on the capitalistic basis means a ceaseless struggle for new and ever new fields of capitalist exploitation" (1973: 22–23).

Marx (1974: 539) also described how capital must not only eliminate spatial boundaries in order to develop a world market, but that it also must seek to reduce time as a factor in this development, thereby promoting the most expansive market possible. The underlying motivation for this development of capitalism to become an increasingly global phenomenon is the expansion of capital accumulation, the quest for profit and the ever-growing need to at least maintain the level of profit. The dynamism of such economic development across the globe has both positive and negative implications, at once polarising wealth and poverty, while still allowing for capital accumulation and the development of abundance (Dunn 2009: 158).

A key factor in the drive to globalisation lies in a fundamental argument of Marx; described as the law of the falling rate of profit (1986c: 211–231). Among a range of options that capital can employ to remove such an obstacle, or at least to postpone and forestall the worst outcomes, is to continually expand and to internationalise its relations. This means, in effect, a continual motion and an endless battle to survive. This inherent contradiction between the need to expand and the tendency for falling rates of profit has been and remains central to globalisation.

Two related propositions of Marx, pertaining to the development of capitalist globalisation, are worthy of note. The first is that merchant capital is inherently destructive to colonial economies while industrial capital constructs new economies (Marx 1969b: 107). The second, that capitalism as an inevitably expansionary process, must destroy older, pre-existing economic systems in order to create new ones (Marx and Engels 1975b: 200–201). These arguments eloquently describe the effects of colonialism and imperialism in the 19th and early 20th centuries. Marxism was clear in its assessment that imperialism served to promote the spread of capitalism into non-capitalist areas of the world. Imperialism, in this historical context, can be regarded as a step towards industrialisation and therefore the proletarianisation of the world. It was an inevitable feature of an expanding capitalism that is at once both destructive as well as progressive.

Such arguments, under conditions of 21st-century capitalist globalisation, unsurprisingly become areas for dispute. Petras and Veltmeyer (2000) argue that globalisation is far from a progressive factor of economic reality, as it extends global power to imperialist states and subjugates less developed economies. In contrast, Silver (2006: 3–23) describes the situation whereby global capital flows serve to actively build new industrial working-class movements, as capitalism constructs new industrial bases across the world. Understanding the processes of capitalist globalisation and the motivations for such a rapid rate of development in recent decades is intimately connected to both Marx's description of the unfolding of global capitalism and of imperialism as a means for that development.

Rosenberg (1996) outlines the general thrust of capitalist development as anticipated by Marx and Engels, whereby all societies would ultimately conform to the model of the then existing capitalist states. He then argues that the reality has proven to be somewhat different. He cites Trotsky (1965: 23–24) and his arguments surrounding the historical unevenness within social development among nations and that capitalism develops from very different starting points. Late developing capitalist states need not necessarily follow the same path of capital accumulation of their more advanced counterparts. The theory of uneven development has been used to explain how newly developing capitalist states exhibit 'different' forms of capitalism. However, it needs to be remembered, that the rapidity of capitalist globalisation, even when operating under conditions of uneven development, essentially conform to Marx's conception of capitalism "creating a world in its own image" (Marx 1977: 71). Lenin (1977e: 678–679) commented on the inevitably uneven rate of development of capitalism across the world but that the export of capital "influences and greatly accelerates the development of capitalism in those countries to which it is exported" (1977e: 681). Capitalism it is argued:

> aims at economic expansion, at the penetration of new territories, the surmounting of economic differences, the conversion of self-sufficient provincial and national economies into a system

> of financial interrelationships. Thereby it brings about their rapprochement and equalizes the economic and cultural levels of the most progressive and the most backward countries (Trotsky 1970: 19).

Capital flows, as described by Silver (2006), are elements of a constant drive to maintain a high degree of profitability. The period since the economic crisis years of the 1970s is undoubtedly a period marked by stagnating profits, and a general decrease in wages across states. Smith (2006: 10) describes the dynamic of globalising capitalism, of the quest not simply for power but of the necessity to seek to maintain profitability as a means of survival. The very *raison d'etre* of capitalism as an economic formation is to expand.

The rapid expansion of capitalist globalisation from the 1970s was accompanied by a dramatic shift in manufacturing from industrialised countries to the developing world. Western capitalism sought to ameliorate the growing crisis that had been presented by rapid economic downturn and a reduction in profit levels. Berberoglu (2003: 97) describes how US capital reacted to the crisis it was facing by transferring production overseas but that this had the obvious effect of producing mass unemployment along with a general reduction in wages. Martin and Schumann (1997: 7) similarly show how wages in the industrial world have tended to fall. Capitalism, in its quest to maintain its growth-centred sense of equilibrium, inevitably creates 'winners' and 'losers'.

As globalisation of the economic and political structures has quickened, so too has the role of the developing global institutions been scrutinised. The neo-liberal economic agenda has been facilitated, in the estimation of many writers, by the increased power of the International Monetary Fund (IMF), the World Bank and significantly with the inception of the World Trade Organization (WTO). Chossudovsky (1998: 35) regards the WTO's role as effectively supervising national trade policies in the interests of the transnational corporations. An even more strident accusation is that the WTO is "the archetypal transnational institution of the new epoch" (Robinson 2004: 117).

The continuing globalisation of capital and the political ramifications that this represents has long been a feature of capitalist relations. Robinson (1998: 567) draws the conclusion that the development of an interstate capitalist system was an historical inevitability and that those relations are being superseded by a globalisation of capitalism. The changes in capitalist relations that are evident are revolutionary in character. It is in the financialisation of capital that changes in capitalism are best observed. Peet (2009: 245) describes the fundamental logic of financialisation, as capital operating with a greater degree of abstraction from its original productive base. Capital has increasingly been removed from production as well as from any confining link to the national state. This continuing separation of capitalism from the restrictions of state structures is but one indication of elemental changes in capitalist relations. These relational changes are inescapable for capitalism as it seeks to overcome the inherent contradictions and tendency toward crisis.

Measuring qualitative change in capitalism

Capitalism is changing and has changed. Wood (1997) argued that capitalism has 'universalised' through its incessant drive to globalisation. She viewed this as a sign of inherent weakness in capitalism as well as a contradictory process that destroys even as it builds and that as capitalism has enveloped the world, it has universalised social polarisation and exploitation. She then immediately contradicted such an analysis by arguing that the working class can only effectively combat this by activism that remained based within a national framework. Whether capitalism is essentially the same as it ever was, or that it has undergone a qualitative change, or that the changes are simply part of an evolutionary process within capitalist development, needs to be regarded in relation to the question of the implications for the working class and its allies.

Arguments for or against capitalist change are inevitably connected to perceptions of capitalist globalisation. Capitalism has always had a globalising character. In this sense, capitalist globalisation can be regarded as 'evolutionary' and an inescapable part of capitalist development. To speak of capitalism undergoing a qualitative change, however, is by no means, contradictory. The processes by which capitalist globalisation occurred certainly brought about the conditions by which such a qualitative change can be observed.

Liodakis (2010) proposes four criteria to 'prove' that qualitative changes are occurring. These include technological developments that have had intense significance, a radical restructuring of capitalism as a means of limiting or reducing the fall in profits and the internationalisation and financialisation of capital. Liodakis' fourth criterion links the preceding ones:

> On the one hand, rising concentrations of economic and political power, the exacerbating crisis and the deadlocks facing contemporary capitalism imply authoritarian ... political and social practices. On the other hand, the requirements of transnational capitalism ... have led to a radical differentiation and indeed internationalization of states (2010: 25–26).

While there is broad acknowledgement of change in capitalism, the idea that capitalism has, in any real sense entered a qualitatively new stage is less well regarded. Wood (1998) noted that capitalism has been compelled to employ a new form of imperialism that becomes evident through financial control, and the manipulation of markets and debt while still maintaining that this in no way indicates any qualitative change in capitalism.

Robinson and Harris (2000), argue that such qualitative changes are already well established. They regard these changes as heralding the arrival of a new global capitalist class. Murray characterises this 'new' capitalism in terms of "the rise of transnationalised capital, the hegemony of a transnational capitalist class, the emergence of a transnational apparatus, and the appearance of new forms of power inequality" (2012: 199). Wood (1998) acknowledged that dramatic changes have occurred in capitalism but argued that these changes are simply part of the process of capitalist development that began with the birth of capitalism.

Capitalist development is an on-going process. Its development has, in large part been a response to the contradictions that imperil its very survival. For Wood, the processes under way are simply 'continuities' between Marx's world and our own. Capitalism exists by the constant "revolutionising of production, uninterrupted disturbances of all social conditions, everlasting uncertainty and agitation … All fixed, fast-frozen relations … are swept away, all new-formed ones become antiquated before they can ossify. All that is solid melts into air" (Marx and Engels 1977: 39). Ultimately these observations are not tied to an 'epoch' of capitalism but are descriptors of capitalism itself. Wood (1997) maintained that globalisation opens up new possibilities for socialist politics but as is so often the case retreated into an argument that stressed that such possibilities remained firmly based within a national perspective. It is an argument that reverberates across much of the literature of contemporary Marxism. It is a limiting and ultimately defeatist position that argues for a national solution to what is a global problem. The reality is that the dislocation and atomisation of the working class and the integration of its organisations into state structures are all elements of an intensification of capitalist crisis and of the contradictions between globalised capitalism and its relationship with the nation-state.

Robinson asserts that we are entering a new 'epoch' in the development of capitalism. What needs to be remembered is that capitalism is first and foremost an economic structure and that the nation-state, as political 'administrator', acts to serve the interests of capital. For Robinson, the nation-state has effectively been displaced by a globalised ruling class. Objective reality would suggest that the nation-state maintains an intensely important place in the administration of capitalism and that capitalism exists both in transnational as well as national forms. It remains an important instrument for the maintenance of a sense of social and class harmony. This assumes greater relevance when factors reflecting the changes in capitalism are considered and, in particular, the financialisation of capitalism.

Foster (2007: 1–7) readily acknowledges that the financialisation of capitalism has changed capitalist relations. He also stresses that monopoly-finance capital is a fundamentally different phenomenon from that which Hilferding and others described in the early 20th-century as the age of 'finance capital' (2007: 7). But at the same time Foster argues that this does not indicate a 'new' stage of capitalism.

Hilferding's (1981) exposition of finance capital did offer a valuable insight into how globalisation was to play out. He showed how profit was increasingly being derived, less from manufacture, and more from investment and trade in currencies. Brewer (2011: 51), writing a century after Hilferding's 1910 work on finance capital, speaks of an increasing tendency within global capitalism toward capital accumulation. This is achieved through a growth of finance capital at the expense of industrial capital. One ramification of this has been the rise in inequality, and particularly as capital accumulation has become concentrated into fewer and fewer hands.

> Over the last thirty years, capital has abstracted upwards, from production to finance; its sphere of operations has expanded outwards, to every nook and cranny of the globe; the speed of its movement has increased, to milliseconds; and its control has extended to include 'everything.' We now live in the era of global finance capitalism (Peet 2011: 18).

It is a tendency that late 19th- and early 20th-century Marxist writers had foreshadowed. The Bank for International Settlements (2016) reported that in 2013, on an average day, currency to the value of $5.3 trillion changed hands. A significant global integration of capitalism has been taking place.

This integration of global capitalism is further highlighted when considered in relation to growth of FDI. Economic activity had traditionally been conducted between individual states representing national forms of capitalism, but increasingly this is taking place between transnational corporations. FDI outflows have become the effective means for financing industrial production outside the industrialised states. Brooks and Hill (2003) provide figures showing the growth of FDI outflows from $53.7

billion in 1980 to $1.2 trillion in 2000. They also state that FDI grew at a rate of 500 per cent in the decade from 1990 to 2000, whereas total global trade grew at less than 200 per cent. While the Global Financial Crisis resulted in a contraction in the rates of growth, the general tendency remains unchanged. It is in the context of these dramatic changes that the argument for a qualitative change in capitalism is strengthened.

Traditionally capitalist relations were framed by three interconnected uses of capital. Money capital is employed as a base for production or productive capital, which in turn is transferred into commodity capital in a continuously repeating cycle. Productive capital, even while capitalism was internationalising, remained based within the confines of a bordered state. This has changed and with it the mobility of labour has been forced to change.

Marx, in Volume II of *Capital* (1986d), described capital in its three forms – money capital, productive capital and commodity capital. He portrayed these forms as 'circuits' of capital. These forms are dependent upon one another and operate as a cycle. Money capital creates the foundation upon which productive capital can be developed. In short, goods are produced. These goods are translated into commodity capital. This, in turn, produces an increase in money capital. The centuries-old process of capitalist globalisation has seen this cycle replicated, at first on a national and increasingly on a global scale. What is significant is that even as capitalist relations were internationalising, productive capital remained essentially bound by national borders. The expanding world market saw raw materials acquired globally, and commodities exported globally. Productive capital, however, remained based in individual nation-states. Profit, as understood within a Marxist framework, is derived from surplus value. If productive capital remained localised, then labour was similarly localised. It was intrinsically connected with the process of the 'sale' of labour power (1986b: Chapter 25) Immigration and the portability of labour became a more obvious factor as capitalism became a more internationalised system. Workers tended to migrate to where productive capital resided. The reverse can now be observed as productive capital moves to wherever it may derive the greatest financial benefit.

Economics operates as an engine for political movement. The changes that are apparent in capitalism validate the base/superstructure argument of Marxist theory. These changes have had dramatic consequences for states, and for the working class in those states. Studies of OECD states show the ramifications that intensified globalisation has had on the manufacturing base of developed capitalist economies. The period since 1990 has seen manufacturing industries in developed capitalist states continue to shrink. Bernard (2009) focuses on job losses in manufacturing in selected OECD countries with jobs in the UK being reduced by 29 per cent, the USA 25 per cent, Japan, 24 per cent, Sweden, 20 per cent and France, 14 per cent. These figures underwrite Silver's (2006) analysis that the quest for profitability, and the consequent flow of capital, builds working-class movements in developing states. Pilat et al. (2006), in describing the changing nature of manufacturing in OECD economies, notes that manufacturing has become more clearly integrated at the global level. Capitalism's relentless globalisation and the dislocation that accompanies it is intrinsically linked to its striving to maintain profitability in the face of constant threats of falling rates of profit. Empirical evidence indicates a growing degree of inequality, alongside a contraction of profit rates over time (Basu and Manolakos 2010). Maito (2014), in a study of 14 capitalist states, also offers statistical evidence that this is the case.

Capitalism has long sought to overcome its contradictions. However, the inherent contradictions that have driven globalisation have not been eliminated. On the contrary, the most acute contradiction between increasingly globalised economic structures and political formations based on national governments are becoming more evident.

Capitalism has broken the bounds of the nation-state and this has been a fact of economic and political life for a very long time (Trotsky 1996). Productive capital no longer resides within the confines of individual nation-states. At the same time, the nation-state, as an organisational structure, remains an objective reality and a reality that enjoys the emotional support of the great majority of the world's population.

Capitalism is caught in a web of contradictions. It requires stable governance that has been so well delivered by the state system. Simultaneously, capitalism, as a globalising entity, needs to break any fetters that such restrictive structures might present. This problem is further compounded by the constant drive to counter and forestall the tendency for the rate of profit to fall. It is in this context that a qualitatively new stage of capitalism can be observed. The growing influence of finance capital in the face of the crisis of capitalism that erupted in the 1970s acted to develop a new global working class while destroying industrial activity in the developed economies (Silver 2006). The contradictory relationship between individual state structures and an increasingly borderless economic system has prompted some to question the long-term viability of the nation-state and others to question globalisation itself.

Changes in capitalism: implications for the nation-state

The intensification of capitalist globalisation, is a visible reminder of both developmental and structural changes in capitalism. This intensification has prompted more than a little discussion as to the future and viability of the nation-state. Strange (1997a) argued that markets are now more powerful than states. Ohmae (1995) contends that the nation-state has no real role in the global economy. UK economist, Pettifor (2008) calls for the threatened state to be 'upsized' as a means of reclaiming autonomy in the face of globalised capital. Herein lies a paradox. The state must facilitate the development of an increasingly borderless capitalism while simultaneously safeguarding political realities within national borders. As a consequence, the nation-state is regarded by some as obsolete, while others call for its strengthening.

While the role of the state has not fundamentally altered, capitalism's development has necessarily placed a strain on that relationship. This first became apparent as capitalism quickly outgrew the nation-state and, more recently, has transformed itself into a globalised entity. Marx's view of the nation-state and of its future was clear. He maintained that the development and expansion of capitalism would ultimately weaken any semblance of independence for the state.

The state, it is clear, increasingly plays a dual role. A range of inter-connected problems arise. The crisis of capitalism has prompted changes in capitalist relations (financialisation, changes in the productive use of capital, and an increased integration of capitalism). This has led to an intensification of inequality and social disharmony which, in turn has manifested itself in a broad, anti-capitalist, anti-globalisation sentiment. There has been a reaction against austerity, growing poverty, and a general tendency toward diminution of social and economic security. Populist movements have grown and the state has increasingly been engaged in maintaining 'order' and legitimacy. A perceptible rise in nationalist sentiment is the result. The state has fostered this sentiment, with the result that the working class has remained locked into a nationalist framework, with leaderships that maintain a national perspective.

The concept of a national state, in conjunction with national governance and national economic organisation, is an entrenched one. This is despite the fact that it is a construction framed by and in an historical period of time. This needs to be kept in the forefront of debates concerning globalisation and the state. Neither the nation-state nor capitalism are immutable but exist in an historical context. What also needs to be borne in mind is that the nation-state is ultimately a political formation and not a geographical location.

The era of state-based autonomous economies has passed. Capitalism has become increasingly integrated. Strange (1997a) wrote of the retreat of the state and the decline of state authority in the face of globalisation.

She argued that where "states were once the masters of markets, now it is the markets which, on many critical issues, are the masters over the governments of states" (1997a: 4). Strange contended that while individual firms might be described as 'American' or 'British', this ought not obscure the fact of global integration and that dramatic changes in financial structures clearly indicate changes in capitalist production relations (Strange 1997b).

Jotia (2011) is among a number of writers who have sought to explain the political and economic realities facing the nation-state. He argues that the nation-state operates largely to arrange domestic issues as a means of facilitating the overarching needs of global capitalism and that it has come to the point where "global change dictates terms under which the national governments should function" (Jotia 2011: 246). The potential dislocation for states is further highlighted by Tanzi who argues that

> globalization is forcing countries to abide more and more ... by the rules of the market. Countries that ignore these rules are now likely to pay a much greater price than they did when economies were closer ... national governments are likely to see their economic role reduced (1998: 13).

The fact that globalisation is affecting the nation-state is obvious. What is less certain is the intensity of this effect. Robinson's argument, in respect of the implications of capitalist globalisation as evidence of a qualitative change in capitalist relations, points to a future that he perceives to be close at hand, whereby the nation-state and its effective role becomes superseded by a transnational capitalist class (1998: 567). Hirst and Thompson (1999), on the other hand, contend that there is nothing particularly special about capitalist globalisation. The fact remains that globalisation of production equates to an increase in international and global economic activity and especially when considered in the context of economic integration. This inevitably has implications for the nation-state. Hirst and Thompson actively seek to downplay the significance of the globalisation of capitalism. They are clear in their wish to expose the 'myth' of globalisation as a means of persuading "reformers of the left and conservatives who care for the fabric of their societies that we are not helpless before uncontrollable global processes" (1999: 7). Neither of these conflicting views, between hyperglobalists and globalisation sceptics, offer anything like a satisfactory response to questions of paths to emancipation for the working class, nor do they offer any resolution to the question of Marxism's relevance in an era of capitalist crisis. Robinson's (2004) view

that there needs to be a movement towards a 'global democratisation' remains vague and ill-defined. Similarly, to dismiss globalisation as a 'myth', limits working class response to capitalism to nationally based reactions to what are increasingly globalised issues.

Regardless of these divergent perspectives, a number of issues are still to be resolved. Capitalism remains framed by crisis. It is a crisis that has serious implications for a working class that is at once increasingly globalised but still confined and constrained by nationalist sentiments and symbols. The debates as to the health of the nation-state in the face of globalised capitalism must, therefore, take into account questions of nationalism as an ideological response. Ever since the rise of capitalism, the state has sought to engender a sense of unity aimed at crossing class divides. It has been remarkably successful and, as previously noted, has been widely observed in Marxist theory. The class composition of society has been diminished in the thinking of many and this is reflected in the organisations of the working class. As globalisation assumed greater significance, so too did the notion that an 'anti-globalisation' movement might halt the march. Globalisation was effectively de-coupled from capitalism. It was as though the two existed in isolation. Globalisation became the enemy and not the state or capitalism.

The question of nationalism again became an issue of concern in Marxist debate in the most recent past. Calhoun (1997) prominently argues that nationalism is, in essence, a positive and even progressive construct. Munck promotes the view that "nationalism continues to articulate social discontent and is the source of new solidarities" (2010: 51). Hardt and Negri offer a contrasting perspective. They argue that capitalist globalisation, or in their terminology, 'empire', is unstoppable and "a step forward in order to do away with any nostalgia for the power structures that preceded it" (2000: 43). Capitalism is undoubtedly a globalising force, and is compelled to be such a force, but is still firmly connected with individual nation-states. This is seen first and foremost in the political role that the state plays and in the class relations that are evident. The working class has grown dramatically in global terms as capitalism has developed new centres of production. Nationalism has been used to diffuse any sense of potential unity within the global working class. Workers are encouraged to see commonalities with their own bourgeoisies and are pitted against each other. In this sense, there is very little to differentiate early 20th-century expressions of nationalism with that of early 21st-century nationalist sentiments.

Another significant issue is the most recent shift towards economic nationalism. Former US Treasury Secretary Summers (2016) indicated an unease regarding perceptions that people have that 'open' economic policies in recent years are producing a political backlash. The managing director of the IMF, Legarde, remarked that:

> I hope it is not a 1914 moment and I hope that we can be informed by history to actually address the negative impact of globalisation ... because it has historically delivered massive benefits and it can continue to do so (2016).

She was referring specifically to Britain's decision to leave the European Union. Equally significant in this context have been nationalist sentiments in relation to US-Russia relations, US-China relations and the rise of nationalist political groupings across the globe.

The nation-state, as a political institution, will either strengthen or adapt to globalisation and the qualitative changes in capitalism. State structures will, however, be shaped both by external influences stemming from the requirements of globalised capital and from internal factors as individual states respond to the pressures linked to globalisation. The effects of globalisation are being felt across all societies and states. Postone (2007: 7) argues that an almost endemic situation of stagnating and falling profits, a tendency toward decreasing wages share and social and political fragmentation is affecting developed and developing states alike. Inequality has risen sharply. Social cohesion has weakened. This is less a result of political and economic policy and more a result of qualitative changes in capitalist relations that have been determined by the growing crisis in capitalism.

Changes in capitalism: implications for the working class

A range of theoretical positions, broadly defined as sceptical, transformational and hyper-globalist have been addressed in relation to changes that have taken place in capitalism. These have been considered against the proposition that capitalism has entered a qualitative new stage in its development. The issue of the nation-state and its relationship to a changed capitalism has also been discussed. The contending schools within the broadly constituted Marxist milieu generally recognise and accept that inequality and social disharmony are growing. There is a generally held consensus that things are changing. What is frequently overlooked, however, is the connectedness between capitalism's qualitative shift and the dramatic rise in inequality, and of the inevitable social discontent that accompanies inequality. Those most affected, the working class, remain powerless, as a consequence of the lack of independent leadership, in their quest for emancipation. They remain caught in entanglements of nationalist rhetoric and a retreat into national responses to global crises.

Inequality and discontent are connected, and their growth has been linked to the rapidity of capitalist globalisation. The steady rise in inequality can be observed in individual countries and globally. The rise in social discontent has been manifested in both anti-globalisation movements and more recently, in developed economies, in both left and right-leaning political and nationalist movements. Globalised capitalist relations have particularly affected the working class as unemployment remains high, industrial and manufacturing production continues to flow from the industrialised states, and welfare state structures have been eroded. Ultimately, this crisis is a consequence of capitalist globalisation, which, in turn, is a by-product of the qualitative changes that are apparent in world capitalism. The ramifications are obvious.

Dallmayr (2002: 144) cites the UN Human Development Report (1999) to show that just three of the wealthiest families in the world enjoy an income equivalent to the poorest 600 million. These statistics change with alarming rapidity as wealth accumulates into fewer and fewer hands. Pieterse (2002: 1025) uses these same figures to indicate that there has been a steady and significant growth in inequality since the Industrial Revolution from a situation in 1820 which saw a gap between the richest fifth of the world's population and the poorest fifth steadily grow from a ratio of 3:1 to 74:1 in 1997. This trajectory has been steadily accelerating and especially since the 1970s. Oxfam figures show that the world's richest 62 individuals control the same wealth as the poorest 3.5 billion people (Oxfam 2016). Credit Suisse (2015) research reveals that nearly three-quarters of the world's population have a per-capita wealth of less than $10,000. Conversely the richest 8 per cent of the population own 84.6 per cent of global wealth. Pieterse asks, "what kind of world economy grows and yet sees poverty and global inequality rising steeply?" (2002:1036). The answer to his question is not simply a capitalist economy, but a qualitatively changed capitalism that exists in conditions of irresolvable crisis.

International institutions, analysts and activists acknowledge that a fundamentally new stage of crisis has emerged. A report issued by the IMF states that:

> Widening income inequality is the defining challenge of our time. In advanced economies, the gap between the rich and poor is at its highest level in decades. Inequality trends have been more mixed in emerging markets and developing countries (EMDCs), with some countries experiencing declining inequality, but pervasive inequities in access to education, health care, and finance remain (Dabla et al. 2015: 4).

The OECD (2015) has similarly reported that inequality in OECD countries is at its highest since records began. The same report indicates that the rise in inequality has been reflected in a growth of part-time and casualised labour. Joint ILO/OECD (2015) research has shown that for decades, labour's share of income has lost ground to capital. OECD (Cingano 2014) reports are also clear that inequality is growing steadily with wealth differentials between rich and poor at their highest in more than 30 years.

Additional ILO (2015) statistics show that in 2015 as many as 75 per cent of all workers across the globe fell into the informal category – either as temporary or short-term employees. The growth of capitalist globalisation is mirrored in the growth of the global working class. Dobbs et al. (2012) estimate that the global workforce will have reached 3.5 billion by 2030. One factor that the working class in the OECD world and in the developing world have in common is a growing sense of insecurity.

This sense of insecurity is exemplified in the relationship between capital and labour. In responding to the tendency that exists for a fall in the rate of profits, capital has sought, as it always has, and as it always must do, to maximise the levels of surplus value at its disposal. What appear to be 'changes' in the very nature of work are observable as these qualitative changes in capitalism have developed. Traditional labour/capital relationships have been altered. There has been a dramatic rise in the casualisation of labour, 'flexible' working arrangements have been introduced, and workers are increasingly regarded as 'sub-contractors'. Despite these 'changes', the reality of that essentially exploitative relationship between capital and labour remains unchanged.

Bieler, Lindberg, and Pillay (2008: 11) argue that the most important change that has occurred in the last 15 years has been the weakening of the position of labour in relation to capital. United Nations Development Program (2014) figures show the downward trend in labour's share of income over the past 30 years. The dilemma that faces the nation-state, as both administrator of capitalism and simultaneously as competitor against other states and against a transnational capital, is clear. The dilemma for the working class within these nation-states is not always so clearly stated.

There is ample evidence to show a dramatic rise in inequality both within nation-states and between states. Capitalism and inequality are inextricably linked. In Marx's (1986e) assessment inequality is a necessary component of the wages system. It is an argument that goes to the very core of the relationship between capital and labour. Capitalism uses both physical and intellectual labour as a commodity. In even more strident terms Marx declared that:

> the cry for an *equality of wages* rests, therefore, upon a mistake, is an *insane* wish never to be fulfilled … to clamour for *equal or even equitable retribution* on the basis of the wages system is the same as to clamour for *freedom* on the basis of the slavery system (1986e: 208–209 emphasis in the original).

Peet (1975: 570) affirms this perspective, arguing that social equality can be achieved only when the sources of inequality are replaced.

The profound changes in capitalism, and in its quest to maintain profitability, has affected how states operate. This is the case in both developed states and the developing economies. Globalised markets have acted as a motivational force for investors to move capital from the traditionally regulated economic centres to the less regulated. This was initially revealed in accelerated global economic growth but has resulted in increasing instability and insecurity for the working class. What is particularly significant is that the rate of economic growth appears to have stagnated or at least is growing at an unacceptably slow rate (IMF 2016b). While this reflects the underlying problems in capitalism as a crisis-prone system, the fact remains that globalisation was, and is, an attempt to rapidly accelerate economic growth to forestall and circumvent crisis stemming from falling profit rates.

Globalisation has also been accompanied by an unevenness in development. Martins (2011: 12) draws a parallel to the extent that inequality grew with the coming of the industrial revolution. Globalisation has been described in terms of it being the 'second' great transformation within capitalist development as it moves from national to global capitalism and thereby assuming a qualitatively different character (Pieterse 2002: 1024). The first, being the establishment of national capitalist relations. Such a characterisation echoes the past with a growing divide between rich and poor.

Social disharmony and discord is evident, but effective challenges have not materialised. There are a range of reasons why this is so and all remain centred around the key questions that this study raises. The working class remains firmly attached to the physical and psychological boundaries of the nation-state. While Marxism traditionally stressed that the working class, if it was to gain emancipation from capitalism, must accept its internationalism (Marx and Engels 1977: 74), the strength of nationalism and nationalist sentiment has remained. Bereciartu argues that "national sentiment in general and nationalism in particular appears to be profoundly rooted in the consciousness of the European working class … at present nationalism is expanding" (1994: 53). It is a view that not only remains entrenched in the thinking of the working class but in the minds of many whose stated perspective is the struggle against capitalism.

Theorists from the Marxist tradition frequently remain locked into a national response to what is ultimately a global question. Capitalism occupies an international terrain. To wage a primarily localised struggle has serious limitations. Class-based discontent has traditionally been waged through trade union activities which become significantly limited by nationally based responses to global problems. Moody (1997) and Berberoglu (2009) are representative of this nationalist perspective. Yates (2003: 239) goes a step further, arguing that the Canadian Auto Workers Union successfully built an identity around class and radical nationalism. Such a proposition, that 'identity' can be developed by a unity of class and nationalism is dubious at best. The issues that occupied European Marxism in the period immediately preceding World War I clearly defined two separate responses. Marxists called for a class-based response but nationalism and an identification with national bourgeoisies remained the dominant perspective. Working class discontent, in the past decade, has shifted, with less emphasis on overt anti-globalisation, anti-capitalist rhetoric to more pronounced nationalist expressions of dissent. Such responses indicate a serious lack of effective leadership and of the nationalist perspectives that still dominate the thinking of many and which are engendered and promoted by the state.

There is also a tendency among some activists and scholars to offer radical propositions but to ultimately vacillate. Robinson (2004: 178), after building a theory to 'explain' the rise of a transnational ruling class and the end of the nation-state as an organisational unit, concludes his arguments by calling for a broad 'democratisation' of global society. Webster, Lambert, and Bezuidenhout (2008) suggest that there is a 'necessity' to engage in utopian thinking. The central contradictions of capitalism, however, remain.

What is to be done?

Historical disputation and dislocation in Marxism have, unwittingly, assisted capitalism to withstand fundamental crisis. The underlying truth of this assumption can be observed in capitalism's journey through crisis, and to the qualitative changes that have been wrought in capitalism in the decades of intensified globalisation. Capitalism remains defined by crisis and, while inequality and social discontent have grown, no tangible threat to capitalism has emerged.

The contradictions that threaten to tear capitalism apart have historically served to drive it towards globalisation. It is an economic system marked by crisis. Marxist debates revolve around capitalism's ability, or lack of ability, to resolve potential crisis. None of these contradictions have been resolved. On the contrary, they have become more acute. The changes that are observable in capitalism – the financialisation of capital, the change in the use of productive capital, the integration of capitalism into a global market – have all failed to resolve these contradictions. Capitalism's relationship with the nation-state is its most pronounced and irresolvable contradiction. Harris argues that the 'dialectic of globalisation', the "conflict between nationalism and globalization contains the main economic, political and social division in today's world" (Harris 2006: 54). The 'transnational period' is not complete, and both transnational and national forms of capitalism co-exist.

This contradiction, between the globalisation of capitalism and the continued importance and strength of the nation-state, assumes special significance when considered alongside the structural changes that have occurred in capitalism. The nation-state, as administrator of capitalism has been required to 'manage' a reality marked by intensification, both in inequality and in social discontent. The geographic construct that is the nation-state has sought to address these problems. Nationalist symbols and sentiment have been promoted with the view of building a sense of national unity in the face of growing economic and political difficulties and dislocations. Such an exercise, as history has shown, is not without danger.

Much discourse surrounds what is perceived as a 'return' to economic nationalism. Economic nationalism is the antithesis of capitalist globalisation and yet it is growing in direct proportion to capitalism's qualitative changes and its globalisation. Pryke defines economic nationalism as "the attempt to create, bolster and protect national economies in the context of world markets" (2012: 290). There are clear indications that protectionist measures within national economies are being actively promoted. The WTO points to a "relapse in G20 economies' efforts at containing protectionist pressures. Not only is the stockpile of trade-restrictive measures continuing to increase, but also more new trade restrictions were recorded" (WTO 2016: 4). A decade earlier, former Chairman of the US Federal Reserve, Bernanke (2006) cautioned against such an economic shift and the negative consequences it might have for the global economy.

Wolf (2004: 37) describes the attempt by capitalist states to reverse the trend toward globalisation that occurred at the end of the 19th century. He contends that economic nationalism led to militarism and imperialism. Free trade was stifled, and war was the ultimate and inevitable result. The motivations behind national states to enter into such a contradictory position is, in part, a response to economic downturn and also as a means of accommodating and ameliorating the fears and concerns of domestic populations that are increasingly facing difficult economic outcomes.

Nationalism has proven to be a most resilient phenomenon and one that has been carefully and consciously engendered by capitalism. The use of emotive symbolism and the ethos of nationalism is a deliberate act of social control in order to manipulate consciousness. Eric Hobsbawm noted that it is "highly relevant to that comparatively recent historical innovation, the 'nation', with its associated phenomena: nationalism, the nation-state, national symbols, histories and the rest. All these rest on exercises in social engineering" (2004: 13). Greenfeld describes a structure that is:

> inherently egalitarian, nationalism has as one of its central cultural consequences an open – or class – system of stratification, which allows for social mobility, makes labor free ... and dramatically expands the sphere of operation of market forces ... Also, because of ... investment in the dignity of the nation – that is, its prestige – which is necessarily assessed in relation to the status of other nations, nationalism implies international competition (2009: 23).

Nationalism, and in this context, economic nationalism, pits one nation against another and by implication one worker against another There are implicit dangers for national economies and for the working class in such a perspective. Using the case of the post-communist period in Russia, Szakonyi (2007) describes the potential, in the exercising of economic nationalism, to create both internal and external 'enemies' as a means of building a narrow national unity. 'Competition' in this sense becomes a vehicle for domination and subjection. The working class, within nation-states, is similarly locked into a class-based economic and political structure that is promoted as 'mobility'.

The working class, under protectionist conditions, is encouraged to view the working class of 'competing' nations as rivals for jobs. This is often combined with appeals to freedom and the danger of a loss of freedom. Marx (1956: 251) warned against the abstract use of the term 'freedom', reminding people that such a term, in a class society, ultimately refers to the freedom that capital enjoys in maintaining its position of dominance. The promotion of nationalist perspectives echoes political and economic debates dating back a century when free trade and protectionist debates flourished in the lead up to World War I. What is fundamentally different in this 21st-century version of the debate is that protectionism and economic nationalism are even less viable options. Capitalist globalisation will continue. To seek an alternative vision evokes Marx and Engels' response to utopianism and its call to an 'earlier' political and economic foundation and to turning back clocks (Marx and Engels 1977; Engels 1966).

While protectionism offers little prospect for benefit to the working class, the alternative call to free trade has similarly provided few benefits and, in actuality, has promoted inequality. Marxists have often struggled with these alternative paths. Marx once declared that he was a supporter of free trade because it hastened the social revolution. He also argued that free trade was simply the freedom of capital. "It does not matter how favourable the conditions under which the exchange of commodities takes place, there will always be a class which will exploit and a class which will be exploited" (Marx 1956: 250). Marxist theory, as a guide to emancipation for the working class, cannot therefore privilege one economic theory, or policy, over another.

Many Marxists regarded the anti-globalisation movement as an appropriate vehicle to confront capitalism. The anti-globalisation movement that briefly flourished at the time of the 1999 Seattle protests against the WTO drew together an eclectic mix of anarchists, environmentalists, as well as a range of activists who broadly identified themselves as Marxist. For some, the protests 'transcended' nationalism (Wainwright and Kim 2008). For others, it was an indication that any contradictions that might divide groups were able to be overcome and were displaced by anti-globalisation activism (Amin et al. 2002: 5). The optimism on the part of many within the anti-globalisation movement might be regarded as utopian, as opposition to capitalism remains diffused and fragmented, and issues of relevance and utility remain problematic.

A state of confusion as to how best to promote an emancipatory agenda is apparent. As with the Seattle protests, there was a sense of unanimity in response to, and protest at, the failed *Multilateral Agreement on Investment* in the late 1990s. On one hand the 'left' seeks to combat globalisation by promoting nationalism and on the other hand recognise and caution against the dangers of nationalism. Gamble (2009: 149–150) argues that the 'left' had traditionally encompassed protectionism in its various programs and that in recent years both right and left have employed protectionist rhetoric. His analysis is correct. It essentially supports the premise that the consciousness of the working class has been manipulated by the state. It explains how nationalism has been so easily employed by the state, and especially in limiting any sense of class consciousness. Nationalism, as a political manifestation to maintain a sense of unity as an expression of economic response to crisis, has seriously weakened the capacity for independent organisation of the working class.

While economic nationalism is resurgent, the capitalist economy remains globalised and increasingly integrated. Shah (2011) shows that 1,318 transnational corporations account for 60 per cent of global wealth with the most powerful 147 of these corporations controlling 40 per cent of the total global output and wealth. Fifty-one per cent of the biggest 'economies' in the world are individual corporations and 41 per cent of these are based in the US. Capitalism is globalised, integrated and qualitatively different and yet the power of the nation-state remains. The renewal of nationalism, politically and economically, has serious implications.

The contradiction between globalised capitalism and a renewed sense of nationalism is disturbingly apparent in the drift, by major economic powers, toward trade blocs and confrontation between 'competitors'. The original proposal to construct the Trans-Pacific Partnership was a case in point. The bloc while professing to 'unite' numbers of regional economies, would only have served to exacerbate tensions between China and the US (Palit 2014: 97). There are fears that, as the crisis of capitalism intensifies, the threat to global stability will also intensify. Holmes, in the *NATO Review*, cites what he calls an 'adage' that "if goods don't cross frontiers, soldiers will" (2009). He sees a real possibility of a return to the conditions that dominated thinking in the 1930s. Global trade has fallen and he fears a return to protectionist policies. He lists a variety of 'threats' with China and Russia being prominent on his list. What remains the most critical of contradictions facing capitalism remains unresolved and is unable to be resolved. This is so because it is a contradiction of capitalism and while capitalism remains then so too will the contradictions that plague it.

Herein lies a dilemma for Marxism and for the working class. Capitalism has undergone qualitative change. It has globalised. It still requires a strong nation-state as political administrator. Nation-states and residual national capitalism must vie with one another for dominance. Leadership must develop that will have the capacity to combat and effectively confront capitalism. It remains the only realistic means of resolving the contradictions of globalised capitalism and the nation-state.

Capitalism is a globalising system. The history of capitalist relations has revolved around the quest by capitalism to resolve what are a set of inherent contradictions. The most profound of these, in the era of capitalist globalisation, is the contradiction between globalised economic processes and national governance. As the crisis in capitalism becomes more intense, so too does this contradiction intensify.

A qualitative change in capitalist relations has been observed. This does not mean a change in the 'nature' of capitalism or its quest to maintain profitability in the face of a tendency for profits to fall. The change is evident in the reliance on the financialisation of capitalism as a means of concentrating wealth and in the globalisation of productive capital away from nation-based centres, in an increasingly integrated transnational form of capitalism. This means, among other things that labour, rather than flowing to the centres of production in the developed states, becomes a globalised working class.

The crisis of capitalism exacerbates the contradiction between globalised capitalism and the nation-state. This becomes immediately apparent as social inequality and discontent becomes more evident. This, in turn, is leading to a resurgence of economic nationalism and protectionist policies. The working class has, through policies that foster a sense of national unity rather than class unity, become less able to develop a capacity to act as an independent force. There is a growing sense that globalisation, rather than capitalism, is at the core of the problems facing the working class. As a consequence, movements against globalisation are frequently non-class, or supra class movements that have, unconsciously served to further weaken working-class consciousness.

6

RESPONDING TO CAPITALIST GLOBALISATION

One expression of the qualitative changes in capitalism has been the intensification of globalisation. Dissent and reaction to the effects of capitalist globalisation have inevitably resulted. Critical responses have been predominantly aimed at fostering campaigns against globalisation. What is important is to not merely recognise these actions but to appreciate the motivations behind them. Globalisation and capitalism are inseparable, and yet there is often a conscious attempt to decouple globalisation from capitalism. Globalisation of itself is not the problem. Rather capitalism was and remains the underlying 'enemy'. Globalisation is simply the inevitable result of capitalism's unsuccessful drive to resolve its inherent contradictions.

It is important to explore the potential foci for anti-capitalist movements. It must be once again stressed that the working class and its organisations have been incorporated, integrated and legitimised within the nation-state. This is a point frequently overlooked by many Marxists who cling steadfastly to the belief that the trade unions offer a viable platform for struggle against capitalism and that globalised capital can be combatted by a globalised union movement. The central role of the working class in anti-capitalist movements has, similarly, been downplayed by many contemporary Marxist theorists. This has been particularly evident since the 1960s with the rise of identity politics and the development of new forms of social movement activism. Marxist theory developed from the premise that the working class is a potentially revolutionary force because of its central wealth-creating role within capitalism. Recent iterations of Marxist theory have shifted emphasis away from the role of the working class, focusing rather on the middle class as a force for change.

Consequently, we need to consider the rise of identity politics as a conscious attempt to oppose the negative aspects of capitalism, while at the same time recognising the serious limitations that become immediately apparent. The limiting nature of such political manifestations, and the narrow focus that they unwittingly engender, resulted in attempts to broaden these non-class political expressions of dissent.

A serious discussion of these 'new' social movements is required. They have repeatedly shown a capacity to mobilise large numbers, but also a tendency toward dissipation and retreat. This, I argue, is a consequence of a limited programme, a lack of clarity in objectives, and an on-going problem of leadership. An analysis of the strengths and weaknesses of these non-class and supra-class social movements, is therefore needed. I show that these movements often engage large numbers of people, burn brightly, but burn briefly. This is primarily due to the lack of ideological clarity and scope of these movements. Regardless of any potential success of non-class movements, no threats to the rule of capitalism have emerged, and nor could they be expected to emerge under such conditions.

This ultimately brings us to a focus on the relevance of Marxism. Marxism remains the most appropriate vehicle to effect change. But capitalism remains unchallenged, despite the rise of anti-capitalist movements, social movements and anti-globalisation activism. It is in a unity of theory and practice, that a renewed Marxism can provide, that such challenge can be perceived. Marxism's continued relevance is reasserted and confirmed by its capacity to project leadership that can and will confront and challenge capitalism.

Identifying the real enemy

Capitalism and globalisation have always been synonymous. Changes to capitalism, as previously outlined, have made this tendency towards globalisation more obvious and has directly led to conditions of heightened inequality. Consequently, globalisation has become a source of discontent and disquiet. Globalisation has been accompanied by accumulation of wealth and an intensification of poverty. For many, activists and scholars alike, the question is reduced to one of how best to 'resist' globalisation, and how best to promote an anti-globalist agenda. For some it is a question of reversing the tendency of capitalist globalisation: to 'de-globalise'. For others, it is to present globalisation as a political issue that can be separated from overriding economic considerations. What needs to be remembered is that there is an inseparable unity between economic globalisation and capitalism. However, globalisation, of itself, is not the cause of the misery that anti-globalists depict. It is capitalism that is the ultimate source of that misery.

Imperialism dominated Marxist thinking in the late 19th and early 20th centuries. Capitalism was breaking the shackles of national borders. Globalisation was the order of the day. Imperialist rivalry, capitalism, and its relationship to the nation-state, were all central themes within Marxist debates at that time. Contemporary issues within international political economy, regarding capitalist globalisation, the nation-state and the role of the working class, find a resonance within those century-old debates.

Certain truths remain. Luxemburg's (1963: 368–370) argument that capital grows by forcibly developing pre-capitalist economies certainly describes aspects of capitalist globalisation. Lenin's (1977e: 726–727) analysis of imperialism, which saw capital becoming more monopolistic, the rise of finance capital, the increasing importance of the export of capital and a division of the world between associations of capitalism also remains relevant. Bukharin (2003: 130–132) viewed the state as acting in the interests of national capital and that imperialism is, therefore, an expression of state power within an international context. Trotsky (1996), on the other hand, asserted that capitalism had outgrown the restrictions of national boundaries and that imperialism was the proof that this was the case.

There are links that can be traced between the imperialist epoch as described in Marxist literature, and that which can be observed in capitalist globalisation in the early 21st century. O'Brien outlines this connection when he states that imperialism refers to "a process of capitalist expansion and dominance emanating from the advanced industrial states ... it captures the link to a dynamic capitalist process that involves state and non-state actors" (2004: 53–54). Halliday (2002) describes five distinct themes that are pertinent to imperialism and to the development of capitalist globalisation. These include capitalism's historical tendency toward expansion, the militaristic nature of capitalist states throughout the 20th century, the rise of global inequality, even as developing states acquire an industrial base, the growth in importance of institutions of capitalist domination in the form of the IMF and World Bank among others and finally, the seemingly irresistible rise of the world capitalist market.

Among the 'dynamics' or rather the dialectic of capitalist globalisation in the contemporary era is the relationship between the nation-state and a globalising economic reality. Cammack (2003) proposes a 'new' materialist approach relating to globalised capital in the 21st century. He considers the implications for an emerging single capitalist system. Individual governments, he contends, share a collective interest in capital accumulation through an array of multilateral institutions. At the same time, individual states exhibit a more traditional role of seeking advantage over other states.

Such a proposition highlights the contradiction of the nation-state evolving into a component of globalised capital, while still maintaining elements of national capitalism. This, while speaking most directly to the qualitative changes that have taken place in capitalism, is also dangerously reminiscent of the era of imperialist rivalry when capitalism broke out from the limitations of national boundaries and onto a global stage.

Among critics of capitalist globalisation are those who optimistically write of class conflict, but who base such perceptions almost exclusively within the confines of the nation-state. Berberoglu (2009: 47), for instance, sees capital in the US facing an imminent challenge from the American working class. Such an appraisal imposes a serious limitation with action based on a national response to what is an increasingly global question. Sklair (2002: 272–296) represents a quite different current in theorising an anti-globalisation strategy. 'Counter Movements' that include localising anti-globalisation struggles through protectionist policies, identity politics and ecological politics are presented as a means of 'challenging' globalisation. "Slowly, labour, environmental and other movements are being drawn into the non-violent fold" (Sklair 2002: 296). Networks of social change are, in Castells' (2004: 428) estimation, a glimpse of a new society in an embryonic form. These views identify some of the difficulties facing the working class and its relationship, both to the nation-state and to capitalist globalisation, not to mention a confused theoretical response from those who cast themselves in the Marxist mould. Broad, supra-class and non-class theoretical propositions offer what appears to be an enticing potential for activism and for expressing dissent, but have an equally strong potential to be diverted.

Sklair (2000: 82–83) focuses on the crisis facing the working class. He acknowledges that a resolution to that crisis can only come from opposing global capitalism and not simply globalisation. Sklair's perceptions of how such a struggle might unfold, based as it is on social movement politics and an appeal to a broadly defined 'democratisation' of global society, can be criticised from a Marxist perspective, as being utopian. Many opponents of globalisation, and of capitalism, have pointed to the magnitude of the global response to the excesses of capitalist globalisation. They argue that the protests at the WTO meeting in Seattle in 1999, and the creation of the World Social Forum in 2001 are indicators of a global resistance movement that might challenge capitalist globalisation. Robinson (2004: 168–172) describes the chronology of events, of the rise of this anti-globalist movement and, significantly, of a lack of strategy in the opposition movement that led to its failure. The divergence of ideas and of proposed outcomes from such an amorphous grouping was, and remains, an unavoidable obstacle. Dicken (2007: 527) is among those who similarly point to the eclectic array of groups and programmes evident in the protests, ranging from anarchists to socialists, from broadly anti-capitalist activists, to democracy advocates, and green groups. What united these disparate groupings was their belief that globalisation could be, either controlled and countered, or reversed. The tendency toward spontaneity led to what was almost inevitably a downward trajectory within the anti-globalisation movement.

To suggest that globalisation, while undoubtedly linked to the rise in inequality in the world, can still be regarded as having a progressive component, inevitably invites criticism. However, such a perspective can be defended. Marx's construction of an historical materialist conception of history, leaves little doubt that globalisation is an inevitable process. Marx's description (Marx and Engels 1975b: 195–201), of the significance of the introduction of steam and of the railways in relation to the transformations of India, has often been cited as an indication of an almost globalising 'mission' of capitalism. At the same time Marx was implacably hostile to capitalism, as it represented an intensely exploitative system. He once stated that to "prevent any possible misunderstanding, a word. I paint the capitalist and the landlord in no sense *couleur de rose*" (1986b: 20). The vision of a globalised world economy was, in Marx's estimation, a step towards an economic and political formation that would replace capitalism. It would only be replaced by recognising the class nature of society and consciously seeking to advance class struggle. Marx, subsequent Marxists, and especially classical Marxists, have sought to develop that consciousness as an integral element in changing and challenging an ever-globalising capitalism.

The working class and opposition to capitalism

Capitalist globalisation, as an expression of changes in capitalism, has direct implications for the working class. The working class arose in conjunction with the development of national capitalism. Working class organisation and concepts of emancipation from capitalism were framed by this reality. The relationship between labour and capital is central to Marxist theory. This relationship has traditionally been an antagonistic one, affected by irreconcilable class interests.

Any analysis of 'anti-capitalist' movements, or of potential challenges to capitalism, needs to consider the working class and its organisations. To defend and strengthen their position, workers historically organised themselves at the point of production. Economic and political alliances of the working class were at first rigorously combatted by capital but, over time, these manifestations of working-class consciousness were increasingly and actively incorporated into the mechanisms and structures of the nation-state. A consequence of this integration appears to answer Luxemburg's famous question of whether the working-class movement should adopt a 'reform or revolution' approach. Marxist views of a revolutionary path to emancipation became a minority perspective. Reformist ideology became dominant, but as the 21st century dawned, neither reform or revolution appear on the agenda of the leadership of working-class organisations.

The primary organisations of the working class have long been social-democratic political parties and the trade unions. However, it is the trade unions that are most frequently the subject of discussion when considering working-class responses to capitalist globalisation. Marxist attitudes to the unions have shifted as the capitalist state has developed. Hyman (1975) identifies a range of Marxist interpretations, from the optimistic view of the early writings of Marx, to the more pessimistic position adopted by Engels' and Marx's later work, as well as those of Lenin and Trotsky. Marx's earlier work (1956: 150–151) envisaged a real potential for unions to play a decisive political role in the overthrow of capitalism. Engels (1984) also regarded the union movement as a powerful force for change. At the same time Marx (1986b: 226) warned the working class that it was confronting the effects of oppression but not the cause, which was capitalism. Lenin (1977c) articulated the view, in his response to the issue of 'economism' in the working-class movement, that unions are not and cannot be a threat to capitalist rule and that the unions had effectively been incorporated into the state. Trotsky took this analysis a step further when he wrote of:

> the degeneration, of modern trade union organizations in the entire world: it is their drawing closely to and growing together with the state power. This process is equally characteristic of the neutral, the Social-Democratic, the Communist and "anarchist" trade unions. This fact alone shows that the tendency towards "growing together" is intrinsic not in this or that doctrine as such but derives from social conditions common for all unions (1972: 5).

Classical Marxism has recognised this tendency towards a growing accommodation with the state. Despite this, political activists and theoreticians, often from within the Marxist tradition, maintain that trade union activity is an effective path toward resistance to capitalism. Marxist orthodoxy, as presented through the lens of Stalinist literature, portrayed the role of the unions not only as organisations of revolutionary potential, but as active class-conscious organisations. The work of Lozovsky (1976) is illustrative of this tendency. The unions become, in the thinking of many, a consciously radicalised and oppositional force. Such an optimistic view is widespread, but flawed. It is well represented in the work of Fairbrother and Yates (2003), Berberoglu (2003, 2009) and Gordon and Turner (2000) among others. They acknowledge the fundamental changes to political and economic realities that are being wrought by capitalist globalisation, but still regard trade unions as the most appropriate vehicle for opposition.

There is also a strongly held view that the working class can best respond to capitalist globalisation by developing trans-national union organisations. Hyman (2004) and Haworth (2005) are both representative of this perspective. Such views ascribe to working-class organisations an independence that is largely imaginary. Selwyn (2013: 50) introduces a more realistic outlook. He regards the integration of labour into the capitalist state as being a two-fold process. Labour's role and 'power' have been diminished due to the threat and prospect of the dispersal of production. At the same time, global integration is seen to offer labour new potential for growth. It is a proposition that echoes Silver (2006), who argues that capital mobility weakens state sovereignty, while simultaneously promoting the growth of a global working class. This globalised working class, however, remains confined, geographically and politically, within the borders of the nation-state.

The capacity of the working class to develop an independent class consciousness is, in Gramsci's estimation, limited by the hegemony enjoyed by the ruling class. He described the actions of the state as "the entire complex of practical and theoretical activities with which the ruling class not only justifies and maintains its dominance but manages to win the active consent of those over whom it rules" (Gramsci 1971: 244). The ability to engage in defensive struggle, let alone to promote an independent offensive against the capitalist state, has further diminished since the intensification of capitalist globalisation from the 1970s. Leisink (1999: 19) cites ILO figures from the *World Labour Report* of 1997–1998 to show a general decline in union membership. Later statistical research from the ILO (2008, 2015; OECD 2014) indicate that this tendency has not abated, but rather has continued apace. A diverse range of opinions are offered as to why this has occurred. Moody (1988: xviii–xx) describes how the American union movement has lost its way and has become increasingly bureaucratic, and undemocratic. Piazza (2001) argues that the breaking of the bargaining power of the unions and of the fall in union density, is linked to the development of globalisation and a general weakening of ‘left’ and social democratic parties. Strange (1997a: 59–60) maintained that there has been a transference of management of labour relations and bargaining from state to larger corporations that have developed within a global framework. She further argued that by the 1990s unions had become effectively powerless in the face of multinational corporation (MNC) organisational practices.

Resistance is an inevitable outcome of a class-based society and of capitalist state rule. Leadership, or rather its absence, is very much a determining factor in the success or failure of that resistance. Another factor is the end result to which such resistance aspires. For some (Yates 2003: 236–237) it becomes a matter of importance that trade union leaderships should respond, not merely to traditional structures and issues, but that they ‘adapt’ to accommodate a diversity of needs within their unions. Gills and Gray (2012) describe what they regard as an upsurge of revolt in the form of ‘people power’ in the face of the assault of globalisation. Rocamora (2012) enthusiastically promotes the view that what effectively remain largely spontaneous actions can achieve lasting results and that uprisings are inevitable because capitalism continues to produce victims. While a range of perspectives might be evident regarding questions of labour leadership, it remains clear that with integration into the state, the working class has become increasingly less well equipped to engage in independent struggle for emancipation.

Van der Pijl (2002: 142) writes that while every ruling class claims ‘universality’ for itself, the reality is that social conflict is what marks out all class-based societies. Social conflict, while an inevitable part of class society, should not, however, be confused with the development of class consciousness. Koo (2000) notes that a sense of growing union identity, and even a strengthening of union influence and militancy, does not necessarily indicate class consciousness. Mann (1973) identifies a hierarchy of class consciousness ranging from identification with the class, to recognition of capitalism as an antagonistic opponent, to finally accepting a goal to be attained through struggle.

Issues of leadership, of capacity, of vision, are all central to the overriding question, not merely of resistance to, but also eventual emancipation from capitalist state structures. While Moore Jr (1978: 474) is able to paraphrase Marx’s critique of industrialisation and the theory that this brings with it a potential revolutionary consciousness, the scope of contemporary Marxist literature tends to be limited when addressing the questions of leadership and its significance. Lenin’s (1977c: 113–114) assessment that strike action is but an embryonic form of class consciousness is worth noting in this context. The problems associated with spontaneity as opposed to consciously constructed actions remains valid today.

Identity politics and anti-capitalist mobilisation

Marxism historically placed particular emphasis on the centrality of the working class in effecting economic, political and societal change. This emphasis, however, has become increasingly muted as the crisis in Marxism has developed. The trajectory of Marxism and its retreats in the last 80 years have been more than adequately traced. The growth of identity politics highlights an important aspect of the ideological dilemma faced by Marxism since the 1960s and the development of New Left politics.

Identity politics came to prominence in the 1970s. This followed the heightened radicalism of the late 1960s. The 'left' and many in the divergent Marxist movement were seeking a route to relevance. The 'revolutionary potential' of the working class had been disputed and apparently discredited. New forms of struggle were adopted. The politics of identity seemed to offer a new hope. Identity politics has been prominently described as a quest to belong. Castells in promoting this perspective has remarked that "identity is people's source of meaning and experience" (2004: 6). To seek identity, to belong, in the face of an intensely alienating society is understandable and especially so as capitalist globalisation is rightly presented as destructive of identity and autonomy. A deepening sense of alienation is observable. Marx in his *Economic and Philosophic Manuscripts of 1844* outlined this process of alienation that is so inherently a part of capitalist relations:

> What constitutes the alienation of labour? First, the fact that labour is external to the worker, i.e., it does not belong to his essential being … The worker therefore only feels himself outside his work, and in his work feels outside himself … His labour is therefore not voluntary, but coerced; it is forced labour. It is therefore not the satisfaction of a need; it is merely a means for satisfying needs external to it … the external character of labour for the worker appears in the fact that it is not his own but someone else's … it is the loss of self (1969a: 110–111).

The working class under such conditions, is inevitably estranged, not just by capitalist relations but from capitalist society and from the state itself. The middle class, too, is more and more affected by this sense of alienation.

Castells (2004: 7–8), in addressing the theory of identity politics, outlines three connected issues that are associated with 'identity'. These are 'legitimising', 'resistance' and 'project' identity. It is in the area of resistance identity that the theory assumes special significance. Resistance identity, in this framework, is generated "by those actors who are in positions/conditions devalued/stigmatized by the logic of domination, thus building trenches of resistance and survival on the basis of principles different from, or opposed to, those permeating the institutions of society" (Castells 2004: 8). Identity, therefore, is seen to assume a political character and is portrayed as a means of rallying like-minded individuals, as well as presenting a means of combatting the 'institutions' of society that form the basis of oppression. Castells also argues (2000) that working-class decline can be partially attributed to the rise of identity politics in the 1960s and 1970s and that the working class can no longer be regarded as the primary actor that will precipitate change. There is a certain logic that may be ascribed to such a proposition but it is a most unsatisfactory logic.

The working class was no longer regarded as pivotal to change. Identity politics appeared to offer itself as a suitable vehicle in seeking to construct a political framework that might confront broadly defined institutions of 'oppression'. It marked a shift in focus, described by Bernstein (2005: 49), as a movement more closely concerned with culture than with challenging class structures. Kauffman describes the process of identity politics as expressing:

> the principle that identity – be it individual or collective – should be central to both the vision and practice of radical politics ... Identity politics also expresses the belief that identity itself – its elaboration, expression, or affirmation – is and should be a fundamental focus of political work (2001: 23).

It is hardly accidental that the political identification with culture and identity, rather than with issues of class and class exploitation dramatically rose in conjunction with the rise in capitalist globalisation and the economic, social and political dislocations that accompanied globalisation of capitalist relations.

The politics of identity became more influential as the politics of class declined in the theoretical perceptions of many within Marxism. The 1970s saw a dramatic rise in political movements based on race, ethnicity, gender and sexuality. Piven (1995) argues that the expansion of capitalism and its globalising character has acted to weaken and destroy the more traditional working-class politics of resistance. He contends that globalisation was the catalyst for the rise of racial, ethnic, religious and gender conflicts and that identity politics is an inevitable consequence. Piven almost simultaneously makes two interesting but intensely contradictory claims. Identity politics at once "makes people susceptible to the appeals of modern nationalism, to the bloody idea of loyalty to state and flag, which is surely one of the more murderous ideas to beset humankind" (1995: 105). He then goes on to describe the politics of identity as "a potentially liberating and even equalizing development, especially among subordinate groups, and the more so in a political culture already dominated by identity politics" (Piven 1995: 106). In other words, identity politics is useful when identity politics already exist.

Feminist politics, and particularly the debates around patriarchy, have fuelled the growth in identity politics. Pateman (1988) succinctly encapsulates much of feminist theory, arguing that patriarchy long pre-dates capitalist oppression, and that the relationship of sexual domination is a separate oppressive structure to that of capitalism. Pateman rejects the notion that individuals 'freely' engage in property exchange or, more significantly, in the sale of labour power. This is true to an extent. There is more coercion than freedom employed. Pateman's view is that such a conception is a 'fiction' that masks patriarchal domination. A more satisfactory argument is that with the division of labour, and with the emergence of class-based societies, patriarchal organisation dominated. Capitalism, as it developed, simply used that which was already the norm (see Engels *The Condition of the Working Class in England*, 1984 and *The Origin of the Family, Private Property and the State*, 1986). While there have been any number of attempts to unify Marxist analyses of patriarchy with feminist critiques, the results have hardly been a resounding success. Yes, patriarchy is deeply rooted in society and yes, it is older than capitalism. Whether it is 'more fundamentally oppressive than capitalism' as some maintain is a debatable issue. What is salient and what needs to be remembered is that capitalism remains the central issue and problem. Capitalism's use of ideology to promote illusions that patriarchy, or race, or ethnicity, are separate issues and detached from capital itself allow it to maintain divisions among people.

This is equally true in relation to what is an issue of immediate importance – the issue of environmental destruction and climate change. Naes (1973) advanced the concept of 'ecophilosophy' as an expression of 'deep ecology'. He argued that both exploiter and exploited are equally unable to achieve self-realisation and that therefore an 'anti-class' posture is required to achieve an ecological egalitarianism. It was a construction that separated class and people and which ultimately failed to challenge capitalism as the cause of environmental degradation. It would seem wiser to remember Weston's (1986: 2–3) arguments against portraying the people as being a cause of the problems facing the environment rather than seeing them as victims of destructive capitalist processes. In other words, capitalism, not the people remain the guilty parties. Capitalism has brought the planet to the brink. It is not the people that are driven to return increasing profits, or who must out-perform rivals, find bigger markets and newer ways of extracting resources. Challenges to capitalism from such an 'ecophilosophy' are unlikely, despite the claim that "with the decline of socialism, environmentalism becomes the major vantage point of opposition to business-as-usual" (Hay 2002: 341).

The development of identity politics was at first criticised among Marxists whose engagement was primarily in political activism. Smith (1994) argues that identity politics fail to offer a realistic framework for those wishing to transform society. Mandle (no date) argues that the politics of identity are zero-sum and ultimately the politics of despair with one 'group' advantaged at the expense of another. There is more than a hint of irony in this. Much of what constitute 'activist politics' in recent decades, have developed a conscious focus on the politics of identity, despite having initially decried the ideology. The programmes and policy statements of virtually all political parties with a Marxist orientation (Communist Party of Australia 2016; Socialist Alternative 2007; Socialist Alliance 2015) all declare that they stand for the replacement of capitalism. These political statements do not stand in isolation but are reflected in the programmes of most parties that claim alignment to Marxism around the world. At the same time, these parties strongly advocate for gender, sexual orientation, racial, and ethnic policies. While not seeking to diminish such advocacy, the question as to how capitalism is challenged by waging campaigns around, what are essentially, non-class issues remains unanswered.

Non-class political movements, in the form of identity politics, have built strong constituencies. They have achieved concessions from state institutions, while not eroding state power or capitalism. A consequence of the shift to identity politics has been the realisation that identity, as a political focus, can and does limit the potential to present any real challenge to underlying conditions. It is intensely difficult for activists to conform to the boundaries that identity politics appear to erect. Struggles are often arranged around issues of colour, of ethnicity, of religion, of sexuality. Some of these have an immediate sense of connectivity. Others do not. There are times when the separation and then integration of differing identity foci verges on the absurd. Ignatow, for instance, describes the work of the African-American Environmentalist Association whose goals are "to increase African-American participation in the environmental movement, promote an African-American point of view in American environmental policy ..." (2007: 1). Such absurdities have become clear for some theorists who have recognised how some single-issue, identity movements are inescapably interconnected with other movements. Such realisations have led to moves to link movements and to discover what unites movements.

This realisation gave birth to the concept of *intersectionality* in radical political movements. The concept of intersectionality is often attributed to Crenshaw. She argues that "the problem with identity politics is not that it fails to transcend differences ... but rather the opposite – that it frequently conflates or ignores intragroup differences" (1991: 1242). She uses the issues of race and gender as a case in point and seeks to broaden the argument to become potentially more inclusive of differences in primary focus. While this theory does take account of the limiting nature of identity politics it remains locked into a non-class approach to understanding inequality. However, regardless of the web of interwoven identities, a problem remains. Marx described the advent of a distribution of labour and the class nature of society, whereby each person "has a particular, exclusive sphere of activity, which is forced upon him and from which he cannot escape" (Marx and Engels 1964: 44). Marx wrote of the limiting nature of workers being identified by trade or the 'type' of work undertaken. Identification within a much greater group offers a greater capacity to effect change. In this case class identification becomes immensely stronger than that of individual trades. A narrow political alignment based on personal identification, like a designated role in the production process, limits the potential for change and emancipation. The idea of intersectionality certainly goes some way toward recognising this fact. At the same time, it is still a limited response to what are broader issues of exploitation that stem, ultimately, from capitalism itself.

Political responses to capitalism, globalisation and the alienation that this generates are inescapable. The position of the working class as a force for fundamental change has been relegated, in the thinking of many, to a position of relative insignificance. Prominent Marxist thinking, in the period from the 1960s, has turned more toward the role that social movement politics can play in the development of a broad anti-capitalist movement. Broad, non-class and supra-class movements have mobilised huge numbers of people and have united diverse sections of the population. For many, social movement politics offers a vehicle to successfully confront capitalism. For others, the very supra-class nature and limitations of programme, inherent in such movements, become clearly defined.

Social movement politics and anti-capitalist mobilisation

As an extension of identity-based politics, social movement activism consciously seeks to broaden the scope for resistance. While social movement politics have flourished in the period of capitalist globalisation, they have a long and sometimes contentious history. Well over a century ago, Small described social movement activism and activists as "a confusion of fussy, fidgety folk, blocking each other and everybody else" (1897: 340). It was an intentionally benign criticism. The general thrust of his argument was supportive. "The task which society today imposes upon its members is direct and conscious effort so to organize personal relations that the masses ... may together realize their common humanity" (1897: 353–354). Social movement activism also seeks to build a sense of collective identity that is perceived to be broader than class identity. Traditional expressions of these processes, based as they were on class as a defining element, are described as 'old' social movements, which most usually take the form of trade union activism. The 'new' forms have tended to carefully and deliberately move away from any overt identification with the working class.

Social movement politics have, for many, replaced the centrality of the working class as a force for change. "In a sense collective identity replaced class consciousness as the factor that accounts for mobilization and individual attachments to new social movements" (Hunt and Benford 2007: 437). The capacity for social movements to mobilise large numbers is evident. The civil rights movement in the US in the 1960s, the anti-Vietnam, anti-nuclear, environment, the 'occupy', anti-globalisation and anti-capitalist movements, are all testimony to the success that these broad movements have in building a constituency. Sustaining constituencies becomes far more difficult. These movements often share things in common. They are inevitably political, in the sense that they make demands upon the state (Rootes 1997: 71) and make conscious efforts at effecting social change (Guigni 1999: xxi). The efficacy of these movements becomes an issue that is contested:

> In their aim of changing the status quo, social movements face a fundamental dilemma. If they ask for short-term policy changes, they have a greater chance that such changes will occur, but they will not alter, in a fundamental way, existing structures and practices. If instead, movements demand long-term institutional changes, they will encounter more difficulties in realizing such changes ... Social movements rarely alter political institutions and only under very restricted conditions (Guigni 1999: xxiv).

Fundamental questions of political theory emerge. They are the questions that Marxists debated a century ago. They are the questions of reformist or revolutionary paths to emancipation.

Social movement theory refers both to reforming and revolutionary movements. Goodwin and Jasper (2009: 4) differentiate between the two forms. They define a 'revolutionary' movement as a social movement that actively seeks to overthrow the state, while a broader social movement, deemed to be a reforming instrument, "is a collective, organised, sustained, and non-institutional challenge to authorities, powerholders, or cultural beliefs and practices" (2009: 4). There is a broadly accepted view that the purpose of social movements, and the political agendas they pursue, are aimed at moving society and institutions within that society to a less oppressive position. There is a distinct and ringing echo in such an ideological construct to debates of more than a century ago between Marxist and social-democratic theorists.

Social movements are "natural self-evident successors of the labour movement" (Olofsson 1988: 16). Such a perspective has won wide support and particularly since the 1960s and 1970s and the rise of New Left and identity politics. Olofsson argues that the labour movement, as a representation of 'old' class-based politics, is a symbol of social movements whose time has passed. It is a logic that is very much in keeping with the move away from class as a defining point in the social and economic relations of capitalism. Social movements have become, as a consequence, non-class or supra-class organisations. This can be regarded as a strength but is also very much a limiting factor. Diani describes these movements as "networks of informal interactions between a plurality of individuals, groups and/or organizations, engaged in political or cultural conflicts, on the basis of shared collective identities" (1992: 1). Proponents of new social movement activism describe them as replacing older social movement forms. Within this lies an inherent assumption that there has been a greater degree of success with the new as opposed to the older 'obsolete' movements. It also presupposes a fundamental difference in approach that is not always apparent.

The labour movement activism that the 'new' social movement advocates describe and critique suffered from a process of integration into the capitalist state structure. Wheelwright (1953) traced the trajectory of the trade union movement and of state responses to union activism. He noted three phases in the relationship between the unions and the capitalist state. The first is one of hostility and attempts at suppression on the part of the state. The second is a position of tolerance but sees the state offering little cooperation to the unions. The third phase is one whereby the unions enter into a period of cooperation and partnership with the capitalist state. This incorporation was long ago noted by Trotsky who described the situation in Europe in the 1920s whereby there "is a powerful international organisation of the trade union bureaucracy. It is thanks to it that the whole structure of capitalism stands upright" (1974: 247–248). Macionis (2007), in discussing newer forms of social movement activism, outlines four stages that constitute the 'life-cycle' of a social movement. These are success, co-optation, repression, or establishment within the mainstream of society. There are striking similarities between his description and that of Wheelwright. That there are clear points of connection between 'old' and 'new' social movements indicate that problems associated with programme and intent remain unresolved. It raises significant questions as to the perceived purpose of the 'movement'. Bernstein's (1975: 202) controversial claim that the eventual destination (socialism) is of less importance than the 'movement' is once more played out.

Capitalist globalisation and the rise of social movement politics have evolved together. These protests have been both national and international in scope. Some have adopted an 'anti-capitalist' perspective. Others have focused on war, poverty, or environmental issues. Organisers have successfully been able to draw millions of people into protest and political action. The World Social Forum and the 'Occupy' movement, among others, highlighted the discontent that many people were and are feeling. These, often supra-class or non-class actions, have assumed a growing significance as the globalisation of capitalism has progressed and are clearly a reaction against globalisation. Political responses, either at a state level or between actors at the sub-state level, frequently share a view that economic actions and outcomes can be separated from the globalisation of capitalism – that capitalism and globalisation can be regarded as separate entities. Anti-globalisation becomes, for some, a euphemism for 'deglobalisation'. This has become more apparent since the anti-World Trade Organisation protests in Seattle in 1999 (Smith 2001: 1–20, Ayres 2001: 55–68). Bello (2004) promotes the idea that globalisation can be reversed and that the nation-state is the vehicle through which such a reversal can be effected. Evans (2005) argues for a movement that will effectively democratise and shift the hegemonic structure of globalisation. Sklair (2002: 273–277) identifies a range of challenges to globalisation including protectionism, social movements and the green movement. The result is a conscious promotion of nationalism in the face of capitalist globalisation.

Sutcliffe (2002) identifies a problem that goes to the heart of the anti-globalisation, anti-capitalist movement. Many critics of globalisation can see no way forward and therefore the only path appears to be backwards, often to nationalist political forms:

> If history is a straight line and we do not like the road ahead there is nowhere to go but back ... If the problem is identified as capitalism and not globalization and if capitalism is global, then that suggests that anti-capitalism is the solution and that anti-capitalism must also make itself global, producing counter

> proposals not to globalization as such but to global capitalism and capitalist globalization (2002: 56).

The term anti-capitalist has a range of interpretations and has the potential to confuse and diffuse ideas and arguments. For some, anti-capitalism can denote a movement that seeks to transform society along socialist lines. For others, it might be a movement based upon ecological principles that may, in turn, look to a pre-capitalist means of production. While Sutcliffe's broad interpretation of the term would indicate a forward movement beyond capitalism, the prospects for confusion remain. Harvey (2010b), for instance, outlines a range of potential lines along which anti-capitalist movements might run, including anarchist and autonomous movements, traditional labour/socialist political expressions, social movement politics effectively promoting local issues, and identity politics including those of gender, sexuality, ethnicity and race. Ultimately the issue of social movement politics, whether 'old' or 'new' becomes a question of purpose, of motive, of determining what result is either desired or required.

The purpose and utility of social movement politics is fundamentally connected to the relevance of Marxism in an era of capitalist crisis. It is a question of determining the most appropriate way forward. This has been the central issue surrounding Marxist debates for a century. Marxists argued as to the various merits of reform or revolution. The issues surrounding identity politics and the broader social movements echo those debates. This is not to suggest that social movement activists have not had spectacular successes in mobilising millions of people. These mobilisations have cut across class lines and have drawn attention to the inequalities inherent in capitalist globalisation. It is in analysing the relative strengths and weaknesses of these movements, that the relevance of Marxism as an organisational model can be tested.

Strengths, weaknesses and the tendency toward dissipation

The globalisation of capitalism has evoked a growing number of critical responses. The anti-capitalist, anti-globalisation aspects of these responses are most obviously seen in the development of social movement politics. Some within the Marxist movement have sought to draw these movements into a broadly defined ideological perspective. However, the movements that oppose capitalist globalisation must ultimately contend with the issue that Marxist and non-Marxist theoreticians have struggled with for more than a century. The point of difference is whether a reforming or revolutionary practice provides the best course of action. Social movements have been described as 'old' or 'new' and these differentiations revolve around the issue of the working class and its role in effecting social, political and economic change.

The primary ideology surrounding working-class action in the face of capitalist globalisation revolves around the trade unions. The unions remain the most obvious and elementary organisations of the working class. There is a problem in such an interpretation. It largely ignores the integration of working-class organisations into the structure of the state. While proposing a globalised union response to globalised capitalism, there is a tendency to rely on national institutions and structures which fails to adequately present a challenge, either to globalised capitalism or to individual capitalist nation-states.

Bieler, Lindberg and Pillay (2008: 264–269) isolate two challenges for contemporary labour movements. The first of these is the globalised nature of capitalism and the tendency for workers, based within national borders to become 'competitors' against workers elsewhere, while the second relates to a growing global army of unemployed and an intensifying of the informal or casual workforce in all countries. They acknowledge that union attempts to minimise attacks on wages and conditions that stem from international 'competitiveness' is less likely to succeed within a nationalist framework and similarly it is all but impossible to act against the trend to an informal global workforce. Unions, in their analysis, act in a defensive capacity at best. Bieler, Lindberg and Pillay (2008: 276) maintain that there needs to be a greater degree of global solidarity between unions and the working class. They describe a need to build transnational links between the trade unions, to organise on behalf of the 'informal' sector and to forge links between the unions and other social movements.

The proposition of building global links and uniting union struggles with social movement politics has been widely supported. Wills (2004: 87) calls for unions at all levels to foster democratic social movements. The call for social movement unionism is similarly proposed by Haworth (2005: 195) who urges unions to move beyond the 'economism' of traditional union activity. Such calls for unions to broaden their scope as a means of incorporating social movement issues need to be considered in the context of a crisis of 'relevance' or at the least in membership. Union density across OECD countries has been decreasing for decades. It has been widely acknowledged that the unions have been successfully co-opted into the state. It is unrealistic, in such a context, to suppose that the union movement is in any position to offer a challenge to capitalist globalisation. The call for labour movements to actively engage in the non-class and supra-class social movements would undoubtedly strengthen those social movements, but it is unlikely that capitalism, or globalisation, would in any way be threatened.

For the unions to accommodate the agenda of social movements is to take a further step away from class identification. Moody (1988: 249–250) makes a point of difference between a 'black' and 'white' American working class. While he accepts that black and white workers have class in common, the very point of referring to a separation between members of the working class is a problem for Marxists. Moody argues that:

> in addition to the massive gap between black and white, the working class in the United States is criss-crossed by social, racial, national and sexual differences reflecting the distinct forms of oppression that affect these groups beyond the shared experience of working-class life (1988: 271).

Accommodation to social movement ideology tends, in such analyses, to focus on specific aspects of oppression, rather than acknowledging that capitalism is the common denominator in an alienating society. What needs to be remembered is that capitalism is a class-based system. Oppression is ultimately rooted in the class nature of society. To separate black from white, or men from women, is to ignore this fact.

Capitalist globalisation from the 1970s has resulted in the retreat of the working class and its allies. Struggles have been waged, but a feature of these struggles has been a lack of focus and leadership. The amorphous nature of the anti-globalisation movement appeared to be a strength, but both the anti-WTO campaign in Seattle in 1999 and the 'Occupy' movement of 2011 predictably ended in dissipation. The Seattle protests garnered widespread support. A brief unity existed between human rights activists, students, environmentalists, unions, anarchists, Marxists and protectionists. They agreed on what they did not want but little else. Waterman (2001: viii–x) argues enthusiastically that Seattle was the formation of a movement that crossed ideological boundaries. The fact remains that despite the capacity to mobilise large numbers of people from a wide range of backgrounds, the protests were short-lived and had little lasting impact.

The capacity for social movements to quickly grow and to quickly dissipate was abundantly clear in the 'Occupy Wall Street' movement. Its 'Declaration and Manifesto' identifies a broad range of issues including housing, health, race and sexual oppression, environmental, animal rights, the rights of workers, legal, press freedom and militarisation. The declaration then issues the following appeal:

> To the people of the world,
> We, the New York City General Assembly occupying Wall Street in Liberty Square, urge you to assert your power.
> Exercise your right to peaceably assemble; occupy public space; create a process to address the problems we face, and generate solutions accessible to everyone.
> To all communities that take action and form groups in the spirit of direct democracy, we offer support, documentation, and all of the resources at our disposal.
> Join us and make your voices heard! (Declaration and Manifesto of Occupy Wall Street Movement 2011)

This was an appeal to protest and to mobilise but failed to advance a programme beyond mobilisation. Roberts reviews a range of literature relating to the Occupy movement. He concludes that the authors were energised:

> by the spirit of the moment. Unfortunately, they are also blinded by it. The prevailing theme is that OWS has fundamentally changed American politics. A more sober assessment is that OWS has exposed the limitations on popular protest against the failures of the neoliberal project (2012: 754).

The 'life cycle' of social movement failure has already been discussed (Robinson 2004, Guigni 1999, Macionis 2007). The successes of social movement politics in mobilising large numbers are countered by disappointment when the *status quo* has not been seriously challenged. An emphasis on finding ways to combat globalisation has also drawn social movement activists, including some Marxists, into campaigns that either seek to reject globalisation or to 'de-globalise'. If the purpose of a social movement is to change the existing political or economic reality, but lacks clarity and programme beyond that of mere protest, then it has a very real potential to dissipate and to drift. Bernstein's (1975) argument that the movement is everything returns as a haunting echo. It is a continuation of the disputation between Marxist and non-Marxist theories of reform or revolution.

What does anti-globalisation mean and how does it equate with any move towards emancipation? The campaigns against globalisation have frequently evolved into campaigns that give tacit support for a resurgent nationalism. The US Presidential campaign of 2016 moved this a step further. Left and right populism, as expressions of nationalist responses to globalisation, dominated the early stages of the campaign, as Sanders and Trump vied with each other to promote economic nationalist 'solutions' to the crisis that American workers were experiencing. By the time the election campaign concluded, Trump was able to manipulate and harness working-class discontent and manoeuvre the hostility of the working class to serve his particular agenda.

Bello argues that deglobalisation "is not about withdrawing from the international economy. It is about reorienting economies from the emphasis on production for export to production for the local market" (2004: 113). While writers such as Bello seek to dress their arguments in radical clothing, his position is a simple and direct appeal to economic nationalism. Populist politics, and in Bello's case, left populist politics, argues for a position that seeks to promote 'progressive' ideology, opposition to the 'elites' and which acts as a voice for the 'people'. Muddle characterises populist political ideology as:

> a thin-centred ideology that considers society to be ultimately separated into two homogenous and antagonistic groups, 'the pure people' and the 'corrupt elite' and which argues that politics should be an expression of the *volonte generale* (general will) of the people (2007: 23).

Muddle's definition fits equally with either left or right populist politics and it is in such a characterisation that ultimate weaknesses in the logic of populism appear. It almost inevitably offers immediate national responses to what are effectively global problems. In focusing on an often-amorphous elite, broader understandings of class and internationalism become blurred. The issue of leadership again reasserts itself. Organised manifestations of discontent all too quickly dissipate. 'Left' and 'right' expressions of disaffection frequently appear to merge. The 'enemy' in such ideological construction can be foreign workers, economic competition from other nations, or an ill-defined globalisation. Herein lies a dilemma for those seeking to combat globalisation while not firmly integrating globalisation and capitalism. Capitalism, by default, remains unchallenged and effectively embraced by left and right populists alike.

Capital remains unchallenged

The shift in Marxist theory, from its focus on the centrality of the working class, to broader, non-class approaches, has seriously limited the potential to oppose capitalist rule. This is shown in a diffused Marxist organisational response to capitalist crisis and, particularly since the 1960s, in social movement theories that do not present an effective challenge to capitalist rule. The attitude of Marxism to social movement politics has often been ambivalent, although Marxists traditionally sought to provide an understanding of the role of capitalism and class. This has been less evident in recent decades. Flacks observes that "one of Marx's central analytic strategies ... is missing from contemporary theories [of social movements] – namely, his effort to embed power relations in an analysis of the political economy as a whole" (2004: 138). This shift is due to a lack of theoretical clarity that emerged from the crisis in Marxism and from capitalism's ideological ability to obscure and cloud what would otherwise have the potential to invigorate a class-conscious appraisal of issues.

The ability to persuade people that legitimacy rests within a class-based society is enormously enduring. The concept of 'false consciousness' or 'social hegemony' have already been discussed, but Piven and Cloward's analysis of social movements further attests to the validity of this theory. They argue that power is:

> rooted in the control of coercive force and in control of the means of production. However, in capitalist societies this reality is not legitimated by rendering the powerful divine, but by obscuring their existence ... [through] electoral-representative institutions [that] proclaim the franchise, not force and wealth, as the basis for the accumulation of power (1977: 2).

Any attempt to seriously challenge capitalism and, therefore, to fundamentally alter the economic structures of society must confront this reality. Hetland and Goodwin (2013: 86) acknowledge that recent studies of social movement politics effectively ignore the power of capitalism in this regard. This artificial legitimisation creates the optimum conditions to render movements that seek to oppose capitalism and globalisation, powerless. This is despite the often-large numbers of people that are drawn into political action.

There is an inability to successfully channel discontent. Bonefeld (2006) questions the capacity of anti-capitalist, anti-globalisation movements if they do not espouse a socialist alternative as a means to emancipation. Responses are frequently conflicting. Harvey states that:

> there is no resolute and sufficiently unified anti-capitalist movement that can adequately challenge the reproduction of the capitalist class and the perpetuation of its power on the world stage ... but just because there is no political force capable of articulating let alone mounting such a program, this is no reason to hold back on outlining alternatives (2010b: 250).

Harvey (2010b) argues for what he describes as a 'co-revolutionary' theory to build opposition to capitalism. However, he concludes his appeal by effectively disregarding Marxist organisational 'party' structures. Instead he remarks that whereas "traditional institutionalized communism is as good as dead and buried, there are ... millions of de facto communists active among us, willing to act upon their understandings, ready to creatively pursue anti-capitalist imperatives" (2010b: 260). These 'understandings' may vary dramatically. What is clearly lacking, but what is required, is a leadership that can develop and unite disparate forces and ideas into a movement that can effectively challenge globalised capitalism.

Without such a leadership, the actions of the many who are drawn into activity are, ultimately, in vain. Capitalism and its structures remain intact. Capitalism and the state can accommodate such actions and even portray them as indications of the 'health' of society. Trotsky (1965: 17) used the analogy of energy being dissipated like steam not enclosed in a piston box. However, while there might be an objective necessity to confront capitalism in the cause of emancipation, capitalist ideology and a weakness in much that constitutes contemporary Marxist theory combine to obscure that perception. This is by no means a new phenomenon. Marx, over 160 years ago, wrote in his *Address of the Central Committee to the Communist League* that:

> the democratic petty bourgeois, far from wanting to transform the whole society in the interests of the revolutionary proletarians, only aspire to a change in social conditions which will make the existing society as tolerable and comfortable for themselves as possible (cited in D'Amato 2006: 104).

Herein lies a problem for Marxism in the 21st century. The role of the working class, once regarded as pivotal to anti-capitalist ideological and organisational movements has, over time, been relegated and diminished. Anti-capitalist and anti-globalist movements have increasingly assumed a non-class and supra-class emphasis. The 'middle class' nature of many of these movements, while briefly mobilising large numbers, has not developed into a movement that would confront and challenge capitalist rule.

The 1960s saw the rise of a more overtly radicalised middle class. This fuelled the ideological shift by many within the Marxist movement away from the working class. The focus and motivations underlying expressions of middle-class radicalism were highlighted by Parkin (1968) when he drew a distinction between working-class and middle-class radicalism. The middle-class variant, in his estimation, was geared less to questions of economic reforms, and more to social reforms which he described as being 'moral' in nature. Such a characterisation of middle-class radicalism from Parkin's perspective in the late 1960s, closely mirrors those of Marx from the 1840s. Parkin was essentially paraphrasing Marx and Engels' comments regarding 'German or true socialism' that they represented:

> not true requirements, but the requirements of Truth; not the interests of the proletariat, but the interests of Human Nature, of Man in general, who belongs to no class, has no reality, who exists in the misty realm of philosophical fantasy (Marx and Engels 1977: 65–66).

This raises important questions. Marxism makes the claim that the working class is a potentially revolutionary force. How can this claim be justified in the face of a weakening of working-class strength and consciousness?

Marxism has long argued that the working class is a revolutionary class, or at least a class with revolutionary potential. Such attribution separates it from other classes and groups in society. The claim is based primarily on the premise that the source of all wealth, all profit in capitalist relations, is derived from labour, from the surplus value produced by labour. Lebowitz proposes the argument that the working class becomes a 'revolutionary subject' precisely from the struggles that it is forced to undergo:

> and, those struggles bring us up against capital. Why? Because capital is the barrier that stands between us and our own development. And it is so because capital has captured the fruits of all civilization, is the owner of all the products of the social brain and the social hand, and it turns our products and the products of workers before us against us—for one sole purpose, which is its own gain, profit. If we are to satisfy our needs, if we are to be able to develop our potential, we must struggle against capital and, in doing so, we working people create ourselves as revolutionary subjects (2012a: 35).

While this is undeniably the case, the growth of middle-class radicalism since the 1960s remains a fact, and a fact that must be taken into consideration. Wright is among a number of theorists who recognise that to arbitrarily separate the middle class from the working class is an error. "Workers cannot be defined simply as wage-labourers, but as wage-labourers who also do not control the labour of others within production and do not control the use of their own labour within the labour-process" (Wright 1979: 73–74). As the crisis in capitalism intensifies, so too does the middle class become threatened.

How relevant is Marxism in the age of capitalist crisis? Therborn (2012) speaks of the 20th century as the century of the working class while the 21st century represents a shift to the middle class. It is a construction that is broadly accepted by many theorists and by many who claim the title of Marxist. Therborn accepts that capitalist exploitation and oppression continue and asks who will put their stamp upon the new century and the struggles against capitalism – the 'new' middle class or those he describes as the 'plebeian' masses. Having declared the century of the working class to be over, Therborn ultimately offers a defeatist and demoralised perspective. Marxism, cannot simply ignore this or that section of the population, but nor can it be permitted to equivocate. The class nature of society has not changed. The potential and capacity of a globalised working class remains strong. The middle class has increasingly been brought into direct confrontation with capitalism. D'Amato (2006: 100) generalises the different perspectives by stating that the world view of the working class is broadly collectivist while that of the middle class is individualist. These perspectives differ, but they do not preclude a radicalised middle class from playing a significant role, alongside a class-conscious working class. This is possibly an optimistic assessment given the apparent lack of class consciousness that exists within the working class today and the obvious lack of leadership that entrenches capitalist rule while it remains riven by crisis. Marxism remains the only viable structure to achieve that optimistic outcome.

The significance of the rise of non-class social movement and identity politics and the strengths and weaknesses of such approaches to emancipatory politics cannot be underestimated. Future attempts by Marxism to provide a cogent leadership that will confront and challenge capitalism must take these movements into consideration. This, however, needs to be balanced with an understanding that the role of the working class as the source of capitalist profit remains pivotal due to its labour and extracted surplus value.

Capitalism remains unchallenged. Marxism remains divided. Marxism, however, is the most appropriate vehicle to offer the required leadership to challenge capitalism. Marxism's relevance is not the issue, but it first must overcome the theoretical and practical problems that have plagued it for decades.

7

THE PROMISE OF MARXISM

It is time to return to the issue of Marxism's role in an era of capitalist crisis. Despite the depredations that come from capitalist crisis, and of the parallel crisis of Marxism, there is more than a little room for optimism. What follows is an optimistic perspective for the future of Marxism in the 21st century. Regardless of arguments to the contrary, it has been shown that economic issues drive political responses and the class nature of capitalist economic structures remain pivotal. Crisis remains elemental to capitalist development. Interpreting the development of capitalism and its changes remains central.

We need, first, to re-focus attention to the question of whether Marxism can address the problems that are posed by 21st-century capitalism. Marxist responses to capitalism need to reflect the qualitative changes that are apparent, but the additional problem of multiple 'Marxisms' needs to be resolved. This problem is reflected in the decades-long debates of 'reform or revolution', as well as the disputed issue of the decisive role of the working class. These issues are further developed when I briefly explore the rich empirical analysis of Piketty, whose work, regardless of its limitations almost unconsciously acts to reinforce the core values inherent in Marxism. However, despite the depth of his analysis on the correlation between capitalist development and the growth of social inequality, Piketty is unable to move beyond a position of making capitalism 'fairer', more 'democratic' and more regulated.

This brings us once more to the 'crisis' in Marxism, and whether a resolution to the crisis is either possible or even desirable. Polemic and debate allow for theory and ideas to grow, but it has come at the cost of the 'practice' of Marxism. Marxism's relevance is inescapably connected to the success or failure of the development of a political movement of the working class. The most significant and fundamental question is what form of political expression this will be.

It is for this reason that attention is turned to the issue of the working class as a 'revolutionary subject'. There is a broad consensus among the various strains of Marxism that a new society is required and that the world needs to change. There is, at the same time, a reticence in offering a view of how change might be effected. This is understandably connected to a sense of fear of failure that the long shadow that Stalinism has cast. Questions of spontaneity and leadership are explored, as is the potential to harness the spontaneous events of protest into more overt class-conscious activity.

There is, in the variants of Marxist theory an on-going and nagging debate between the conflicting positions of class and identity as springboards for action. I argue that class analysis and the role of the working class must remain the essential priority of Marxist theory. At the same time, it is an objective reality that identity and social movement politics have mobilised large numbers of people into an often amorphous 'anti-capitalist' sentiment. It may be that some form of principled unity might be developed that acknowledges the potential for identity politics to become more directly connected to deeper issues of class as a means of confronting capitalism. At the same time, there is a central truth that must be borne in mind. Capitalism survives and reproduces itself via the class nature of the system – by the use of labour, and by convincing the working class that it needs capitalism to survive.

This brings us to the final and ultimately defining question of Marxism's purpose and future. In responding to this question, I re-iterate the central arguments that run through this book – of Marxism's relevance in an age of capitalist crisis and of Marxism's central purpose. It is accepted that Marxism has proven to be a valuable analytical tool and has the capacity to trace the trajectory of capitalism. This, however, is not enough. Marxism's ultimate purpose is to combat and challenge capitalism, with a view to fundamentally changing the world.

Marxism and 21st-century capitalism

Marxism has historically sought to respond to changes in capitalism. This has led to disputation and dislocation within Marxist theory and practice. Marxist theorists have shown an enduring capacity to analyse developments within capitalism, but this has often been at the expense of what remains the central function of Marxism; an organisational and leadership role that can effectively challenge capitalism. This is not to belittle the rich analytical and intellectual history of Marxism. From the Stalinisation of the Russian Revolution and the limitations this imposed on the development of Marxist thought, to the subsequent crisis in

Marxism, there has been an on-going movement to develop a Marxist ideology that would remain relevant. The various schools of Marxist thought have responded to capitalist development. They have acknowledged the ideological questions that 21st-century capitalism poses and have sought to analyse and answer those questions. What has remained uncertain is Marxism's current capacity to respond and to finally resolve these questions, and in so doing, challenge the continuation of capitalist rule.

There have been dramatic changes in capitalism. These are particularly evident in the financialisation of capitalism, changes in the productive use of capital, and in increased capitalist integration. This demands a conscious and constant re-appraisal of Marxist theory and practice. These changes in capitalism are said to indicate that "we are living in a Marxist moment" (Laffey and Dean 2002: 90). Such a statement leads to a question of enormous significance. Which Marxism? Wallerstein (1986) famously refers to a 'thousand Marxisms'. Laffey and Dean (2002: 92) describe the difficulty, in the face of a multiplicity of Marxisms, of making choices between them. Can the claim that Marxism can address the questions that 21st-century capitalism raises be credible if it is first necessary to 'choose' between Marxisms?

This dilemma of choice needs to be addressed. A suitable starting position is to regard the problem from the perspective of Marx and the Marxist method of analysis. Marx (1974) proposed that what was of singular importance was to make observations that move from the simple to the complex – from labour, value, exchange and ultimately leading to globalised capitalist relations and the world market. It was the inter-relationship of all component parts that was paramount. What can be observed in much contemporary Marxist theory is an unwillingness to acknowledge those simple truths. Issues of class, exploitation, and economics as the engine of political movement, are routinely downplayed.

It remains a truth that capitalism and its development is predicated on the appropriation of surplus value. Capitalist society is based on the notion of an economic base, upon which rests a political and social superstructure. The state, as facilitator of the dominant economic ideology, is rooted in class and class divisions. These are some of the key issues that define Marxism. Ultimately there is one capitalism that essentially conforms to that pattern. It adapts to changes in prevailing conditions as a means of seeking escape from its inherent contradictions, but remains the obstacle to emancipation of the working class and its allies. There is one Marxism, albeit a dislocated Marxism, that seeks to challenge capitalist rule. This often-fractured Marxism still seeks to answer the questions of capitalism. What it has often failed to do, precisely because of its perceived fracture, is to promote a practice that will challenge and replace capitalism.

Capitalism, in the 21st century, is mired in crisis. Tabb (2010: 320) makes an unexceptional point, arguing that capitalism has always disregarded any interests apart from those that serve its development and that this disregard of communities and of the working people is heightened in periods of crisis. Tabb cites Brenner's comments that "the basic source of today's crisis is the declining vitality of the advanced economies since 1973 and especially since 2000" (2010: 317). This assessment indicates that crisis, rather than abating, will deepen. Experience validates such a view.

Brenner's assessment, however, does little to resolve the problem. Perspectives that consciously seek to articulate the need to challenge capitalist hegemony remain muted. Lebowitz describes the situation whereby the predominant response to capitalist 'abuses' is to seek ways to regulate and ameliorate its worst and most evident excesses.

> We see the same pattern when it comes to the current financial crisis of capitalism. New regulations, new limits, new forms of oversight are seen as a solution to abuse and excess ... Bad capitalists, rather than capitalism itself are identified as the evil (2012b: 59).

Capitalist crisis, of itself, has not led to effective challenge. Marxism, in the 21st century, can and does answer the questions of capitalism but, truth be told, has done little to effectively resolve the problem. For many, capitalism remains an almost immutable force. Once more the Luxemburg/Bernstein polemic returns as a haunting refrain: reform or revolution? Marxism may lay all manner of claims to an intellectual, moral, analytical high-ground but the words of Luxemburg are still bitingly fresh:

> As long as theoretic knowledge remains the privilege of a handful of 'academicians' in the party, the latter will face the danger of going astray. Only when the great mass of workers take the keen and dependable weapons of scientific socialism in their own hands will all the petty bourgeois inclinations, all the opportunist currents, come to naught. The movement will then find itself on sure and firm ground. 'Quantity will do it' (1988: 10).

Luxemburg's call for 'quantity' appears even more remote than when she uttered those words in 1900. Influential Marxist theorists of the late 20th and early 21st century have, in their quest to remain 'relevant' and to respond to capitalism's attempts to adapt, unconsciously weakened the movement that might 'change the world'. There have been numerous departures from the essence of Marxist theory, but the most telling, from the perspective of presenting a serious challenge to the dominance of capitalism, has been the relegation of class as a pivotal issue.

Class, and an acknowledgement of the potential of a globalised working class, is essential to making Marxism relevant in the age of capitalist crisis. The continuing growth of the working class is such that by 2030 it is estimated that globally there will be 3.5 billion members of the working class (Dobbs et al. 2012). It is necessary for Marxism, both as a theoretical construct, and as an organising force, to recognise that the core components of Marxist theory remain valid.

Capitalism poses questions for the working class and for those who seek emancipation. Burgmann (2016: 240) sums up one enduring response to these questions when using the example of austerity programs in Greece. That response is to repeat the mantra that the unions react by re-forming themselves and taking up new forms of struggle. The problems with such a perspective are immediately clear. To assume that trade union struggles alone can challenge capitalism is to invite defeat. Nothing much has changed in this regard since Lenin (1977c: 109) described how the unions were engaged in economic struggle but fundamental change requires an ideological and theoretical position that trade union politics could not offer. What also remains relatively unchanged is the battle of ideas within the anti-capitalist movement. It is a battle between those who seek an accommodation with capitalism in the hopes of making capitalism more responsive to the needs of the people – to democratise capitalism – and those who seek to fundamentally reorganise society and the economy to serve the interests of the working class and its allies.

Contemporary Marxist theory has tended to promote the merits of identity politics, and social movement politics ahead of the working class. The essence of the arguments that I have pursued is that the working class remains the central force for effecting fundamental change. To relegate the working class to a position of relative insignificance is a position that is deeply flawed. At the same time, it is an objective reality that social movement politics have the capacity to engage large numbers. Marxist approaches to the issues of 21st-century capitalism and its crisis need to recognise the value of incorporating both trends. The organisation and leadership of anti-capitalist movements will necessitate a confluence of these two forces. This can only be achieved by resolving the issue of leadership. The 20th century can be characterised as a century of crisis, revolution and war. The conditions are no different in this century. The decisive questions are the same as they were a century ago. What forces can be marshalled to challenge the economic and political system? How can the world be transformed? It is a question that has been debated for decades. A successful resolution to that question also offers the definitive answer to the question of whether Marxism can address the questions that 21st-century capitalism poses. Central to achieving such resolution is the requirement to re-focus attention to just what constitutes the essence of Marxism.

An effective theory for the 21st century

It should not be a difficult task to establish and isolate the core values of Marxism. A range of analyses of capitalist development can be used as a means of finding 'common ground' and agreement on what constitutes the essence of Marxist theory. The central contradictions that are observable in capitalism have already been described. These include:

1 the private nature of ownership and the public nature of the production process,
2 the necessity to globalise economic relations while maintaining a reliance on the nation-state as a political foundation, and
3 the drive to maximise profits and surplus value while facing a tendency to see profit rates fall.

While the theory of the falling rate of profit remains contested and divisive, points 1 and 2 tend to resonate among all schools of Marxist thought. An even more elemental perspective is the proposition that economic issues drive political outcomes – the base/superstructure thesis. However, this idea, so central to Marxist theory, is perhaps the most divisive. Even so there are a great many values that are shared.

Burawoy and Wright describe what they term the 'centrepiece' of Marxist theory in the depiction of capitalism as "a particular kind of class society" (2006: 461). Such a proposition is regarded as a potentially unifying factor within Marxism. Burawoy and Wright (2006: 461) explain that the central arguments of Marxist theory fall within three theoretical 'clusters'. These are: a theory of the trajectory of capitalist development, a theory of the reproduction of capitalism, and the emancipatory theory of socialism and communism. Such a premise certainly allows for a sense of optimism, and particularly from the point of view of developing and articulating a Marxist theory for the 21st century. Theory develops, according to the objective conditions at hand. Capitalism continues to exist in conditions of crisis. It has been shown that this crisis not only continues but has become increasingly acute. Marxist theorists are largely in accord with such an observation. It is in the integration of a growing theory with a neglected practice that Marxism's on-going significance rests. Burawoy and Wright's work is important in that they identify those areas of commonality. The next steps, of linking a developing theory to practice, assume an even greater significance. While these 'clusters' remain at the very centre of Marxist theory, the question of the emancipatory program, of fundamentally changing the world, remains the most problematic for Marxism in the 21st century. Once more we return to that most divisive but defining question of reform or revolution.

Finding common ground within what appears to be a range of 'Marxisms' is difficult. This is particularly the case when considered alongside the idea of advancing an emancipatory program for the working class and its allies. The 'crisis' of Marxism that Korsch (1931) identified has not been resolved. On the contrary, it has deepened. At the same time, Marxist theory has continued to develop. Its capacity for analysis and observation has remained its strength. Drawing together those elements of Marxist theory that serve both to promote a class-based analysis and to seek ways to organise a class-based resistance to capitalism becomes a central task. The role and importance of the working class remains central to the idea of Marxist relevance, to resolving the 'crisis' in Marxism, and in challenging capitalism. This role is reinforced as a working class is formed in developing economies. Silver comments that:

> The insight that labor and labor movements are continually made and remade provides an important antidote against the common tendency to be overly rigid in specifying who the working class is ... our eyes are open to the early signs of new working-class formations as well as 'backlash' resistance from those working classes that are being 'unmade.' A key task becomes the identification of emerging responses from below to both the creative and destructive sides of capitalist development (2006: 20–21).

Silver's analysis of the 'making' and the 'unmaking' of the working class in different parts of the world, reinforces earlier Marxist perspectives on one of the defining characteristics of the general crisis in capitalism. This is the growth of the working class. While trade union density in industrialised nations has shrunk and manufacturing jobs have declined, the global working class has expanded (Dobbs et al. 2012). Capitalism, as Marx explained, promotes the growth of the working class, and importantly, as capitalism develops, the growth of a global working class. An inevitable feature of an expanding capitalism is that it is both destructive as well as progressive (Marx 1969b: 107; Mark and Engels 1975b: 200–201). The working class and the importance of class remains at Marxism's core. Marxism is a means to an end. That end is to challenge capitalism and to change the world.

To state that Marxism's purpose is to change the world can hardly be regarded as antagonistic to Marxism's other theoretical 'clusters' as identified by Burawoy and Wright. I have broadly discussed the trajectory of Marxism and have been critical of its development. At the same time, the analytical capacity of contemporary Marxism has contributed to an understanding of how capitalism operates and has developed, even as it effectively ignores the need to challenge capitalism. Attempts by the Regulation School to re-build aspects of Marxist theory serve as just such an example.

Marxist theory argued that capitalism was prone to 'breakdown' under the weight of internal contradictions. The 'golden age' of capitalism after World War II appeared to throw the breakdown theory into confusion and disarray. Regulation Theory "set its eyes on the analysis of the crisis-ridden process of capitalist development. It argued that crises, far from leading to the demise of capitalism, generate structural transformations that facilitate its survival and longevity" (Mavroudeas 2012: 3). Jessop describes Regulation Theory as a way to:

> integrate the analysis of political economy with that of civil society and the state to show how they interact to 'normalize' the capital relation. It examines the social processes and struggles that define and stabilize modes of economic calculation and norms of economic conduct (2001b: 216).

Aglietta correctly asserts that "theory is never final and complete, it is always in the process of development" (2000: 15). However (in the sense that Regulation Theory claims an alignment with Marxism), theory ought to generate activity that will lead to change. The fundamental position of the regulation theorists is that capitalism remains a self-regulating system. If this is true then theory becomes a circle not unlike the cyclical nature of capitalism, resulting in equilibrium rather than change. The ultimate point of departure between classical Marxism and Regulation theory rests on the regulationists' acceptance and insistence that capitalism is both resilient and enduring, whereas the classical Marxist perspective is that capitalism is crisis-prone and liable to breakdown.

Running along a not altogether dissimilar pathway is Marx's concept of the reproduction of capital. This, for Burawoy and Wright, is one of the theoretical 'clusters'. Lebowitz has argued that the working class play a central role in this cycle of reproduction and that they have come to see the existence and reproduction of capital as essential to their own existence. He describes a 'vicious circle' beginning with:

> (a) people who are separated from the means of production and with needs that they must fulfil, we see that these people (b) must go into the labour market to sell their labour power – competing with other people in the same situation. They (c) enter into capitalist production, that process which yields as its result impoverished workers with the need and the means to consume. Having (d) consumed the products they are able to purchase, however, these workers are once again without the means to maintain themselves and must present themselves again to capital (2012b: 63–64).

This cycle of dependence serves not merely to reproduce capital but to reproduce the class relationships within capitalism itself.

Burawoy and Wright's first two theoretical 'clusters' – theories of the trajectory of capitalist development and of the reproduction of capitalism, become the focus of Piketty's *Capital in the Twenty-First Century*. His book evoked intense discussion, with the *The Economist* describing him as 'a modern Marx' (The Economist 2014). This is despite Piketty's own assertion that he is not a Marxist. Indeed, Piketty (2014: 1–13) seeks to chart a course between what he describes as Marx's 'apocalyptic' theory of capitalist breakdown and collapse and Kuznets 'fairy-tale' of a link between the growth of capitalism and a diminution of inequality. Kuznets' theory (1955) assumed that as an economy developed there would be an initial intensification of inequality but, as that individual economy and market grows and matures, then so too does inequality diminish. Kuznets' view appeared to be validated by post-World War II capitalist stabilisation and relative economic growth. The period from the 1970s and heightened capitalist crisis has led to a re-assessment of this theory and, consequently, a reappraisal of the Marxist breakdown theory.

Piketty's exhaustive and thorough empirical study validates the claim that inequality and capitalism are inseparable. It is one thing to 'prove', through diligent use of statistics that this is the case. The question remains of what to do with the data and how to redress that visible and growing inequality. Piketty (2014: 569) argues that capital must be brought under 'democratic' control and that the problems of economic and social inequality that he so painstakingly exposes, can be resolved by "a progressive annual tax on capital. This will make it possible to avoid an endless inegalitarian (sic) spiral while preserving competition and incentives for new instances of primitive accumulation" (Piketty 2014: 572). While he in no way seeks to present a challenge to capitalism, his work and research was still attacked and the fact that growth in inequality is both quantifiable and verifiable was questioned (Giles 2014).

Piketty's work, and the reactions to it, show that inequality has risen in direct proportion to the growing crisis in capitalism which in turn serves to reaffirm the relevance of Marxism. The threat of crisis hangs in the air. However, stating this is one thing. There are many contending schools of Marxist thought and the trajectory of Marxism has done little to eliminate, let alone limit contention within the anti-capitalist movement. It is in the process of re-building a theory, of returning to the core issues that can unite Marxists, that optimism can be found. The most central of values, the deepest core of Marxism, lies in its oft-stated call to 'change the world'. That can only come from people engaged in concerted struggle to effect fundamental change.

Resolving the crisis in Marxism

Realising Marxism's stated objective of challenging capitalism has been made more difficult by division and crisis. However, a resolution of the crisis in Marxism is both possible and necessary. Marxism, it has been shown:

1 is the antithesis of capitalism,
2 offers a thorough analysis of capitalism's trajectory,
3 exists to challenge capitalism and to change the world, and
4 promotes the view that the working class is the force that has the potential to overthrow capitalism.

Marxism has, since its formation, been engaged in intense polemic and contention. To expect that the divergent trends within Marxist theory could be expected to find common cause or principled unity is, in the immediate future, unlikely. This observation is not made from a position of pessimism. Marxism offers a rational path to emancipation. The promotion of an emancipatory path is what most significantly divides Marxism and, paradoxically, offers a means of by-passing, if not resolving the crisis that has long afflicted Marxist thought.

Describing 'problems' in Marxism, from a Marxist perspective, has a long history. Plekhanov (1976) Korsch (1931), the theorists of the Frankfurt School, Western Marxism, the 'New Left', the neo-Marxists, post-Marxists, have all focused on the problems. What has become almost commonplace is the claim that the "crisis is ultimately not one of

Marxist philosophy but of Marxism as revolutionary social theory" (McCarney 1990: 189). It is an idea that gained currency as post-modernist and post-Marxist theories developed.

As a consequence, reactions to the Marxist concept of the 'revolutionary potential of the working class' assume importance as either a means of seeking a path towards renewal of Marxism, or of resolving the crisis within Marxism. The working class, regardless of poor leadership, or periods of indifference, remains a potentially revolutionary force. Three interconnected elements validate this proposition. First, the working class is the class that, by their labour, produce and reproduce capitalist production and class relations (Marx 1986b: 529–530). Second, the needs of opposing classes remain intensely contradictory (Marx and Engels 1977: 35–36). Finally, the working class has become an increasingly globalised class as capitalism itself has become a globalised economic structure (Silver 2006). Recognition of these three facts becomes pivotal when considering the prospects for Marxist renewal.

Class formation, in Marx's view, had little to do with aspirations or desires. "Men make their own history, but they do not make it just as they please; they do not make it under circumstances chosen by themselves, but under circumstances directly encountered, given and transmitted from the past" (Marx 1986a: 97). It is a view that needs to be considered in the light of much contemporary Marxist scholarship. 'Identification' with a group, rather than a place in a set of economic arrangements has become a dominant perspective. The role and potential power of the working class has been diminished within the broad scope of this scholarship.

The issue of class and the role of the working class continues to be among the most vexatious in terms of finding that elusive 'common ground' among Marxists. Despite evidence to the contrary (Silver 2006, World Bank 1995, Dobbs et al. 2012) some Marxist analysts maintain that a global 'proletarianisation' has not occurred and it is unlikely that it will do so (Sitton 2010: 15). Sitton does not deny that struggles against capital are a fact of life. He argues that:

> Multiple forces of opposition are gathering in the world today. Some are trying to protect their jobs, their culture, the environment, or their families. Others are simply asserting human dignity in the face of crushing circumstance. Overthrow by a self-conscious proletariat has never been the only possibility … whatever their motives, they will be determined that economies exist to serve people, not people to serve economies (2010: 26).

There remains, however, a reluctance to acknowledge the potential power of the working class. At the same time, the need for 'change' is broadly accepted. Fuentes-Ramirez (2014: 142), for instance, argues that change can be brought about by influencing the state to empower institutions that might, in turn, cause 'ruptures' within capitalist institutions. To separate state institutions from capitalist institutions and to use one set against another would seem an unlikely scenario. Harvey (2012: xiii) shifts the focus again when he speaks of a revolutionary working class being constituted from urban rather than 'exclusively' factory workers. Harvey argues that 'glimmers' of hope are visible. He bases these hopes on the left-populist movements in Spain and Greece and on what he describes as 'revolutionary impulses' in Latin America (2012: 157). It is an argument that is strongly influenced by the *Occupy Wall Street Movement*. He proposes that the anti-capitalist movement should connect with the alienated and discontented and that this 'movement' "be democratically assembled into a coherent opposition … an alternative political system, and, ultimately, an alternative way of organizing production, distribution, and consumption for the benefit of the people" (Harvey 2012: 162–163). While recognising the need to effect change and 'revolutionary' change, two factors remain obscure and understated. How is this change to be brought about and which forces will bring about change? They are questions that go to the heart of any real chance for Marxist realignment or resolution to the theoretical differences within Marxist theory.

The potential for realigning Marxist theory, or of resolving the differences within Marxist theory, must be seriously considered if Marxism is to fulfil its historical role. None of capitalism's historical contradictions have been resolved but, rather, have become more obvious.

Areas of accord among anti-capitalist activists and theorists can be identified, but contemporary Marxist theory remains divided in the area of forging anything remotely resembling a unity of purpose between theory and practice. I have argued that among those elements that constitute a Marxist core, the working class and its identification as revolutionary subject, remains pivotal. The shift in Marxist theory, from the centrality of the working class to non-class issues, has limited Marxism's capacity to oppose capital. Theory is enhanced by considering and reconsidering the historical context that contributes to the present and future movement of social forces.

Which forces, then, are most likely to bring about this change? Marxist theory was built upon the premise that an organised working class is central to challenging capitalism. The development of class consciousness and organisation of the working class is not something that develops spontaneously. A degree of coyness exists when describing this channelling of discontent. The organisational structure that would seem to be inevitable under conditions of class rule is an overtly political organisation – a political party framed by Marxist theory. The reluctance of many Marxists to speak in terms of political organisation is perhaps, at a glance, understandable. The history of Marxist political parties throughout the 20th century has been mired in Stalinism. Non-Stalinist Marxist political expressions have been dogged by problems associated with perceived irrelevance that afflict small and often powerless organisations. To speak, therefore, of a Marxist party that might organisationally arm the working class, is often derided.

The idea of a political expression of Marxism through the vehicle of a political party is very nearly as old as Marxism. The strength of such parties has appreciably weakened. "In the capitalist world, self-described Marxist parties have become noticeably weaker or have ceased to be potent political forces at all" (Allen 2004: xii). There is an irony in such analysis. On the one hand, a resurgence of interest in Marxism and an appreciation of capitalist crisis is acknowledged and yet, on the other hand, political expressions of Marxist theory have become weaker. The relevance of Marxism in the face of capitalist crisis must be gauged by its capacity to challenge the rule of capitalism. The means of organisation has traditionally been through a party-political organisation.

Marxism has long espoused the need for a political movement of the working class. It is regarded as the most appropriate means of leading a movement that seeks to change the world. To this end Marx and Engels produced the *Manifesto of the Communist Party* as a guide to the embryonic *Communist League*. Sitton laments that Marx never "clarified what would be the form of the proletariat organized as the ruling class" (2010: 12). It is a curious lament. All too often classical Marxists are berated for regarding Marx's words as something akin to 'holy writ' and yet their critics seem to demand that an almost prescriptive formula for change be presented. Marxists in a capitalist world can, justifiably seek to create the conditions by which such a transformation might be enacted, but not to determine what and how that future society would operate. The role and purpose of such a party in the 21st century is central to clarifying what Marxism is 'for' in this century, its claim to relevance and what forces are best suited to promote the emancipatory project of the working class.

What that form of political organisation takes is necessarily dependent upon the objective conditions that exist. What is clear is that the essential formation of any such political organisation could not be limited by national boundaries and nor could it hope to exist under the 'patronage' of the state that it ultimately would seek to challenge. Rees argues that:

> A revolutionary organization remains the indispensable tool ... Without the struggle to build such an organization, the danger remains that the dialectic of capitalist development will remain ... but if the struggle to build such an organization is successful, we have a chance – not more, not less – to make the leap from the realm of necessity to the realm of freedom (1998: 301–302).

It is around this 'call to arms' that Marxism, in the age of capitalist crisis, can assert its relevance and, if not re-group and realign itself, then discover ways to resolve the crisis that has been a feature of its development for the better part of a century.

New organisational structures and overcoming the crisis of leadership

An essential step in resolving the perceived crisis in Marxism is to overcome what has been described as a 'crisis of leadership'. Such a proposition is predicated on a number of assumptions that have their basis in classical Marxist theory. The first is that the working class is the class most capable of bringing about fundamental change. For this to occur there needs to be a high degree of class consciousness. This class consciousness needs to be guided to action that will result in both challenge to capitalism and to its replacement as a ruling idea. The most capable form of such leadership is one based in Marxist theory and practice. This premise is at the basis of Marxist theory and yet many contemporary Marxists appear reluctant to broach the issue of how change can be effected. This becomes an even greater problem when so many Marxist theorists reject the idea of the working class as a 'revolutionary' subject. Mann (1973: 71) argues that the working class in developed capitalist states is unlikely to develop 'revolutionary' class consciousness and therefore is unlikely to become an agent for radical change. Subsequent decades have seen this assumption grow in strength.

While there is a reluctance to consider how change can be implemented there is no shortage of calls for a different future. Badiou typifies these, often amorphous calls to the future:

> The communist hypothesis is that a different collective organization is practicable, one that will eliminate the inequality of wealth and even the division of labour. The private appropriation of massive fortunes and their transmission by inheritance will disappear. The existence of a coercive state, separate from civil

> society, will no longer appear a necessity: a long process of reorganization based on a free association of producers will see it withering away (2008: 42).

Badiou, while 'wishing' for a better future, essentially maintains a position of antipathy towards the working class. What is evident is a desire to break from capitalism and a wish for 'something better'. What is not evident is how to go about it. The difficulties are exacerbated when the working class is relegated to a position of insignificance by so many who claim some adherence to Marxism. What needs to be considered, but is ignored by Badiou and post-Marxism in general, is a fundamental premise of Marxism. This is, that capitalism is a system framed by alienation of labour, upon which its continued future and profitability rests. While this is the case, there is an understandable fear of the past and of the distortions in Marxism that stemmed from the experience of Stalinism. Swyngedouw succinctly describes the situation whereby the "fear of failing has become so overwhelming that fear of real change is all that is left; resistance is as far as our horizons reach – transformation, it seems, can no longer be thought, let alone practiced" (2010: 317). However, even while acknowledging the problem that 'fear' remains, he fails to move beyond the call, in principle at least, for change. This 'revolutionary' change requires two conditions to occur. Productive forces need to be highly developed and the working class and its allies must assume political power. In other words, what is required is a coming together of objective and subjective conditions for fundamental change.

If change is merited and capitalism is to be confronted, then there needs to be a mechanism by which to approach that change. Political organisation has already been briefly discussed, as has the importance of the working class as an agent for change. Historical moments have arisen when change might successfully have been achieved and yet capitalism remains the obviously dominant paradigm. The failures of the working-class movement can be attributed, as Trotsky (1974) forcefully did, to a failure of leadership of the working class. Such a proposition has been criticised with Beilharz (1987: 72) seeking to dismiss the idea as being 'Jacobin' in its style with its focus being almost exclusively on leadership and leadership alone. What is important to remember in such debates is that Marxist theories of radical change have traditionally been formulated on the need for a focused and consistent theory that is not subject to the dissipations of effort that so often mark spontaneous activity.

The issue of spontaneity and Marxist responses appear quite unequivocal. Lenin bluntly focused on this issue stating that the task was to "*combat spontaneity, to divert* the working-class movement from this spontaneous, trade unionist striving to come under the wing of the bourgeoisie, and to bring it under the wing of revolutionary Social-Democracy" (emphasis in the original 1977c: 122). At the same time situations arise that can be regarded as spontaneous moments of radical upsurge and these cannot be discounted. The point is how to channel these moments as a means of challenging capitalism. In recent years, there have been numerous examples of mobilisations that have withered for want of leadership and program. The Seattle protests, anti-WTO actions, the 'Occupy' movement and the widespread protests in the US in the aftermath of the 2016 presidential elections are just some examples. Discontent is apparent but these manifestations of unrest remain disconnected and isolated and inevitably without conscious leadership.

Inevitably, it would seem, the question returns to how to unify the broad anti-capitalist sentiments that exist. Marxism's relevance in the 21st century will be judged by its capacity to answer that question, theoretically and practically. It is a task of some magnitude and many obstacles stand in its way. The working class as revolutionary subject needs to be re-affirmed. The flawed concept of identity politics needs to be addressed. The issues and discontents exhibited in such protest movements need to be brought into a class perspective that allows for an integration of separate grievances into the broader anti-capitalist movement. The debilitating problem of nationalism needs to be overcome in the face of a relentless globalisation of capitalism. The global, international nature of the burgeoning working class needs to be recognised and harnessed in order to issue any successful challenge to the rule of capital. Political organisation is required and a consistent leadership is necessary. Overcoming the problems appears a daunting task, but not an impossible one.

The requirement of a global response to the global problem of capitalism has long vexed socialist and Marxist theorists. It has framed the articulation of an ideology of global trade union responses, to movements for a global human rights and socialist globalisation and as Sklair states:

> the many radical movements … feed into an emerging anti-globalization movement. As this movement inspires ever larger numbers of people to become active in the pursuit of human rights and the social responsibilities that are an integral part of them, we can begin to work out alternatives to capitalist globalization. Socialist globalization is one of many alternative paths (2002: 319).

Sklair recognises class as an issue but remains a captive of identity politics, arguing that conflicts effectively revolve around issues of personal identity and that “there is no adequate theory of how class relates to race, religion, and nationalism in the economic, political and culture-ideology spheres, nationally or transnationally” (2002: 324). A starting point in isolating such a ‘theory’ would appear to be a return to Marx. The *Communist Manifesto*, might allay some of Sklair’s fears. “Does it require deep intuition to comprehend that man’s ideas, views and conceptions, in one word, man’s consciousness, changes with every change in the conditions of his material existence, in his social relations and in his social life?” (Marx and Engels 1977: 57).

Marx and Engels (1977: 49) declared that the essence of a communist organisation is that it operates in the interests of the working class, regardless of nationality and in the direct interests of the movement as a whole. For them, emancipation and the challenge to capitalism was, necessarily, to be organised through the auspices of a political organisation and that this organisation could only be a political party organised at the global level. This is all the more relevant today as capitalism has assumed an intensely global character. The difficulties are enormous but the capacities to link and unite working class struggles, with the issues that have been promoted through divisive identity politics and non-class social movements offers a chance to change the world. The significance of Marxism in the era of capitalist crisis lies in its insistence upon its organisational capacity, its internationalism, its analytical abilities and a capacity to merge theory and practice. It is possible, if not altogether probable, that the divergent schools of Marxism that have developed in the past century can unite around such a perspective. It is a possibility that is fraught with difficulties, but regardless, the era of capitalist crisis requires an ideological opposition that can mount a concerted and committed challenge.

Lebowitz (2004) seeks to explain how and why capitalism keeps going. In his concluding remarks, he argues that for change to be effected more is required than simply explaining the nature of capitalism or its history. It is necessary for people to believe that something better is possible. He concludes by asserting that,

> to the extent that those of us on the left are not actively attempting to communicate the nature of capitalism and working explicitly for the creation of a socialist alternative, we are part of the explanation as to what keeps capitalism going (2004: 25).

Such a proposition requires a consistent and lucid theory and practice as a way to either resolve the crisis in Marxism, or to re-invigorate Marxism.

Reinterpreting class and social identity

The question posed, a little earlier, about which forces might transform the world brings us back to issues of class and social identity. The two concepts are inextricably linked and yet, in contemporary literature, often stand apart and in an often-antagonistic relationship. Class and social class for Marx was the foundation-stone of economic and political structures. The "history of all hitherto existing society is the history of class struggles" (Marx and Engels 1977: 35). Historically there has been a strong identification with class, although this often becomes somewhat subjective. Class identification remains difficult to discern. However, Sheppard and Biddle (2015) indicate that over 50 per cent of Australians regard themselves as 'middle-class' while 40 per cent still identify as 'working class'. Figures from the United States (Newport 2015) show that identification with the working class has risen rapidly in direct proportion to the rise of inequality.

While class identification may be a subjective affair, Marxist understanding of class is more solidly defined. It is a division determined by position in relation to the process of production (Lukacs 1976: 46). Class can be simply described on the basis of the ownership of the means of production, distribution and exchange. "It is always the direct relationship of the owners of the conditions of production to the direct producers" (Marx 1986c: 791). Marx briefly elaborated on this, differentiating between:

> the owners merely of labour-power, owners of capital, and landowners, whose respective sources of income are wages, profit and ground-rent, in other words, wage-labourers, capitalists, and landlords, constitute then three big classes of modern society based upon the capitalist mode of production (Marx 1986c: 885).

Such divisions are necessarily antagonistic and constitute the basis of the concept of class-consciousness as well as social inequality.

A class-based society and economy inevitably engenders a sense of inequality. Marx employed the analogy of a house to describe this feeling:

> A house may be large or small; as long as the surrounding houses are equally small it satisfies all social demands for a dwelling. But let a palace arise beside the little house, and it shrinks from a little house to a hut … the occupant of the relatively small house will feel more and more uncomfortable, dissatisfied and cramped within its four walls (1986f: 83).

It is a situation that has become the norm and, as such, is little remarked upon. What has happened, over time, has been a concerted and successful ideological offensive waged by capitalism and the state. It has, through engendering a sense of national unity and commonality, been able to successfully foster a belief among many that there are shared interests based not on class, but on national identity. Marx's (1986c: 83) argument, that the working class remains dependent upon capital rather than there being any 'community' of interests between worker and capitalist, remains as valid today as it did in 1849.

The crisis in Marxism that has been evident for a century serves to highlight this dilemma of class and class identification. Faced with such a tightly constructed and maintained ideological shield, many activists and theorists alike have sought to construct a framework that advantages identity over class. While this has already been discussed, it remains an objective reality that supra-class approaches to capitalism enjoy a position of dominance and, as such, need to be seriously considered in seeking a way forward for Marxism in the 21st century. This is said, not in any sense of acquiescence or accommodation to those who reject the leadership role of the working class, but rather to find, if possible, any sense of accord between the non-class activist approach and the classical Marxist class-based path to challenge capitalism.

Increasingly identity politics (Castells 2004: 11–12) has been presented as the only 'valid' response to inequality. It is a claim that directly challenges the essence of Marxist class-based politics. It is an argument that is based, in Castells' view, on the premise that the "ideological emptiness created by the failure of Marxism-Leninism to actually indoctrinate the masses was replaced, in the 1980s, when people were able to express themselves, by the only source of identity … in the collective memory: *national identity*" (2004: 43 italics in the original). Setting to one side his emotive language, it remains that for large numbers of people, identity has continued to be central. Herein lies a problem for identity as a political expression. Castells (2004: 6–7) outlines the potential array of identities that any one person may have including that of worker, parent, sportsperson etc. The needs of one identity group are not necessarily in concert with the needs of another and yet Castells argues that identity politics has become the most appropriate vehicle by which to respond to inequality. Such a perspective is held, despite the fact that identity politics inevitably runs along a line of potentially diverging interests.

Moran (2015: 165) also argues that identity politics can challenge issues of inequality and the distribution of resources within capitalist societies. However, he queries whether such a political framework can challenge the 'logic' of the capitalist system. This brings us to a dilemma that identity politics ultimately faces. It is said that the politics of identity is capable of providing a 'challenge' to aspects of capitalism but not the 'logic' of the system itself. This has led some theorists to seek to merge what are separate issues. They seek to discover a commonality between class and identity political movements. This is despite the fact that identity politics invariably takes a non-class approach as its initial premise. Fraser (1998) argues that the struggle for social justice has increasingly become polarised. Choices are variously made between class and identity. Fraser maintains that this is a false division and that 'justice' demands a redistribution across class lines and with a recognition of identity in close embrace. Such a position seeks to challenge the view of those whose perspective is either rooted in class as the determining factor or those who regard identity as the only valid vehicle that can combat capitalism.

Such a view is advanced by Kelley (1997) who argues that the rise of identity politics advances and strengthens class politics. His perspective is that any call to subsume issues of race, ethnicity or gender into broader 'class' issues weakens the movement for emancipation. Kelley, while advocating a broad class struggle infused with the recognition of identity politics, also supports the concept of 'radical humanism' which opposes a Marxist worldview. Kelley and Fraser seek a mechanism by which to fuse class and identity politics. They may well argue that such a fusion is possible, but their arguments need a far greater degree of clarity. There possibly may be, from the point of view of a reformist political program, a unity of working class and identity-based politics that would, at best, advance a call to make capitalism more tolerable. Walker (2015), president of the Ford Foundation, argues that capitalism is obliged to improve and strengthen the economic and political system. He oversaw a financial contribution of $100 million to the 'Black Lives Matter' (BLM) movement. Many of the activists in BLM would describe themselves as anti-capitalist. The Ford Foundation do not share such an anti-capitalist perspective and assiduously work to limit any rise in class antagonisms.

The capitalist state has sought to diminish expressions of working-class identity. This has driven the 'anti-capitalist' movement to assume a broad, non-class identity. What needs to be remembered is that those who maintain an anti-capitalist perspective frequently share class as well as identity. To deny class is to ignore the magnitude of the global working class and, in large measure to ignore Marxism. To ignore identity as a motivating factor is to ignore its capacity for mobilisation. Identity-based movements ought, with conscious leadership, to be able to be incorporated into class politics. However, a coming together of these elements needs first to recognise that it is not sufficient to make capitalism a more palatable system. The Ford Foundation president asks: what 'kind' of capitalism do we want? It is a question of the utmost relevance and especially when considered alongside an enduring perception that there is no real alternative to capitalism.

Lebowitz (2004) argues that capitalism's ability to 'keep going', or more precisely to reproduce itself, is due in large part to the acquiescence of the working class. He speaks of a dependency that workers feel for capitalism. They come to believe that capitalism meets their needs and that the worker needs capitalism.

> As long as workers have not broken with the idea that capital is necessary, a state under their control will act to facilitate the conditions for the reproduction of capital ... Capitalism produces the working class it needs. It produces workers who look upon it as necessary ... A system where the reproduction of capital is necessary for the reproduction of wage laborers. What keeps capitalism going? Wage laborers (2004: 24).

Lebowitz also separates what is 'necessary' for capitalism to survive from what is 'useful' for its survival. Capitalism requires an exploited working class to survive. It is a *necessity*. A working class and that is divided across often arbitrary lines of race, gender, ethnicity, and sexuality becomes *useful* for capitalism. Resolving any of these non-class issues would not, of itself, undermine the rule of capitalism. It has often been eloquently shown to be the case. The Ford Foundation's largesse to the anti-racist movement is a case in point. This assumes a particular significance when re-assessing the core values of Marxism and its relevance in an age of capitalist crisis. Such a re-assessment focuses, in the final assessment, on the fundamental question of Marxism's purpose.

Marxism's purpose and future

An article appeared in *Time Magazine* in 2013 entitled 'Marx's Revenge: How Class Struggle Is Shaping the World'. The article acknowledged that the global economy is in crisis and that workers around the world are experiencing a stagnation and decline in income, growing unemployment and debt. The author reminds his readers that "Marx theorized that the capitalist system would inevitably impoverish the masses as the world's wealth became concentrated in the hands of a greedy few, causing economic crises and heightened conflict between the rich and working classes" (Schuman 2013). The article also cites French philosopher Ranciere's argument that working-class organisations today are calling, at best, to reform an unequal system, and that "virtually all progressive or leftist parties contributed at some point to the rise and reach of financial markets, and rolling back of welfare systems in order to prove they were capable of reform" (Ranciere cited in Schuman 2013). The article is particularly relevant. It at once accepts the potential for class struggle to assume increasing significance in conditions of acute crisis for capitalism but that the organisations of the working class have acted against these very interests. The *Time Magazine* article neatly sums up the dilemma facing the working class today and how capital profits from acquiescent and institutionalised working-class organisations.

Questions of the relevance of Marxism ultimately depend on perceptions of capitalism's efficacy and whether it can be sustained, or, indeed whether it can confront and overcome its elemental contradictions. Gilpin enthusiastically speaks of a new age of global capitalism. "Americans, other citizens of the industrialized world, and many people in other parts of the international economy have entered what the financial expert and economic commentator Hale has called 'The Second Great Age of Global Capitalism'" (2000: 15). Unfortunately, or possibly fortunately, such extravagant claims have a tendency to rapidly become outdated. The Global Financial Crisis, as an expression of the deepening crisis in capitalism, the retreat into economic nationalism, the clearly irresolvable contradictions between globalised capitalism and the nation-state, make such exaltation questionable in the extreme. Gilpin (2000: 51) further argues that economic efficiency and the ambitions of dominant nation-states will determine the future power and prosperity of global capitalism. If he is correct, then Marxism has no future and therefore no purpose. On the other hand, Marxism has not been disproven. On the contrary, the very problems within capitalism attest to the validity of Marxism. Marxist analysis, however acute and accurate it might be, has not led to change. Is Marxism to simply be a useful tool to analyse that which is observable, or a vehicle by which to bring about change?

For Marx, the very point of understanding the world was to change it. It was the very point and purpose of his work. For this to be accomplished, a close interplay between theory and practice was considered a necessity. Gouldner (1980: 1–7) describes the coming to power of the Bolsheviks in 1917 and closely attends to the importance of a theoretical underpinning to the revolutionary practice that 'shook' the world. Pannekoek, writing during World War I and on the eve of the 1917 Revolution, stated what was, for Marxists, an unarguable reality. "Man is only the agent of economic needs; but these needs can only be changed thanks to his activity. Both parts are equally correct and important, and together they form a complete theory" (Pannekoek 1915). Marxism remains a philosophy that is integrally and dialectically connected to the economy. It is a philosophy that is fundamentally connected to the world, while simultaneously seeking to construct a new world.

Marx (Marx and Engels 1964: 31–32) built his method of analysis on the premise that the first historically significant moment for human development was the production of the economic means to satisfy material requirements and needs. Eagleton extrapolates from this, stating that:

> Marxism, however, wants to claim more than this. It wants to argue that material production is fundamental not only in the sense that there could be no civilisation without it, but that it is what ultimately determines the nature of that civilisation (2011: 108).

Marxist theory rests on the notion that economic factors largely determine social and political actions and reactions. Gray rejects Marxism as a failed attempt at social engineering. Even so he is compelled to concede that "in market societies ... not only is economic activity distinct from the rest of social life, but it conditions, and sometimes dominates, the whole of society" (2002: 12).

The future of Marxism and the question of what Marxism is for, is intimately connected with Marx's own emphasis on economics. For many critics of Marx, both non-Marxist and from within the broad Marxist milieu, the issue of Marx's 'economism' becomes the nub of Marxism's 'problems' and therefore an obstacle to a 'future' for Marxism. Gamble argues that:

> Marxism in the end has to stand by the claim that the economic power which accrues to the class which controls productive assets is a crucial determinant of the manner in which political, cultural and ideological power are exercised. Many kinds of sophisticated concepts can be deployed to understand the intricacies of the relationship, but in the end if the primacy of the economic is lost, then Marxism loses its distinctiveness and its value in social theory (1999b: 143).

Much of the on-going crisis within Marxism stems from a perceived need to distance Marxism from its 'economism' and its 'determinism'. Western Marxism and its variations have, for decades, sought to reconstruct Marxist theory. This has been at the expense of core Marxist considerations of the centrality of economics. In its place, has grown a misplaced acceptance that societal and political issues inform economic questions. Despite this, the crisis of capitalism has continued to indicate that economic issues do, indeed, play a central role in determining social and political outcomes. Marxism offers a theoretical and analytical framework from which to build resistance to capitalism. This resistance must, necessarily address the primacy of economic questions. Ultimately a fundamental difference within schools of Marxist thought remains unresolved. This is the issue of base and superstructure. The economic structures of society and capitalism constitute the base. Social and political activities and the institutions of the state (the superstructure) rest on this economic base. Elemental change can only be effected by changing the base. If the purpose of Marxism is to change the world then the economic structures of that world must be addressed, understood and fundamentally changed.

Change, according to Marxist theory, takes place within the context of class conflict. The working class and its allies assume an historical role. Cockshott and Zachriah (2012: 17) promote the idea of an historical 'project' of the working class. They assert that success can only be achieved if the working class espouses its own political vision for the future. The development of such a political vision can only be advanced alongside a leadership that is independent from the structures of the state and has the support of the class that is expected to 'espouse' a political vision. In this context, Marxism's intent, as envisaged more than a century ago becomes central to the issues of the 21st century. Lebowitz in an interview on the relevance of Marx in the 21st century remarked:

> I think that there is absolutely no question that Marxism enables us to understand the nature of the capitalist crisis today. For non-Marxists, everything is an accident or the result of bad decisions. They are not able to distinguish between causes and effects and often see symptoms as the source of problems. In contrast, Marxism permits us to consider capitalism as a whole and to understand the underlying factors which characterize not only its crises but also its periods of uninterrupted expansion.
>
> However, I think it is an error to think that Marxism can solve the crisis. Marxism is a theory – it is a way to understand. Ultimately, the only way to end capitalist crises is to end capitalism. And that requires more than a theory; it requires a commitment and determination to put an end to this perverse economic system (2013).

If Marxism is no more than a theory and a guide to understanding how the world turns, then it remains and must remain incapable of effecting change. Marxism has historically sought to present a theoretical response to capitalism while simultaneously promoting a practice that would enable an ideologically armed working class to bring about its own emancipation. Such has been the 'theory' of Marxism. The 'practice' has often been quite a different matter. Deutscher (1973: 18) described a rift between theory and practice that divided classical Marxism from Western Marxism and the New Left. It was a reminder of two of Marxism's more famous aphorisms – that without revolutionary theory there can be no revolutionary movement and that practice without theory is blind and that theory without practice is sterile.

In much the same sense that Cox (1981: 128) argues that theory is always for someone and for some purpose, then so too is Marxism for a particular purpose. That purpose is to promote a theory and practice that will equip the working class to confront and combat capitalism. Central to this purpose is Marxism's capacity to respond to, address and provide answers to the questions that capitalism, in the 21st century, raises. Marxism, then, has relevance, it has purpose and it has a future. It exists to counter capitalism in an age of capitalist crisis.

8

CONCLUSION

The fundamental question of Marxism's relevance in an age of capitalist crisis has been answered. In reaffirming its claim to relevance, and situating this alongside Marxism's historical exhortation to confront and challenge capitalism, I consciously engaged in an exercise in theory-building. The theoretical propositions outlined by Marx and subsequent Marxists have, over time, become mired in dislocation and disputation. This has been an exercise in re-focusing attention to the central, pivotal values espoused by Marxism. This has also involved exploring what, if any grounds there might be for a realignment of Marxist thought in the face of on-going and intensifying capitalist crisis.

A statement of intent was made in the introduction, of an intent to explain the connection between contemporary Marxism's endemic problems and capitalism's continued survival. It was also stated that questions of Marxism's relevance in the 21st century would be raised. There has, consequently, been a close engagement with an interconnected question of how broad, non-class and supra class social movements, as well as the politics of identity, could be expected to respond to the intensification of capitalist crisis.

The trajectory of capitalism became an early focus in the analysis. This, in turn, was linked to a discussion of the development of Marxist theory as it responded to the unfolding processes of capitalism and of its globalising nature. Capitalism is an economic system riven by contradiction and crisis. Marxism, for the past 100 years, has been embroiled in disputation. Running along parallel lines to questions of Marxism's on-going relevance, is the contention that the crisis in Marxism has, to a significant extent, aided and abetted capitalism's continued existence.

It was argued that capitalism's capacity to survive crisis and avoid fundamental breakdown has little to do with any inherent strength of capitalism and more to do with an inability on the part of Marxism to seriously threaten capitalism. This is due, in large part, to on-going schisms that weakened Marxism from the early 20th century. The split in Marxism, as a reaction to resurgent nationalism on the eve of World War I, the rise of Stalinism, the subsequent development of Western Marxism, the New Left, post-Marxism and the growing emphasis on the politics of identity rather than class, all served to weaken the capacity of the working class to struggle for emancipation. Marxism's ability to play a central leadership role in such emancipatory projects was seriously limited. For many Marxists, the working class, as a revolutionary subject, was deemed to no longer have any particular significance.

Attention was drawn, in advancing the claim of Marxism's continued relevance, to the 'purpose' of Marxism, and attention was refocused on the issue of just what Marxism is for. In so doing, this work was able to assert its own relevance. It is important to reflect on the relationship between previous research and the contributions made in the preceding pages to on-going research.

Marxist theory exists within a broadly constituted battle of ideas. This battle is never over. The arguments that have been presented represent small steps in a process that will continue. The argument for the relevance of Marxism in the 21st century has been clearly established. However, there is no prescriptive path that Marxism must adhere to. Debates as to how capitalism is to be confronted are necessarily pertinent to 'today' and consequently assume a sense of immediacy. What a 'post-capitalist' society might look like is a question for the future. This project is simply a part of that on-going process.

A backward glance

It was argued that Marxism still enjoys a sense of purpose and relevance for the 21st century. I further argued that in an era of capitalist crisis, Marxism, as a theoretical construct and a guide to action, assumes an even greater degree of significance. The first of these claims – of the continued relevance of Marxism – should not be especially contentious. There is much within contemporary Marxist literature that points to the on-going importance of Marxist analysis and of its capacity to interpret and understand the world. Issues such as the state and its relationship with capitalism, the inherent crisis of capitalism, and responses to capitalist globalisation are all well-documented. Marxism provides a sound and rational means to analyse and observe these historical processes as well as providing a mechanism by which to consider future prospects for the development of capitalism. There is a growing literature that admirably traces the trajectory of capitalism and it clearly shows that Marxism, as a vehicle for analysis, retains its claim to relevance in the 21st century.

While this is undoubtedly the case, I maintain that Marxism must be more than merely an analytical tool.

The second claim – of Marxism's increased and heightened significance, not only as a source of understanding capitalism, but importantly as a guide to action that would challenge capitalism – reveals serious limitations in much contemporary Marxist research. It is in this area that this work, and its stated role of theory building, assumes significance. A prolonged 'crisis' in Marxist theory and practice has unconsciously assisted capitalism's capacity to remain unchallenged. Marxist scholarship is replete with analysis of the developing problems within Marxism but largely fails to address this interconnected issue.

These problems were apparent from Marxism's earliest days. Marxism suffered a blow with the split that centred on support for national bourgeoisies at the time of World War I. The Russian Revolution offered hope and renewal, but the logic of the Marxist theory of 'permanent revolution' was replaced by Stalinism and the deeply flawed concept of 'socialism in one country'. The Stalinisation of Marxism and the geographical shift in its centre of gravity from Western Europe to the East led to fissures in Marxist theoretical development. Western Marxism and the various schools of Marxist thought that followed struggled with ways of overcoming problems, but a process of turning away from core, elemental Marxist values became increasingly apparent. The role of the working class as revolutionary subject was downplayed. The fundamental premise of Marxism, that political and social institutions rested upon an economic base was, at first questioned, and subsequently ignored. Social movement and identity politics became the perceived vehicles by which to advance anti-capitalist campaigns. While many Marxist writers focus their work on these issues, there are few calls to reassert Marxism's historic call to 'change the world' and even fewer proposals as to how that change might be effected.

It is not enough to simply state that Marxism enjoys on-going significance. Such a claim needs to be validated and, as a means to that end, an uncompromisingly Marxist methodological approach was employed. While acknowledging the depth of Marxist scholarship, criticisms cannot be overlooked or disregarded. There is a tendency that can be observed, towards a one-sided and, at times impressionistic perspective, rather than a dialectical analysis of issues and events. Each of the component parts that have been isolated in the literature describing particular 'problems' that assailed Marxism are analysed by many contemporary Marxist theorists and in great depth. However, those same Marxists all too frequently discuss historical moments and changes in perspective and trajectory as isolated phenomena, which is a departure from the Marxist analytical approach.

The adoption of a consistent Marxist method of analysis permitted a synthesis of the component parts that constitute a 'crisis' in Marxism. In so doing the problems in Marxism, were described, the strengths and weaknesses that exist in the theory were isolated and a perspective that would allow for a reinvigorated Marxism that can challenge capitalism was promoted. Marx's method, and its application for today, was described in some detail. In that discussion, I noted that Marx argued that what was essential was to make observations that move from the simple to the complex and that show the inter-relationship of all component parts and how:

> simple conceptions such as labour, division of labour, demand, exchange value, and conclude with state, international exchange and world market ... The concrete is concrete because it is a combination of many determinations, i.e. a unity of diverse elements. In our thought it therefore appears as a process of synthesis, as a result, and not as a starting point, although it is the real starting point and, therefore, also the starting point of observation and conception (1974: 100–101).

A fundamental contradiction exists between capitalist globalisation and the continued role and significance of the nation-state. While this is broadly recognised, it also exposes limitations in contemporary Marxist thought and practice. The reluctance to move beyond national responses to global issues needs to be overcome if the working class is to successfully struggle for emancipation.

The overarching issue that framed the preceding arguments was of Marxism's pivotal role in an age of capitalist crisis. It was necessary, in responding to this to deal, in some detail, with the ideologically charged question of whether Marxism, apparently fragmented and riven by dislocations, can present an effective challenge to capitalism and offer leadership in the quest for emancipation from capitalism. In seeking to resolve these problems, and satisfactorily answering the questions raised, Marxism was reaffirmed as an ideological, theoretical and practical force capable of effecting fundamental change.

There was, therefore, a focus on divergent trends within contemporary Marxist theory and an exploration of mechanisms by which *rapprochement* might be possible. For this to happen there needs to be a re-commitment by Marxists to core, unifying elements of Marxism. This includes the acceptance of the concept of the working class as a revolutionary subject, and on the primacy of economics as the central force that drives social, political and societal developments. From such a position, it is possible to incorporate identity politics and social movement politics into class-based movements that are, and must remain, independent from the state.

Capitalism has survived potential breakdown, growing endemic crisis, and immense and destructive internal contradictions. I actively sought to expose the limitations that exist in the literature of contemporary Marxism and pointed to areas that deserve attention in the future. Naturally the parameters of such an analysis are limited. This is, after all, one contribution to on-going debates and polemics. Such contributions will support the development of a theoretical and practical platform upon which new research can build. They will allow Marxism to reconnect with its core, classical premise, while still being able to adapt in order to meet the challenges that capitalism presents. This work, in consciously seeking to contribute to Marxist theory in the 21st century, has implications for future research. It invites criticism. Marxist theory, however, has been built on critical appraisals and disputation.

Implications and limitations

My research was conducted within a very specific framework and with a particular purpose in mind. It is a modest contribution to a 'battle of ideas' within Marxism that is as old as Marxism itself. Mention was made earlier of Cox's famous observation that theory is always for someone and for some purpose (1981: 128). I remarked that Marxism, too, is for a particular purpose, arguing that this purpose is to promote a theory and practice that will equip the working class to confront and combat capitalism. Central to this purpose is Marxism's capacity to respond to, address, and provide answers to the questions that capitalism, in the 21st century, raises. As a consequence, the arguments and research that comprise the essence of this work need to be accountable and with it an acknowledgement that these arguments have implications.

The trajectory of Marxism during the 20th century was, to a large degree, inconsistent with the professed purpose and aims of Marxism as it was first constructed. The call, to not simply interpret the world but to change it, became muted. Few theorists within the milieu of contemporary Marxism care to be reminded of that injunction. This, perhaps, is not altogether surprising. Such a reluctance can be explained from historically identifiable problems that have besieged Marxism for a century. However, many who have acted in the name of Marxism have effectively, if unconsciously, done Marxism a great disservice. It all comes down to the question of just what Marxism is for, and in so doing to emphasise the two interlocking elements of Marxism – the dialectical unity of theory and practice. Two of Marxism's most oft-repeated aphorisms; that without revolutionary theory there can be no revolutionary practice, and, that practice without theory is blind while theory without practice is sterile, are worth repeating and reconsidering. Deutscher's view that a rift between theory and practice had divided classical Marxism from Western Marxism and the New Left is also repeated here. The historical shifts in Marxism, were responses to capitalist crisis and development. This work, in arguing that Marxism needs to re-engage in a fundamental way with its classical roots, moves beyond merely engaging with this or that 'Marxism', or in highlighting what has been left unstated, but consciously contributes to that literature and to Marxist theory.

There is a need to re-invigorate Marxism. This has been argued from the point of view of the historical purpose of Marxism and its stated aim of fundamentally challenging capitalism and, in so doing, changing the world. Similarly, a re-engagement with the working class as revolutionary agent is essential, as is the acceptance of classical concepts of Marxism. These concepts include the base/superstructure formation of society, the class nature of capitalist society and the point that capitalist reproduction is only possible within the framework of a class-based system that co-opts and incorporates the working class. The trajectory of contemporary Marxist theory, however, has been to promote non-class and supra-class social movements and the politics of identity. These, almost polar opposites, would indicate that any serious potential for a re-forged and united Marxism is unlikely. Such a scenario is not necessarily a negative thing. At the same time, it is not inconceivable that the 'broad' non-class movements can be integrated and incorporated under an encompassing class-centred umbrella that accepts the primacy of the working class and of its revolutionary potential. I have also argued that there is little to be gained by offering prescriptive approaches. The necessity of an alignment of all Marxist schools is not of primary importance. What is required is the return to the core values upon which Marxism was built.

There are implications for future research and in the development of theory. In a broader context, there are long-term implications for such a theoretical perspective. Marxism's relevance relies on its ability to initiate a challenge and to effect change. This, it has been argued, can only be achieved if theory and practice complement each other. A political expression of Marxist theory is required. One significant factor in the seeming inability for the working class and its allies to combat capitalism, is that the traditional organisations of the working class have been increasingly incorporated into the institutions of the state. An equally significant factor has been the historical crisis of leadership that is similarly connected to this reliance upon those same institutions of the capitalist state.

On-going discussions and polemics around expressions of Marxist theory and practice are essential. This sits comfortably within classical conceptions of Marxism and of its purpose. At the same time, such a proposition invites criticism. I have engaged with a range of divergent Marxist schools of thought. To promote an activist view of Marxism with an overt perception of its historic role of organiser, is necessarily to come into conflict with much of contemporary Marxist thought. However, the intent was to respond to the overriding question of Marxism's relevance in an age of capitalist crisis. The relevance of Marxism must be and can only be gauged by its capacity to challenge capitalism and that capitalism's longevity can be traced, in part, to Marxism's inability to present such a challenge.

Any research that seeks to play a part in the development of a theoretical proposition is, inevitably limited by a range of factors. These include time and the scope of the project, the polemical nature of the arguments that are presented, and a separation between theoretical premises and empirical evidence to validate those same premises.

The scope of the study was deliberately broad and encompassed a sweep of time and space. This approach was undertaken to better provide an historical and theoretical overview and employed a Marxist Historical Materialist approach. A range of separate but interconnected issues were analysed. I remain critical of a widely-held tendency to isolate and separate individual elements of a whole. It may be argued that these elements deserved a depth of analysis that the structure of this project was unable to provide. Equally it can be argued that avenues are being opened for further research and analysis.

Elemental contradictions within capitalism were both isolated and analysed. These included an exposition of the arguments that presented evidence of qualitative changes that have occurred in capitalism. These changes are most evident in the globalisation of capitalism. It was argued that among the factors that have intensified capitalist globalisation was a tendency toward a falling rate of profit. Evidence was presented to validate this core aspect of Marxist theory. It drew attention to a range of scholarship that provides a deeper and broader use of empirical evidence to support the claims made in this book. This central aspect of Marxist theory deserves on-going attention and needs to become the substance for future research.

A forward glance

Issues within capitalist development as well as approaches designed to combat capitalism have been confronted. The analysis that was conducted warrants on-going research. Four specific areas for future research present themselves and are all interconnected. The first involves the relationship between state and capital and the conflicted roles of the nation-state within globalised capitalism. The second relates to the return of economic nationalism in the face of an intensification of global capitalism. A third area for future research concerns the role of the working class under conditions of an intensification of capitalist globalisation. The fourth is directly related to the previous issue and relates to the organisation of a global working class and its political response to the global crisis of capitalism. While these four issues have been analysed, they require much further work. Each of these potential research paths may be the focus of separate research projects, but more importantly they become component parts of a broader work that would significantly expand the outcomes that have been offered here.

There is an extensive, almost exhaustive literature surrounding the state and capitalism. Marxist theory has, however, often been criticised for not developing a clarified, unified, theory of the state. Despite such criticisms, Marxism is essentially united in the view that a central role of the state is to facilitate capitalist development. This relationship becomes increasingly contentious for the state as it is burdened with the dual roles of political organiser in a local setting, and facilitator of ever-increasing global requirements of capitalism. This growing contradiction is evident in the growth of economic nationalism, with its call to tariffs, protectionism, trade blocs and trade wars. Politically this dilemma has given rise to right and left populist movements. Capitalism cannot be expected to stop its march to globalisation, but equally unrealistic is the demand, by sections of capital, to rely on nationalism in order to promote their own interests and security. How Marxists respond to such a challenge, and how the working class, both within the traditional confines of national borders and as a global force, respond, become important questions.

Capitalist reproduction requires a working class that is often unconsciously complicit in that very act of reproduction. The importance of class, and the working class as a revolutionary subject, should not be downplayed. The development of capitalism has required a growing proletarianisation of the world. Many contemporary Marxist analysists question that this is the case. The importance of the working class has continuously been diminished. This is despite the more than ample empirical evidence showing that the working class, as a global force, has grown and continues to grow at a remarkable rate. This has been particularly evident since the intensification of capitalist globalisation. There has been no shortage of research undertaken concerning the possibilities of developing global union struggles to defend workers' conditions and of developing ways to link working-class struggles across states. What remains unclear, however, is how such global expressions of working-class unity within the limitations of a trade union ethos can be expected to successfully promote the interests of the working class, let alone challenge the rule of capitalism. Research that would link the evidence of a growing working class, and of the casualisation of this global working class, with a re-focused Marxist analysis of potential working-class emancipation, would inevitably merge into another future scope for research – future organisational structures for working-class political action.

The concept of working-class political organisations that move beyond the limitations of national borders is an area that deserves special and urgent attention. The period of Stalinism and the negative experience that Marxist political parties, both as ruling parties and as working-class parties in the capitalist world, has had a lasting and negative legacy. This is evident, from within Marxist theory and from the point of view of many within the broad working class and anti-capitalist movements. Feelings of antipathy towards political parties that proclaim themselves to be Marxist are entirely understandable when considered against the backdrop of recent history, and yet it is in the realm of political activity that an alternative to capitalist rule can best be envisaged.

There is an undeniable need of political organisation among the working class that could offer a real challenge to the rule of capital. The collapse of the USSR and its 'fraternal' political organisations around the world was heralded by many as marking the death knell of organised Marxist politics. A contrary perspective is, that with the passing of Stalinism and the false perception that it represented a legitimate expression of Marxism, a potential exists for a rebuilding of the idea of Marxist political organisation within the working-class movement. This, by implication, would occupy a different terrain to that of its predecessors and would necessarily be a global organisation operating in a unified manner across states. Such an organisation currently exists, although in embryonic form as Marxism remains divided and the working class essentially remains tied, geographically and psychologically to concepts of nationalism and the nation-state. However, such a form of political organisation deserves serious consideration and can act as a means of either overcoming, or by-passing, the ideological and theoretical differences within various schools of Marxism.

Future research also needs to consider the role of the working class and the rise of identity-based political movements. The decades-long move by many Marxists to relegate the working class to a position of obscurity in favour of identity politics and social movement activism has been discussed and its limitations exposed. Further analysis is required that re-positions the working class as revolutionary subject while still acknowledging the energy and activism that these non-class movements engender. Finding ways of bringing these movements under the aegis of an ideologically conscious working class needs serious consideration. In doing so, Marxist theory and practice for the 21st century would become enriched. A significant effect of such action would be a step toward resolving the divisions within Marxist theory. The perspective that the working class has been relegated to a position of irrelevance would also be categorically renounced.

This work has consciously acted to expose the limitations that are evident in much of the literature of contemporary Marxism. The tendency to diminish the importance of economic factors, to downplay the class nature of society, and to dismiss the working class as a revolutionary subject have all been critically analysed. A rational, Marxist analysis of the crisis that exists both in capitalism and in Marxist responses to that crisis has been offered. The areas for future research that have been described above are examples of those limitations. This does not imply that work has not been done, but rather, that future research, framed by a consistent Marxist analysis, allows for a unified approach to the problems to which this study has responded and is an objective requirement in resolving the crisis of capitalism.

These potential areas for research and analysis stand as separate issues, but importantly reflect a dialectical unity. This highlights the Marxist method that has been employed in these pages. This method of analysis has been outlined in some detail but it may be paraphrased as a system of analysis that regards individual elements or events, not as episodic or isolated issues, but as part of a broader process. Such an approach eliminates a tendency toward developing impressionistic responses to economic or societal developments. It allows for the development of Marxist theory and practice that is best suited to challenge capitalism in an age of crisis.

And in the end …

This book set itself a particular task. It was to re-affirm the relevance of Marxism in an age of capitalist crisis. An apparent irony might be observed. No Marxist would seriously countenance the notion that Marxism was anything but relevant. That, after all, is the province of non-Marxist or anti-Marxist theoreticians who have repeatedly, in the past 100 years, written obituaries for Marxism. However, what becomes clear, from a close analysis of the crisis in capitalism, as well as the crisis that has been perceived in Marxist thought, is a direct correlation between capitalism's ability to withstand what are existential threats to its survival, and Marxism's inability to present a fundamental challenge to the rule of capitalism. Herein lies the question of Marxism's 'relevance' and of its very purpose.

Marxism's claim to relevance has been defended but a degree of conditionality remains. Marxism can only claim to be relevant if it challenges capitalism and actively promotes a practice that would effect change. The trajectory of contemporary Marxism has been one of a growing distance from the norms and mores of traditional, or classical Marxist perspectives. It has seen the role of the working class downplayed along with a range of central Marxist premises. Consequently, I considered both the potential for the divergent trends within Marxism to become aligned, whether such a realignment was possible, necessary, or indeed a requirement in any real sense.

I have engaged in a process of theory building. This, in no way suggested that Marxism lacks a rich and encompassing theoretical framework. What became clear was that the various schools of Marxist thought have progressively distanced themselves from many of the values that give the theory its flavour and its relevance. This book, therefore, consciously promoted the case for classical Marxism in the 21st century and to advocate for a return to, and reflection upon, those core values of class and class struggle, of developing theory to drive practice and to politically arm a growing global working class.

The claims that have been made are contentious, but respond in a positive manner to what are critical moments as the 21st century develops. As Antonio says in the *Tempest*: 'what's past is prologue'. This discussion began by stating that "there has to be something better and it is that something better that we must search for". We live in an age of capitalist crisis. Marxism offers resolution to that crisis. And so, to the future.

BIBLIOGRAPHY

Aglietta, M. 1998 'Capitalism at the turn of the century: regulation theory and the challenge of social change', *New Left Review*, I/232 (November–December)

Aglietta, M. 2000*A Theory of Capitalist Regulation: The US Experience*, Verso, London and New York

Allen, A.W. 2004 *Karl Marx*, Routledge, Taylor & Francis, London and New York

Amin, S. 2011 *Ending the Crisis of Capitalism or Ending Capitalism?*, Pambazuka Press, Capetown, Dakar, Nairobi and Oxford

Amin, S., Hardt, M., Lundberg, C. and Wennerhag, M. 2002 'How capitalism went senile', *Eurozine April*. Retrieved 22 July 2016. www.eurozine.com/articles/2002-05-08-amin-en.html

Anderson, C. 1974 *The Political Economy of Social Class*, Prentice Hall Inc., New Jersey

Anderson, P. 1979 *Considerations on Western Marxism*, Verso, London

Anderson, P. 1983 *In the Tracks of Historical Materialism*, Verso, London

Anderson, P. 1998 *The Origins of Postmodernity*, Verso, London

Aronowitz, S. 1992 *The Politics of Identity: Class, Culture, Social Movement*, Routledge, New York

Ayres, J.M. 2001 'Transnational political processes and contention against the global economy', *Mobilization: An International Quarterly*, 6(1) Spring: 55–68

Badiou, A. 2008 'The communist hypothesis', *New Left Review*, 49, January–February: 29–42

Bank for International Settlements 2007 *77th Annual Report*, BIS Press and Communications, Basel, Switzerland. Retrieved 30 March 2016, www.bis.org/publ/arpdf/ar2007e.pdf

Bank for International Settlements 2016 *Press Release, 30th March 2016*, Triennial Central Bank Survey of Foreign Exchange and OTC Derivatives Markets. Retrieved 10 July 2016, www.bis.org/press/p160330.htm

Banerjee, A.V. and Duflo, E. 2008 'What is middle class about the middle classes around the world', *Journal of Economic Perspectives*, 22(2)

Bannerjee, D. and Goldfield, M. 2007 'Neoliberal globalization, labour and the state', in D. Bannerjee and M. Goldfield (eds), *Labour, Globalization and the*

State: Workers, Women and Migrants Confront Neoliberalism, Routledge, Oxon and New York: 1–18

Basu, D. and Manolakos, P.T. 2010 'Is there a tendency for the rate of profit to fall? Econometric evidence from the US economy, 1948–2007', *University of Massachusetts - Amherst ScholarWorks@UMass Amherst*, Working Paper 2010–2004. Retrieved 17 May 2015, http://scholarworks.umass.edu/cgi/viewcontent.cgi?article=1098&context=econ_workingpaper

Beasley, W.G. 1989 *Japanese Imperialism 1894–1945*, Clarendon Press, Oxford

Beilharz, P. 1987 *Trotsky, Trotskyism and the Transition to Socialism*, Croom Helm, London and Sydney

Bello, W. 2004 *Deglobalization: Ideas for a New World Economy*, Zed Books, London and New York

Bello, W. 2013 *Capitalism's Last Stand: Deglobalization in the Age of Austerity*, Zed Books, London and New York

Berberoglu, B. 2003 *Globalization of Capital and the Nation State: Imperialism, Class Struggle, in the Age of Global Capitalism*, Rowman & Littlefield Publishers Inc., London, Boulder CO, New York and Oxford

Berberoglu, B. 2009 *Class and Class Conflict in the Age of Globalization*, Lexington Books, Plymouth

Berberoglu, B. 2012 *Beyond the Global Capitalist Crisis: The World Economy in Transition*, Ashgate Publishing, Surrey and Burlington VT

Bereciatru, G.J. 1994 *Decline of the Nation-State*, University of Nevada Press, Reno, Las Vegas, NV and London

Bernanke, B.S. 2006 *Global Economic Integration: What's New and What's Not?* Speech at the Federal Reserve Bank of Kansas City's Thirtieth Annual Economic Symposium, Jackson Hole, Wyoming. Retrieved 23 July 2016, www.federalreserve.gov/newsevents/speech/bernanke20060825a.htm

Bernard, A. 2009 'Trends in manufacturing employment', *Perspectives*, Statistics Canada, Retrieved 10 July 2016, www.statcan.gc.ca/pub/75-001-x/2009102/article/10788-eng.htm#a1

Bernstein, E. 1975 *Evolutionary Socialism: A Criticism and Affirmation*, Schoken Books, New York

Bernstein, J. 1994 *Frankfurt School: Critical Assessments*, Routledge, London

Bernstein, M. 2005 'Identity politics', *Annual Review of Sociology*, 31: 47–74

Beynon, H. 2003 'Globalization, trade union organization and workers' rights', in P. Fairbrother and C.A.B. Yates (eds), *Trade Unions in Renewal*, Routledge, Taylor & Francis, London and New York: 263–281

Bidet, J. and Kouvelakis, S. 2008 'Introduction: Marxism, post-Marxism, neo-Marxisms', in J. Bidet and S. Kouvelakis (eds), *Critical Companion to Contemporary Marxism*, Brill, Leiden and Boston: 23–38

Bieler, A., Lindberg, I. and Pillay, D. 2008 'What future strategy for the global working class? The need for a new historical subject', in A. Bieler, I. Lindberg and D. Pillay (eds), *Labour and the Challenges of Globalization: What Prospects for Transnational Solidarity?*Pluto Press, London and Ann Arbor, MI: 264–286

Bina, C. and Davis, C. 2015 'Globalization, technology, and skill formation in capitalism', in R. Baiman, H. Boushey and D. Saunders (eds), *Political Economy and Contemporary Capitalism: Radical Perspectives on Economic Theory and Policy*, Routledge, Taylor & Francis, London and New York: 193–202

Blackledge, P. 2006 'The New Left's renewal of Marxism', *International Socialism: A Quarterly Review of Socialist Theory*, 112. Retrieved 20 May 2016, http://isj.org.uk/issue-112/

Bloch, E. 2015 'The principle of hope', *Marxists Internet Library*. Retrieved 22 January 2016, www.marxists.org/archive/bloch/hope/introduction.htm

Bonefeld, W. 2006 'Anti-globalisation and the question of socialism', *Critique*, 31(1): 39–59

Boucher, G. 2012 *Understanding Marxism*, Acumen Publishing Ltd., Durham

Boyer, R. 2002 'The origins of regulation theory', in R. Boyer and Y. Saillard (eds), *Regulation Theory: The State of the Art*, Routledge, London and New York: 13–20

Braudel, F. 1977 *Afterthoughts on Material Civilization and Capitalism*, Johns Hopkins University Press, Baltimore

Brenner, R. 2006 *Economics of Global Turbulence: The Advanced Capitalist Economies from Long Boom to Long Downturn, 1945–2005*, Verso, London

Brenner, R. and Glick, M. 1991 'The regulation approach: theory and history', *New Left Review*, I/188July–August

Bresser-Pereiro, L.C. 2010 'The global financial crisis and a new capitalism?', *Levy Economics Institute*, Working Papers No 592. Retrieved 3 January 2016, www.levyinstitute.org/pubs/wp_592.pdf

Brewer, B.D. 2011 'The long twentieth century and the cultural turn: world-historical origins of the cultural economy', *American Sociological Review*, 17(1): 39–57

Bronner, S.E. 2011 *Critical Theory: A Very Short Introduction*, Oxford University Press, New York

Brooks, C. 1994 'Class consciousness in comparative perspective', *Social Science Research*, 23(2): 167–195

Brooks, D.H. and Hill, H. 2003 'Divergent Asian views on a multilateral framework for FDI', *OECD*. Retrieved 10 September 2016, www.oecd.org/dev/pgd/20354697.pdf

Bukharin, N. 2003 *Imperialism and World Economy*, Bookmarks, London and Sydney

Burawoy, M. 1990 'Marxism is dead, long live Marxism', *Socialist Review*, 90(2): 7–19

Burawoy, M. and Wright, E.O. 2006 'Sociological Marxism', in J.H. Turner (ed), *Handbook of Sociological Theory*, Springer, New York: 459–486

Burgmann, V. 2016 *Globalization and Labour in the 21st Century*, Routledge, Taylor & Francis, London and New York

Burgoon, B. 2013 'Inequality and anti-globalization backlash by political parties', *European Union Politics*, 14(3): 408–435

Burnham, P. 2002 'Class struggle, states and global circuits of capital', in M. Rupert and H. Smith (eds), *Historical Materialism and Globalization*, Routledge, London and New York: 113–128

Burris, V. 1988 'Reification: a Marxist perspective', *California Sociologist*, 10(1): 22–43

Calhoun, C.J. 1997 *Nationalism*, University of Minnesota Press, Minneapolis MN

Callinicos, A. 1983 *Marxism and Philosophy*, Oxford University Press, Oxford and New York

Callinicos, A. 1990 *Against Postmodernism: A Marxist Critique*, St Martin's Press, New York

Callinicos, A. 1991 *The Revenge of History: Marxism and the East European Revolutions*, Polity Press, Cambridge

Cammack, P. 2003 'The governance of global capitalism: a new materialist perspective', *Historical Materialism*, 11(2): 37–59

Carnoy, M. 1984 *The State and Political Theory*, Princeton University Press, Princeton NJ

Carver, T. 1991 'Reading Marx: life and works', in T. Carver (ed), *The Cambridge Companion to Marx*, Cambridge University Press, Cambridge, New York, Port Chester, Melbourne, Sydney: 1–22

Castells, M. 2000 *The Rise of the Network Society: The Information Age: Economy, Society and Culture, Volume 1*, 2nd edn, Wiley & Blackwell, Oxford

Castells, M. 2004 *The Power of Identity: The Information Age: Economy, Society and Culture Volume 2*, 2nd edn, Wiley & Blackwell, Malden MA, Oxford, and Chichester

Chodos, H. 2007 'Marxism and socialism', in D. Glaser and D.M. Walker, *Twentieth-Century Marxism: A Global Introduction*, Routledge, Taylor & Francis, London and New York: 177–195

Choi, J.C., Berger, R. and Kim, J.B. 2010 'Capitalism's global financial crisis: the role of the state', *The Social Science Journal*, 47: 829–835

Chossudovsky, M. 1998 *The Globalisation of Poverty: Impacts of IMF and World Bank Reforms*, Zed Books, London and New York

Chun, N. 2010 'Middle class size in the past, present, and future: a description of trends in Asia', *Asian Development Bank Working Paper Series No 217*. Retrieved 3 January 2016, www.adb.org/sites/default/files/publication/28421/economics-wp217.pdf

Cingano, F. 2014 'Trends in income inequality and its impact on economic growth', *OECD Social, Employment and Migration Working Papers*, No. 163, OECD Publishing. Retrieved 20 July 2016, http://dx.doi.org/10.1787/5jxrjncwxv6j-en

Claessens, S. and Kose, M.A. 2013 'Financial crises: explanations, types, and implications', *IMF Working Paper*. Retrieved 9 April 2016, www.imf.org/external/pubs/ft/wp/2013/wp1328.pdf

Clarke, S. 1989 'The internationalisation of capital and the nation state', *International Conference on 'New Forms of the Internationalisation of Capital'*, Washington DC. Retrieved 24 April 2016, http://homepages.warwick.ac.uk/~syrbe/pubs/washi.pdf

Clarke, S. 1990 'The Marxist theory of overaccumulation and crisis', *Science and Society*, 54(4): 442–467

Clarke, S. 1994 *Marx's Theory of Crisis*, Palgrave Macmillan, Houndmills, Basingstoke, Hampshire

Cockshott, P. and Zachriah, D. 2012 *Arguments for Socialism*, Amazon. Retrieved 30 September 2016, http://eprints.gla.ac.uk/58987/

Colgan, J.D. and Keohane, R.O. 2017 'The liberal order is rigged: fix it now or watch it wither', *Foreign Affairs*, 96(3)

Collado, E. 2010 *The Shrinking Middle Class: Why America is Becoming a Two-Class Society*, Universe, Bloomington NY

Colletti, L. 1969 *Marxism and Hegel*, Verso Books, London

Colletti, L. 1974 'Bernstein and the Marxism of the second international', in L. Colletti, *From Rouseau to Lenin: Studies in Ideology and Society*, Monthly Review Press, New York: 45–108

Colletti, L. 1977 'A political and philosophical interview', in New Left Review (eds), *Western Marxism: A Critical Reader*, New Left Books, London: 315–350

Communist Party of Australia 2016 *Policies*, Communist Party of Australia. Retrieved 6 August 2016, www.cpa.org.au/policies/index.html

Cox, R.W. 1981 'Social forces, states and world orders: beyond international relations theory', *Millennium: Journal of International Studies*, 10(2): 126–155

Cox, R.W. 1987 *Production, Power and World Order: Social Forces in the Making of History*, Columbia University Press, New York

Cox, R.W. 1993 'Gramsci, hegemony and international relations: an essay in method', in S. Gill (ed), *Gramsci, Historical Materialism and International Relations*, Cambridge University Press, Cambridge, New York and Melbourne: 49–66

Credit Suisse 2015 Global Wealth Report 2015, *Credit Suisse Research Institute*. Retrieved 23 July 2016, www.protothema.gr/files/1/2015/10/14/ekthsi_0.pdf

Crenshaw, K. 1991 *Mapping the Margins: Intersectionality, Identity Politics, and Violence Against Women of Color*. Retrieved 15 November 2016, http://socialdifference.columbia.edu/files/socialdiff/projects/Article__Mapping_the_Margins_by_Kimblere_Crenshaw.pdf

Critchley, P. 1997 *Beyond Modernity and Postmodernity: Vol. 1: Marx on the Postmodern Terrain*, Academia. Retrieved 22 May 2016, http://mmu.Academia.edu/PeterCritchley/Books

Crocker, L. 1980 'Marx's use of contradiction', *Philosophy and Phenomenological Research*, 40(4): 558–563

Cutler, A.C. 2002 'Historical materialism, globalization, and law: competing conceptions of property', in M. Rupert and H. Smith (eds), *Historical Materialism and Globalization*, Routledge, Taylor & Francis, London and New York: 230–256

Dabla, E., Kochhar, K., Suphaphiphat, N., Ricka, F. and Tsounta, E. 2015 'Causes and consequences of income inequality: a global perspective', *IMF Strategy, Policy and Review Department*. Retrieved 20 July 2016, www.imf.org/external/pubs/ft/sdn/2015/sdn1513.pdf

Dahl, R. 1967 *Pluralist Democracy in the United States: Conflict and Consent*, Rand McNally, Chicago IL

Dallinger, U. 2013 'The endangered middle class? A comparative analysis of the role played by income redistribution', *Journal of European Social Policy*, 23(1): 83–101

Dallmayr, F.R. 2002 'Globalization and inequality: a plea for global justice', *International Studies Review*, 4(2): 137–156

D'Amato, P. 2006 *The Meaning of Marxism*, Haymarket Books, Chicago IL

Davidson, A. 2000 'Democracy, class and citizenship in a globalising world', in A. Vandenberg (ed), *Citizenship and Democracy in a Global Era*, St Martin's Press, New York: 110–120

Day, R.B. 1976 'The Theory of the Long Wave: Kondratiev, Trotsky, Mandel', *New Left Review*, I/99, September–October

Dean, M. 1992 'Review: Pateman's dilemma: women and citizenship', *Theory and Society*, 21(1): 121–130

Declaration and Manifesto of Occupy Wall Street Movement 2011 *Declaration Project*. Retrieved 20 August 2016, www.declarationproject.org/?p=166

De Jasay, A. 1985 *The State*, Basil Blackwell, Oxford and New York

della Porta, D. 1999 'Protest, protesters and protest policing: public discourses in Italy and Germany from the 1960s to the 1980s', in M. Guigni, D. McAdam and C. Tilly (eds), *How Social Movements Matter*, University of Minnesota Press, Minneapolis and London: 66–96

Deutscher, I. 1965 'Marxism in our time', *Marxist Internet Archive*. Retrieved 7 February 2018, www.marxists.org/archive/deutscher/1965/marxism.htm

Deutscher, I. 1973 edited by T. Deutscher *Marxism in our Time*, Ramparts Press, San Francisco CA

Diani, M. 1992 'The concept of social movements', *Sociological Review*, 40(1): 1–26

Dicken, P. 2007 *Global Shift: Mapping the Changing Contours of the World Economy*, 5th edn., Sage Publications, London, Thousand Oaks CA and New Delhi

Dobb, M. 2001 'Marxism and the social sciences', *Monthly Review: An Independent Socialist Magazine*, 53(4): 38–54

Dobbs, R., Madgavkar, A., Barton, D., Labaye, E., Manyoka, J., Roxburgh, C., Lund, S. and Madhav, S. 2012 'The world at work, jobs, pay and skills for 3.5 billion people', *McKinsey Global Institute*, McKinsey and Company. Retrieved, 22 July 2016, www.mckinsey.com/global-themes/employment-and-growth/the-world-at-work

Driver, S. and Martell, L. 2000 'Left, right and the third way', *Policy and Politics*, 28(2): 147–161

Dunn, B. 2009 , *Global Political Economy: A Marxist Critique*, Pluto Press, London

Eagleton, T. 1991 *Ideology: An Introduction*, Verso, London and New York

Eagleton, T. 2011 *Why Marx was Right*, Yale University Press, New Haven CT and London

Easterly, W. 2008 'Capitalism works because it is self-correcting', in M. Kinsley and C. Clarke (eds), *Creative Capitalism: A Conversation with Bill Gates, Warren Buffett and Other Economic Leaders*, Simon & Schuster, New York, London, Toronto and Sydney

Elster, J. 1991 *Making Sense of Marx*, Cambridge University Press, Cambridge, New York, Port Chester, Melbourne, Sydney

Emmison, M. 1991 'Conceptualising class consciousness', in J. Baxter, M. Emmison, J. Western and M. Western (eds), *Class Analysis and Contemporary Australia*, Macmillian Australia, Sydney: 246–278

Emmott, B. 2009 'The future of capitalism', *Voice*. Retrieved 8 April 2016, www.billemmott.com/article.php?id=250

Enderwick, P. 2006 *Globalization and Labor*, Chelsea House, Philadelphia PA

Engels, F. 1890 'Engels to C. Schmidt in Berlin', *Marx-Engels Correspondence 1890*. Retrieved 30 April 2016, www.marxists.org/archive/marx/works/1890/letters/90_08_05.htm

Engels, F. 1959 *Anti-Duhring: Herr Eugen Duhring's Revolution in Science*, 2nd edn., Foreign Language Publishing House, Moscow

Engels, F. 1966 *Socialism: Utopian and Scientific*, Progress Publishers, Moscow

Engels, F. 1976 *The Dialectics of Nature*, Progress Publishers, Moscow

Engels, F. 1984 *The Condition of the Working Class in England*, Progress Publishers, Moscow and Lawrence & Wishart, London

Engels, F. 1986 'The origin of the family, private property and the state', in *Marx & Engels Selected Works*, Progress Publishers, Moscow: 449–583

Engels, F. 1999 'Letter to Bloch, Marx–Engels correspondence 1890', *Marxists.org*. Retrieved 3 March 2016, www.marxists.org/archive/marx/works/1890/letters/90_09_21.htm

Engels, F. 2000 'A letter to Franz Mehring', *Marx-Engels Correspondence 1893*. Retrieved 5 January 2016, www.marxists.org/archive/marx/works/1893/letters/93_07_14.htm

Eschle, C. 2005 'Constructing "the anti-globalisation movement"', in C. Eschle and B. Maiguascha (eds), *Critical Theories, International Relations and the 'Anti-Globalisation Movement: The Politics of Global Resistance*, Routledge, Taylor & Francis, New York and London

Evans, M. 2005 'Neoliberalism and policy transfer in the British competition state: the case of welfare reform', in S. Soederberg, G. Menz and P.G. Cerny (eds), *Internalizing Globalization: The Rise of Neoliberalism and the Decline of National Varieties of Capitalism*, Palgrave Macmillan, Hampshire and New York: 69–89

Evans, M. 2006 'Elitism', in C. Hay, M. Lister and D. Marsh (eds), *The State: Theories and Issues*, Palgrave Macmillan, Hampshire and New York: 39–58

Fairbrother, P. 2008 'Social movement unionism or trade unions as social movements', *Employee Responsibilities and Rights Journal*, 20(3): 213–220

Fairbrother, P. and Yates, C.A.B. 2003 'Unions in crisis, unions in renewal?', in P. Fairbrother and C.A.B. Yates (eds), *Trade Unions in Renewal*, Routledge, Taylor & Francis, London and New York: 1–31

Farr, J. 1991 'Science: realism, criticism, history', in T. Carver (ed), *The Cambridge Companion to Marx*, Cambridge University Press, Cambridge: 106–123

Farred, G. 2000 'Endgame identity? Mapping the New Left roots of identity politics', *New Literary History*, 31(4): 627–648

Femia, J. 2007 'Western Marxism', in D. Glaser and D.M. Walker (eds), *Twentieth-Century Marxism: A Global Introduction*, Routledge Taylor & Francis Group, London and New York: 95–117

Flacks, R. 2004 'Knowledge for what? Thoughts on the state of social movement studies', in J. Goodwin and J. Jasper (eds), *Rethinking Social Movements: Structure, Meaning, and Emotion*, Rowman & Littlefield, Lanham MD: 135–154

Forbes, S. and Ames, E. 2009 *How Capitalism Will Save Us: Why Free People and Free Markets are the Best Answer in Today's Economy*, Crown Publishing Group, New York

Forgacs, D. (ed) 2000 *The Gramsci Reader: Selected Works 1916–35*, New York University Press, New York

Foster, J.B. 2007 'The financialization of capital', *Monthly Review: An Independent Socialist Magazine*, 58(11): 1–12

Foster, J.B. and Magdoff, F. 2009 *The Great Financial Crisis: Causes and Consequences*, Monthly Review Press, New York

Foster, J.E. and Wolfson, M. 2010 'Polarization and the decline of the middle class', *Journal of Economic Inequality*, 8: 247–273

Fraser, N. 1998 'Social justice in the age of identity politics: redistribution, recognition, participation', *SSOAR Open Access Repository*. Retrieved 30 October 2016, www.ssoar.info/ssoar/bitstream/handle/document/12624/ssoar-1998-fraser-social_justice_in_the_age.pdf?sequence=1

Fuentes-Ramirez, R.R. 2014 'Marxist perspectives on twenty-first century transition to socialism', *Socialism and Democracy*, 28(1): 123–142

Fukuyama, F. 1992 *The End of History and the Last Man*, Free Press, New York

Gamble, A. 1999a 'Why bother with Marxism?', in A. Gamble, D. Marsh and T. Tant (eds), *Marxism and Social Science*, University of Illinois Press, Urbana IL and Chicago IL: 1–8

Gamble, A. 1999b 'Marxism after communism: beyond realism and historicism', *Review of International Studies*, 25: 127–144

Gamble, A. 2009 *The Spectre at the Feast: Capitalist Crisis and the Politics of Recession*, Palgrave Macmillan, Houndmills, Basingstoke, Hampshire

Giddens, A. 1998 *The Third Way: The Renewal of Social Democracy*, Polity Press, Cambridge and Malden MA

Giles, C. 2014 'Picketty findings undercut by errors', *Financial Times*. Retrieved 5 November 2016, www.ft.com/content/e1f343ca-e281-11e3-89fd-00144feabdc0

Gillman, J.M. 1957 *The Falling Rate of Profit: Marx's Law and its Significance to Twentieth Century Capitalism*, Dennis Dobson, London

Gills, B.K. and Gray, K. 2012 'People power in the era of global crisis: rebellion, resistance, and liberation', *Third World Quarterly*, 33(2): 205–224

Gilpin, R.G. 1981 *War and Change in World Politics*, Cambridge University Press, New York

Gilpin, R.G. 2000 *The Challenge of Global Capitalism: The World Economy in the 21st Century*, Princeton University Press, Princeton NJ and Oxford

Glaser, D. 2007 'Marxist theory, Marxist practice', in D. Glaser and D.M. Walker (eds), *Twentieth-Century Marxism: A Global Introduction*, Routledge, Taylor & Francis Group, London and New York: 196–211

Glynn, A.Hughes, A.Lipietz, and Singh, A. 1990 'The rise and fall of the golden age', in S.A. Marglin and J.B. Schor (eds), *The Golden Age of Capitalism: Reinterpreting the Postwar Experience*, Clarendon Press, Oxford

Goodwin, J. and Jasper, J.M. 2009 'Editors' introduction', in J. Goodwin and J.M. Jasper (eds), *The Social Movement Reader: Cases and Concepts*, 2nd edn., Wiley and Blackwell, Chichester: 3–8

Gordon, M.E. and Turner, L. 2000 'Going global', in M.E. Gordon and L. Turner (eds), *Transnational Cooperation among Labor Unions*, Cornell University Press, Ithaca and London

Gorz, A. 1997 *Farewell to the Working Class*, Pluto Press, London

Gouldner, A.W. 1980 *The Two Marxisms: Contradictions and Anomolies in the Development of Theory*, Seabury Press, New York

Gramsci, A. 1971 *Selections from Prison Notebooks*, Lawrence & Wishart, London

Grant, T. and Woods, A. 2002 *Reason in Revolt: Dialectical Philosophy and Modern Science*, Algona Publishing, New York

Gray, J. 2002 *False Dawn: The Delusion of Global Capitalism*, Granta Books, London

Green, D. and Griffith, M. 2002 'Globalization and its discontents', *International Affairs*, 78(1): 49–68

Greenfeld, L. 2009 *The Spirit of Capitalism: Nationalism and Economic Growth*, Harvard University Press, Harvard CA

Grossman, H. 1992 *The Law of Accumulation and Breakdown of the Capitalist System*, Pluto Press, London

Guigni, M. 1999 'Introduction how social movements matter: past research, present problems, future developments', in M. Guigni, D. McAdam and C. Tilly (eds), *How Social Movements Matter*, University of Minnesota Press, Minneapolis MN and London: xii–xxxiii

Hallas, D. 1970 'Trotsky', *Marxist Internet Archive*. Retrieved 28 February 2018, www.marxists.org/archive/hallas/works/1970/08/trotsky.htm

Halliday, F. 2002 'The pertinence of imperialism', in M. Rupert and H. Smith (eds), *Historical Materialism and Globalisation*, Routledge, London and New York: 75–89

Hamilton, C. 2001 'The third way and the end of politics', *Australian Review of Public Affairs*, 2(2): 89–102

Hardt, M. and Negri, A. 2000 *Empire*, Harvard University Press, Cambridge MA, London

Harman, C. 1991 'The state and capitalism today', *International Socialism*, Summer: 3–54

Harman, C. 1999 *A People's History of the World*, Bookmarks, London, Chicago and Sydney

Harman, C. 2010 *Zombie Capitalism: Global Crisis and the Relevance of Marx*, Haymarket Books, Chicago IL

Harris, J. 2006 *The Dialectics of Globalization: Economic and Political conflict in a Transnational World*, Cambridge Scholars Press, Newcastle

Hartmann, H.I. 1979 'The unhappy marriage of Marxism and feminism: towards a more progressive union', *Capital and Class*, 3(2): 1–33
Harvey, D. 1995 'Globalization in question', *Rethinking Marxism*, 8(4): 1–17
Harvey, D. 2005 *A Brief History of Neoliberalism*, Oxford University Press, Oxford and New York
Harvey, D. 2010a *The Enigma of Capital and the Crises of Capitalism*, Oxford University Press, London
Harvey, D. 2010b 'Organizing for the anti-capitalist transition', *Interface: A Journal for and about Social Movements*, 2(1): 243–261
Harvey, D. 2012 *Rebel Cities: From the Right to the City to the Urban Revolution*, Verso, London and New York
Harvey, D. 2015 *Seventeen Contradictions and the End of Capitalism*, Profile Books, London
Haworth, N. 2005 '"You've got to admit it's getting better ...": organised labour and internationalisation', in B. Hayley, J. Hyman and P. Thompson (eds), *Participation and Democracy at Work: Essays in Honour of Harvie Ramsay*, Palgrave Macmillan, Hampshire and New York: 186–203
Hay, C. 1999 'Marxism and the state', in A. Gamble, D. Marsh and T. Tant (eds), *Marxism and Social Science*, University of Illinois Press, Urbana IL and Chicago IL
Hay, P. 2002 *Main Currents in Western Environmental Thought*, UNSW Press, Sydney
Held, D. 2008 *Models of Democracy*, 3rd edn., Polity Press, Cambridge and Malden MA
Held, D., McGrew, A., Goldblatt, D. and Perraton, J. 1999 *Global Transformations: Politics, Economics and Culture*, Stanford University Press, Stanford
Hetland, G. and Goodwin, J. 2013 'The strange disappearance of capitalism from social movement studies', in C. Barker, L. Cox, J. Krinsky and A.G. Nilsen (eds), *Marxism and Social Movements*, Brill, Leiden and Boston MA: 83–102
Hilferding, R. 1981 *Finance Capital: A Study of the Latest Phase of Capitalist Development*, (ed), T. Bottomore, Routledge and Kegan Paul, London
Hillier, B. 2010 'Australia's resilience during the global crisis, 2007–2009', *Marxist Interventions*, 2: 59–77
Hirst, P.Q. 1993 *The Pluralist Theory of the State: Selected Writings of GDH Cole, JN Figgis and HJ Laski*, Routledge, London and New York
Hirst, P. and Thompson, G. 1999 *Globalization in Question: The International Economy and the Possibilities of Governance*, 2nd edn., Polity Press, Cambridge
Hirst, P. and Zeitlin, J. 1992 'Flexible specialization versus post-Fordism: theory, evidence, and policy implications', in M. Stoper and A.J. Scott (eds), *Pathways to Industrialization and Regional Development*, Routledge, Taylor & Francis, London and New York: 63–101
Hobsbawm, E. 2004 'Introduction: inventing traditions', in E. Hobsbawm and T. Ranger (eds), *The Invention of Tradition*, Cambridge University Press, Cambridge: 1–14
Holmes, P. 2009 'Protectionism: who does it really protect?' *NATO Review*. Retrieved 23 July 2016, www.nato.int/docu/review/2009/FinancialCrisis/PROTECTIONISM/EN/index.htm

Horkheimer, M. 1982 *Critical Theory: Selected Essays*, Continuum Publishers, New York

Hudson, W. 1982 *The Marxist Philosophy of Ernst Bloch*, Macmillan Press, London

Hunt, S.A. and Benford, R.D. 2007 'Collective identity, solidarity, and commitment', in D.A. Snow, A. Soule and H. Kriesi (eds), *The Blackwell Companion to Social Movements*, Blackwell Publishers Ltd., Malden MA, Oxford and Victoria: 433–457

Husson, M. 2008 'The Regulation School: a one-way ticket from Marx to social liberalism?', in J. Bidet and J. Kouvelakis (eds), *Critical Companion to Contemporary Marxism*, Brill, Leiden and Boston: 175–188

Hyman, R. 1975 *Marxism and the Sociology of Trade Unionism*, Pluto Press Ltd., London

Hyman, R. 2004 'An emerging agenda for trade unions', in R. Munck (ed), *Labour and Globalisation*, Liverpool University Press, Liverpool: 19–33

Ignatow, G. 2007 *Transnational Identity Politics and the Environment*, Lexington Books, a division of Rowman & Littlefield Inc., Lanham BO, New York, Toronto, Plymouth

International Labour Office (ILO) 2008 *Global Wage Report*. Retrieved 13 February 2015, www.ilo.org/wcmsp5

International Labour Office (ILO) 2015 *World Employment and Social Outlook – Trends 2015*. Retrieved 21 May 2015, www.ilo.org/global/research/global-reports/WESO/2015/lang–en/index.htm

International Labour Organization/Organisation for Economic Co-operation and Development 2015 'The Labour Share in G20 Economies' *ILO/OECD*. Retrieved 20 July 2016, www.oecd.org/g20/topics/employment-and-social-policy/The-Labour-Share-in-G20-Economies.pdf

International Monetary Fund 2016a 'World economic outlook: too slow for too long', Washington DC, April, *IMF Publication Services*. Retrieved 21 July 2016, www.imf.org/external/pubs/ft/weo/2016/01/pdf/text.pdf

International Monetary Fund (IMF) 2016b 'Subdued demand, diminished prospects', *World Economic Outlook: Update January 2016*. Retrieved 3 March 2016, www.imf.org/external/pubs/ft/weo/2016/update/01/index.htm

Jay, M. 1996 *The Dialectical Imagination: A History of the Frankfurt School and the Institute of Social Research, 1923–1950*, Heinemann, London

Jellissen, S.M. and Gottheil, F. 2009 'Marx and Engels: in praise of globalization', *Contributions to Political Economy*, 28: 35–46

Jenkins, K. 2005 *On "What is History?": From Carr and Elton to Rorty and White*, Routledge, New York and London

Jessop, B. 1982 *The Capitalist State: Marxist Theories and Methods*, Martin Robertson, Oxford

Jessop, B. 1990 *State Theory: Putting Capitalist States in their Place*, The Pennsylvania State University Press, University Park PA

Jessop, B. 1995 'The regulation approach, governance and post-Fordism: alternative perspectives on economic and political change?', *Economy and Society*, 24(3): 307–333

Jessop, B. 2001a *Regulation Theory and the Crisis of Capitalism Vol. 1*, Edward Elgar, Cheltenham

Jessop, B. 2001b 'Regulationist and autopoieticist reflections on Polanyi's account of market economies and the market society', *New Political Economy*, 6(2): 213–232

Jotia, L. 2011 'Globalization and the nation-state: sovereignty and state welfare in jeopardy', *US–China Education Review B*, 2: 243–250

Kaletsky, A. 2010 *Capitalism 4.0: The Birth of a New Economy*, Bloomsbury Publishing Plc., London

Kauffman, L.A. 2001 'The anti-politics of identity', in B. Ryan (ed), *Identity Politics in the Women's Movement*, New York University Press, New York: 23–34

Kelley, R.D.G. 1997 'Identity politics and class struggle', *New Politics*, 6(2) (Winter)

KeynesJ.M. 1932 'The world's economic outlook', *The Atlantic Ideas Tour*. Retrieved 7 April 2016, www.theatlantic.com/ideastour/markets-morals/keynes-full.html

King, J.E. 2013 *David Ricardo*, Palgrave Macmillan, Houndmills

Kliman, A. 2011 *The Failure of Capitalist Production: Underlying Causes of the Great Recession*, Pluto Press, London

Kondratieff, N. 1984 *The Long Wave Cycle*, Richardson & Snyder, New York

Koo, H. 2000 'The dilemmas of empowered labor in Korea: Korean workers in the face of global capitalism', *Asian Survey*, 40(2): 227–250

Korsch, K. 1931 'The crisis of Marxism', *Marxists.org*. Retrieved 6 January 2016, www.marxists.org/archive/korsch/1931/crisis-marxism.htm

Korsch, K. 1950 'Ten theses on Marxism today', *Marxist Internet Archive*. Retrieved 7 May 2016, www.marxists.org/archive/korsch/1950/ten-theses.htm

Korsch, K. 1970 *Marxism and Philosophy*, New Left Books, London

Kotkin, S. 2014 *Stalin: Volume I: Paradoxes of Power, 1878–1928*, Penguin, New York

Krippner, G.R. 2011 *Capitalizing on Crisis: The Political Origins of the Rise of Finance*, Harvard University Press, Cambridge

Kuznets, S. 1955 'Economic growth and income inequality', *The American Economic Review*, 45(1): 1–28

Laclau, E. and Mouffe, C. 2001 *Hegemony and Socialist Strategy: Towards a Radical Democratic Politics*, 2nd edn., Verso, London and New York

Laffey, M. and Dean, K. 2002 'A flexible Marxism for flexible times: globalization and historical materialism', in M. Rupert and H. Smith (eds), *Historical Materialism and Globalization*, Routledge, Taylor & Francis Group, London and New York: 90–109

Lapavitsas, C. 2009 'Financialised capitalism: crisis and financial expropriation', *Historical Materialism*, 17(2): 114–148

Lebowitz, M.A. 2004 'What keeps capitalism going', *Monthly Review*, 56(2): 19–25

Lebowitz, M.A. 2008 *Following Marx: Method, Critique and Crisis*, Brill, Leiden and Boston MA

Lebowitz, M.A. 2012a 'What makes the working class a revolutionary subject?', *Monthly Review: An Independent Socialist Magazine*, 64(7): 35–37

Lebowitz, M.A. 2012b 'Change the system, not its barriers', in M. Musto (ed), *Marx for Today*, Routledge, Taylor & Francis Group, London and New York: 59–72

Lebowitz, M.A. 2013 'The relevance of Marxism today: an interview with Michael A. Lebowitz by Zhuo Mingliang', *MRZine* 21 March. Retrieved 30 September 2016, http://mrzine.monthlyreview.org/2013/lebowitz210313.html

Legarde, C. 2016 'Legarde warns Trump-style protectionism would hit world economy', *Financial Times*. Retrieved 17 July 2016, https://next.ft.com/content/134aac12-4403-11e6-9b66-0712b3873ae1

Leisink, P. 1999 'Introduction', in P. Leisink (ed), *Globalization and Labour Relations*, Edward Elgar, Cheltenham, Northampton MA: 1–35

Lenin, V. 1918 'Prophetic words', *Pravda, no 133 July 2, 1918*. Retrieved 10 March 2016, www.marxists.org/archive/lenin/works/1918/jun/29b.htm

LeninV.I. 1977a 'The state and revolution: the Marxist theory of the state and the tasks of the proletariat in the revolution', in *VI Lenin Selected Works in Three Volumes, Volume 2*, Progress Publishers, Moscow

Lenin, V.I. 1977b 'The three sources and three component parts of Marxism', in *VI Lenin Selected Works in Three Volumes, Volume 1*, Progress Publishers, Moscow

Lenin, V.I. 1977 c 'What is to be done? Burning questions of our movement' outline', in *VI Lenin Selected Works in Three Volumes, Volume 1*, Progress Publishers, Moscow

Lenin, V.I. 1977 d 'Marxism and revisionism', in *VI Lenin Selected Works in Three Volumes, Volume 1*, Progress Publishers, Moscow

Lenin, V.I. 1977 e 'Imperialism, the highest stage of capitalism: a popular outline', in *VI Lenin Selected Works in Three Volumes, Volume 1*, Progress Publishers, Moscow

Lenin, V.I. 2000 'The right of nations to self-determination', *Marxists Internet Archive*. Retrieved 28 March 2016, www.marxists.org/archive/lenin/works/1914/self-det/

Levesque, C., Hennebert, M.-A. and Fairbrother, P. 2013 'Futures of transnational trade unionism', in P. Fairbrother, M.-A. Hennebert and C. Levesque (eds), *Transnational Trade Unionism: Building Union Power*, Routledge, Taylor & Francis, New York and London: 265–280

Liodakis, G. 2010 *Totalitarian Capitalism and Beyond*, Ashgate Publishing Ltd., Surrey and Burlington VT

Little, D. 1986 *The Scientific Marx*, University of Minnesota Press, Minneapolis

Little, D. 2007 'Marxism and method', in D. Glaser and D.M. Walker (eds), *Twentieth-Century Marxism: A Global Introduction*, Routledge, Taylor & Francis, London and New York: 230–246

Lloyd, J. 2001 *The Protest Ethic: How the Anti-globalisation Movement Challenges Social Democracy*, Demos Publishing, London

Lovins, L.H. and Cohen, B. 2011 *Climate Capitalism: Capitalism in the Age of Climate Change*, Hill and Wang, New York

Lowenthal, R. 1964 *World Communism*, Oxford University Press, Oxford

Lozovsky, A. [pseud. for Dridzo, S.A.] 1976 *Marx and the Trade Unions*, Greenwood Press Publishers, Westport CT

Lubasz, H. 1984 'The dialectical imagination by Martin Jay', in J. Marcus and Z. Tar (eds), *Foundations of the Frankfurt School of Social Research*, Transaction Books, New Brunswick: 79–92

Lukacs, G. 1970 *Lenin: A Study on the Unity of his Thought*, New Left Books, London

Lukacs, G. 1976 *History and Class Consciousness: Studies in Marxist Dialectics*, MIT Press, Cambridge MA

Lukacs, G. 2000 *A Defence of History and Class Consciousness: Tailism and the Dialectic*, Verso, London and New York

Luxemburg, R. 1963 *The Accumulation of Capital*, Routledge and Kegan Paul, London

Luxemburg, R. 1988 *Reform or Revolution*, Pathfinder Press, New York

Lyotard, J.-F. 1984 *The Postmodern Condition: A Report on Knowledge*, University of Minnesota Press, Minneapolis MN

Macionis, J.J. 2007 *Sociology*, 11th edn., Pearson/Prentice Hall, New Jersey

MacPherson, C.B. 1989 'Do we need a theory of the state?', in G. Duncan (ed), *Democracy and the Capitalist State*, Cambridge University Press, Cambridge: 15–32

Magdoff, F. 2002 'Capitalism's twin crises: economic and environmental', *Monthly Review*, 54(4): 1–5

Maguire, D. 2010 'Marxism', in D. Marsh and G. Stoker (eds), *Theory and Methods in Political Science: Political analysis*, Palgrave Macmillan, Houndmills, Basingstoke, Hampshire: 136–155

Maito, E.E. 2014 'The historical transience of capital: the downward trend in the rate of profit since XIX century', *Munich Personal RePEc Archive*. Retrieved 20 December 2016, https://mpra.ub.uni-muenchen.de/55894/1/

Mandel, E. 1976 *Introduction to Karl Marx, Capital, Vol. 1*, Penguin, Harmondsworth

Mandel, E. 1978 *Late Capitalism*, Verso Press, London

Mandle, J.D. (no date) 'How political is the personal? Identity politics, feminism and social change'. Retrieved 8 August 2016, https://userpages.umbc.edu/~korenman/wmst/identity_pol.html

Mann, M. 1973 *Consciousness and Action Among the Western Working Class*, Macmillan, London

Marcuse, H. 1972a *Eros and Civilization: A Philosophical Inquiry into Freud*, Abacus, London

Marcuse, H. 1972b *An Essay on Liberation*, Pelican, Harmondsworth

Marcuse, H. 1972 c *One Dimensional Man*, Abacus, London

Martin, H.P. and Schumann, H. 1997 *The Global Trap*, Zed Books, London and New York

Martins, N. 2011 'Globalisation, inequality and the economic crisis', *New Political Economy*, 16(1): 1–18

Marx, K. 1918 *A Contribution to the Critique of Political Economy*, Charles H. Kerr & Company, Chicago

Marx, K. 1956 *The Poverty of Philosophy*, Lawrence & Wishart, London

Marx, K. 1968 *Theories of Surplus Value, Volume 2*, Progress Publishers, Moscow

Marx, K. 1969a *Economic and Philosophic Manuscripts of 1844*, International Publishers, New York

Marx, K. 1969b *Karl Marx On Colonialism and Modernization: His Despatches and Other Writings on China, India, Mexico, the Middle East and North Africa*, (ed with an introduction by S. Avineri), Doubleday Anchor, New York

Marx, K. 1974 *Grundrisse: Foundations of the Critique of Political Economy (Rough Draft)*, Penguin Books, Harmondsworth, Middlesex

Marx, K. 1977 *Critique of Hegel's 'Philosophy of Right'* (edited with an introduction and notes by J. O'Malley), Cambridge University Press, London, New York, and Melbourne

Marx, K. 1986a 'The eighteenth Brumaire of Louis Bonaparte', in *Marx Engels Selected Works*, Progress Publishers, Moscow: 94–179

Marx, K. 1986b *Capital: A Critique of Political Economy, Volume 1*, Progress Publishers, Moscow

Marx, K. 1986 c *Capital: A Critique of Political Economy. Volume 3*, Progress Publishers, Moscow

Marx, K. 1986 d *Capital: A Critique of Political Economy, Volume 2*, Progress Publishers, Moscow

Marx, K. 1986 e 'Wages, prices and profit', in *Marx Engels Selected Works*, Progress Publishers, Moscow: 185–226

Marx, K. 1986 f 'Wage, labour and capital', in *Marx Engels Selected Works*, Progress Publishers, Moscow: 64–93

Marx, K. and Engels, F. 1964 *The German Ideology*, Progress Publishers, Moscow

Marx, K. and Engels, F. 1969 'Speech at the Anniversary of The People's Paper', in *Marx & Engels Selected Works, Vol. 1*, Progress Publishers, Moscow: 500

Marx, K. and Engels, F. 1975a *The Holy Family: Critique of Critical Critique*, Progress Publishers, Moscow

Marx, K. and Engels, F. 1975b *Articles on Britain*, Progress Publishers, Moscow

Marx, K. and Engels, F. 1977 *Manifesto of the Communist Party*, Progress Publishers, Moscow

Mavroudeas, S. 2012 *The Limits of Regulation: A Critical Analysis of Capitalist Development*, Edward Elgar, Cheltenham and Northampton MA

McCarney, J. 1990 *Social Theory and the Crisis in Marxism*, Verso, London and New York

McDonough, T., Reich, M. and Kotz, D.M. 2010 *Contemporary Capitalism and its Crises: Social Structure of Accumulation Theory for the 21st Century*, Cambridge University Press, Cambridge

McNally, D. 2011 *Global Slump: The Economics and Politics of Crisis and Resistance*, PM Press, Oakland CA

Michels, R. 1962 *Political Parties: A Sociological Study of the Oligarchical Tendencies of Modern Democracy*, The Free Press, New York, Collier-Macmillan Ltd., London

Miller, R.W. 1991 'Social and political theory: class, state, revolution', in T. Carver (ed), *The Cambridge Companion to Marx*, Cambridge University Press, Cambridge: 55–105

Milliband, R. 1969 *The State in Capitalist Society: An Analysis of the Western System of Power*, Basic Books, New York

Mills, C.W. 1963 *The Power Elite*, Oxford University Press, New York

Meyer, D.S. 1999 'How the Cold War Was really won: the effects of the antinuclear movements of the 1980s', in M. Guigni, D. McAdam and C. Tilly (eds), *How Social Movements Matter*, University of Minnesota Press, Minneapolis and London: 182–203

Moody, K. 1988 *An Injury to All: The Decline of American Unionism*, Verso, London and New York

Moody, K. 1997 'Towards an international social movement unionism', *New Left Review*, 225(1) (September–October)

Moore, K. 1999 'Political protest and institutional change: the anti-Vietnam War movement and American science', in M. Giugni, D. McAdam and C. Tilly (eds), *How Social Movements Matter*, University of Minnesota Press, Minneapolis and London: 97–118

Moore, B.Jr 1978 *Injustice: The Social Bases of Obedience & Revolt*, Palgrave Macmillan, London

Moran, M. 2015 *Identity and Capitalism*, Sage Publishers, Los Angeles, New Delhi, Singapore, Washington DC

Muddle, C. 2007 *Populist Right Radical Parties in Europe*, Cambridge University Press, Cambridge and New York

Munck, R. 2010 'Globalization and the labour movement: challenges and responses', *Global Labour Journal*, 1(2): 218–232

Murray, G. 2012 'Australia's ruling class: a local elite, a transnational capitalist class, or bits of both', in G. Murray and J. Scott (eds), *Financial Elites and Transnational Business*, Elgar Publishing, Cheltenham: 193–219

Musto, M. 2012 *Marx For Today*, Routledge, Taylor & Francis, London and New York

Naes, A. 1973 'The shallow and the deep, long-range ecology movement: a summary', *Inquiry*, 16(1–4): 95–100

Nash, K. 2000 , *Contemporary Political Sociology: Globalization, Politics, and Power*, Blackwell Publishers, Malden MA and Oxford

Newell, P. and Paterson, M. 2010 *Climate Capitalism: Global Warming and the Transformation of the Global Economy*, Cambridge University Press, Cambridge, New York

Newport, F. 2015 'Fewer Americans identify as middle class in recent years', *Gallup*. Retrieved 27 October 2016, www.gallup.com/poll/182918/fewer-americans-identify-middle-class-recent-years.aspx

North, D. 2015 *The Frankfurt School, Postmodernism and the Politics of the Pseudo-Left*, Mehring Books, Michigan

O'Brien, R. 2004 'Globalisation, imperialism and the labour standards debate', in R. Munck (ed), *Labour and Globalisation: Results and Prospects*, Liverpool University Press, Liverpool: 52–70

Offe, C. 1974 'Structural problems of the capitalist state: class rule and the political system: on the selectiveness of political institutions', in K. von Beyme (ed), *German Political Studies*, Sage Publishers, Beverly Hills CA: 31–54

Olofsson, G. 1988 'After the working class movement? What's 'new' and what's 'social' in the new social movements', *Acta Sociologica*, 31(1): 15–34

Organisation for Economic Cooperation and Development (OECD) 2014 'Focus on inequality and growth', *OECD Directorate for Employment, Labour and Social Affairs*. Retrieved 20 May 2015, www.OECD.Org/Social/Focus-Inequality-and-Growth_2014.PDF

OECD 2015 'In it together: why less inequality benefits all', *OECD Publishing*, Paris. Retrieved 20 July 2016, http://dx.doi.org/10.1787/9789264225120-en

Ohmae, K. 1995 *The End of the Nation State: The Rise of Regional Economies*, Harper Collins, London

Ormerod, P. 2015 'Capitalism is stable and resilient', *City AM*, 9 April. Retrieved 8 April 2016, www.paulormerod.com/category/capitalism/

Overbeek, H. 2004 'Global governance, class, hegemony: a historical materialist perspective', *Working Papers Political Science No. 2004/01*. Retrieved 3 March 2016, www.fsw.vu.nl/en/Images/Global_Governance,_Class,_Hegemony_A_historical_materialist_perspective_tcm250-42721.pdf

Oxfam 2014 'Still the lucky country? The Growing gap between rich and poor is a gaping hole in the G20 agenda', *Oxfam Australia*. Retrieved 15 July 2015, www.oxfam.org.au/wp-content/uploads/2014/06/2014-66-g20-report_fa_web-2.pdf

Oxfam 2016 *An Economy for the 1%: How privilege and power in the economy drive extreme inequality and how this can be stopped*, 210 Oxfam Briefing Paper, January. Retrieved 7 July 2016, www.oxfam.org/sites/www.oxfam.org/files/file_attachments/bp210-economy-one-percent-tax-havens-180116-en_0.pdf

Palit, A. 2014 *The Trans-Pacific Partnership, China and India: Economic and Political Implications*, Routledge, Taylor & Francis, London and New York

Panitch, L. and Gindin, S. 2000 'Rekindling socialist imagination: utopian vision and working class capacities', *Monthly Review: An Independent Socialist Magazine*, 51(10): 36–35

Pannekoek, A. 1915 'Marxism as action', *Marxist Internet Archive*. Retrieved 25 September 2016, www.marxists.org/archive/pannekoe/1915/marxism-action.htm

Parenti, M. 1995 *Against Empire*, City Light Books, San Francisco CA

Parkin, F. 1968 *Middle Class Radicalism: The Social Bases of the British Campaign for Nuclear Disarmament*, University of Manchester Press, Manchester

Pateman, C. 1988 *The Sexual Contract*, Polity Press, Cambridge

Patnaik, P. 2016 'Capitalism and its current crisis', *Monthly Review: An Independent Socialist Magazine*, 67(8): 1–13

Peet, R. 1975 'Inequality and poverty: a Marxist-geographic theory', *Annals of the Association of American Geographers*, 65(4): 564–571

Peet, R. 2009 *Unholy Trinity: The IMF, World Bank and WTO*, ZED Books, London and New York

Peet, R. 2011 'Contradictions of finance capitalism', *Monthly Review: An Independent Socialist Magazine*, 63(7)

Pettifor, A. 2008 'Economies of scale', *The Guardian*. Retrieved 9 August 2016, www.theguardian.com/commentisfree/2008/oct/21/globalisation-brettonwoods

Petras, J. and Veltmeyer, H. 2000 'Globalisation or imperialism?', *Cambridge Review of International Affairs*, 14(1): 32–48

Piazza, J. 2001 'De-linking Labor: Labor unions and social democratic parties under globalization', *Party Politics*, 7(4): 413–435

Pieterse, J.N. 2002 'Global inequality: bringing politics back in', *Third World Quarterly*, 23(6): 1023–1046

Piketty, T. 2014 *Capital in the Twenty-First Century*, The Belknap Press of Harvard University Press, Cambridge MA and London

Pilat, D., Cimper, A., Olsen, K. and Webb, C. 2006 'The changing nature of manufacturing in OECD economies', *STI Working Paper, 2006/9*, OECD Directorate for Science, Technology and Industry. Retrieved 10 July 2016, www.oecd.org/science/innol/37607831.pdf

Piven, F.F. 1995 'Globalizing capitalism and the rise of identity politics', *Socialist Register*, 31: 102–116

Piven, F.F. and Cloward, R.A. 1977 *Poor People's Movements: Why They Succeed, How They Fail*, Vintage Books, New York

Plekhanov, G. 1976 *Selected Philosophical Works, Volume 3*, Progress Publishers, Moscow

Poggi, G. 1990 *The State: It's Nature, Development and Prospects*, Stanford University Press, Stanford CA

Popper, K.R. 1985 *Popper Selections* (ed. D. Miller), Princeton University Press, Princeton NJ

Popper, K.R. 2002 *The Poverty of Historicism*, Routledge, London and New York

Posner, R.A. 2009 *A Failure of Capitalism: The Crisis of '08 and the Descent into Depression*, Harvard University Press, Cambridge MAand London

Postone, M. 2007 'Theorizing the contemporary world: Robert Brenner, Giovanni Arrighi, David Harvey', in R. Albrittin, R. Jessop and R. Westra (eds), *Political Economy and Global Capitalism: The 21st Century, Present and Future*, Anthem Press, London, New York and Delhi: 7–23

Poulantzas, N. 1975 *Classes in Contemporary Capitalism*, New Left Books, London

Pressman, S. 2007 'The decline of the middle class: an international perspective', *Journal of Economic Issues*, 41: 181–200

Pryke, S. 2012 'Economic nationalism: theory, history and prospects', *Global Policy*, 3(3): 281–291

Ramos, V.Jr 1982 'The concepts of ideology, hegemony, and organic intellectuals in Gramsci's Marxism', *Marxists.org*. Retrieved 15 April 2016, www.marxists.org/history/erol/periodicals/theoretical-review/1982301.htm

Ray, L.J. 1993 *Rethinking Critical Theory: Emancipation in the Age of Global Social Movements*, Sage Publications, London

Rees, J. 1998 *The Algebra of Revolution: The Dialectic and the Classical Marxist Tradition*, Routledge, London and New York

Reich, R.B. 2015 *Saving Capitalism for the Many, not the Few*, Penguin, Random House

Renton, D. 2002 *Classical Marxism: Socialist Theory and the Second International*, New Clarion Press, Cheltenham

Renton, D. 2005 *Marx on Globalisation*, Lawrence & Wishart, London

Robbins, R.H. 2011 *Global Problems and the Culture of Capitalism*, 4th edn, Allyn & Bacon, Boston MA

Roberts, A. 2012 'Why the Occupy movement failed', *Pacific Administration Review*, 72(5): 754–762

Robinson, W.I. 1998 'Beyond nation-state paradigms: globalization, sociology, and the challenge of transnational studies', *Sociological Forum*, 13(4): 561–594

Robinson, W.I. 2004 *A Theory of Global Capitalism: Production, Class and State in a Transnational World*, John Hopkins University Press, Baltimore MD and London

Robinson, W.I. 2010 'The crisis of global capitalism: cyclical, structural or systemic', in M. Konings (ed), *The Great Credit Crash*, Verso, London: 289–310

Robinson, W.I. 2014 *Global Capitalism and the Crisis of Humanity*, Cambridge University Press, New York

Robinson, W.I. and Harris, J. 2000 'Towards a global ruling class? Globalization and the transnational capitalist class', *Science and Society*, 64(1): 11–54

Rocamora, J. 2012 'People power is alive and well', *Third World Quarterly*, 33 (2): 201–204

Rodrik, D. 1997 *Has Globalization Gone Too Far?*Institute for International Economics, Washington DC

Rootes, C.A. 1997 'Social movements and politics', *African Studies*, 56(1): 67–95

Rosen, M. 1996 *On Voluntary Servitude: False Consciousness and the Theory of Ideology*, Polity Press, Cambridge

Rosenberg, J. 1996 'Isaac Deutscher and the lost history of international relations', *New Left Review*, I/215, January–February

Rupert, M. and Smith, H. 2002 'Editor's introduction', in M. Rupert and H. Smith (eds), *Historical Materialism and Globalization*, Routledge, Taylor & Francis, London and New York: 1–13

Sayer, D. 1985 'The critique of politics and political economy: capitalism, communism and the state in Marx's writings of the mid-1840s', *The Sociological Review*, 33(2): 221–253

Schenk, C. 2003 'Social movement unionism: beyond the organizing model', in P. Fairbrother and C.A.B. Yates (eds), *Trade Unions in Renewal: A Comparative Study*, Routledge, London and New York: 244–262

Scholte, J.A. 2005 *Globalization: A Critical Introduction*, 2nd edn. Palgrave Macmillan, Basingstoke

Schuman, M. 2013 'Marx's revenge: how class struggle is shaping the world', *Time Magazine*, 25 March. Retrieved 30 September 2016, http://business.time.com/2013/03/25/marxs-revenge-how-class-struggle-is-shaping-the-world/

Scott, B.R. 2012 *Capitalism, Democracy and Development*, Springer Publishers, New York

Selwyn, B. 2013 'Karl Marx, class struggle and labour-centred development', *Global Labour Journal*, 4(1): 48–70

Shah, A. 2011 'Corporate power: facts and stats', *Global Issues*. Retrieved 21 July 2016, www.globalissues.org/article/59/corporate-power-facts-and-stats#Concentrationoftransnationalcompanies

Shandro, A. 2007 'Lenin and Marxism', in D. Glaser and D.M. Walker (eds), *Twentieth-Century Marxism: A Global Introduction*, Routledge, Taylor & Francis Group, London and New York: 15–29

Sharpe, M. 2010 'The crisis of capitalism', *Challenge*, 53(5): 98–119

Sheppard, J. and Biddle, N. 2015 'Social class in Australia: beyond the "working" and "middle" classes', *ANU POLL 19*, Australian National University

Silver, B. 2006 *Forces of Labor: Workers' Movements and Globalization since 1870*, Cambridge University Press, Cambridge

Sim, S. 2011 'Post or past? Does post-Marxism have any future?', *Global Discourse: An Interdisciplinary Journal of Current Affairs and Applied Contemporary Thought*, 2(1): 12–23

Singer, D. 1999 *Whose Millennium? Theirs or Ours?*Monthly Review Press, New York

Sitton, J.F. 2010 *Marx Today: Selected Works and Recent Debates*, Palgrave Macmillan, New York

Sklair, L. 2000 'The transnational capitalist class and the discourse of globalisation', *Cambridge Review of International Affairs*, 14(1): 67–85

Sklair, L. 2002 *Globalization: Capitalism and its Alternatives*, 3rd edn., Oxford University Press, Oxford

Small, A.W. 1897 'The meaning of the social movement', *American Journal of Sociology*, 3(3): 340–354

Smith, D. 2006 , *Globalization: The Hidden Agenda*, Polity Press, Cambridge and Malden MA

Smith, J. 2001 'Globalizing resistance: the battle of Seattle and the future of social movements', *Mobilization: An International Quarterly*, 6(1) Spring: 1–20

Smith, M.E.G. 2014 *Marxist Phoenix: Studies in Historical Materialism and Marxist Socialism*, Canadian Scholars' Press Inc., Toronto

Smith, S. 1994 'Mistaken identity: or can identity politics liberate the oppressed?', *International Socialism Journal*, 62, Spring

Smith, S. 2008 'The politics of identity', *International Socialist Review*, 57, January–February

Socialist Alliance 2015 *Towards a Socialist Australia*, Socialist Alliance. Retrieved 6 August 2016, https://socialist-alliance.org/documents/towards-socialist-australia

Socialist Alternative 2007 *Statement of Principles*, Socialist Alternative, www.sa.org.au/node/3924

Solomon, S. and Rupert, M. 2002 'Historical materialism, ideology, and the politics of globalizing capitalism', in M. Rupert and H. Smith (eds), *Historical Materialism and Globalization*, Routledge, London and New York: 284–300

Spector, A.J. 2013 'The origins and development of the global capitalist economy and capitalist crises', in B. Berberoglu (ed), *Beyond the Global Capitalist Crisis: The World Economy in Transition*, Ashgate Publishing, Burlington VT: 17–33

Stevis, D. and Boswell, T. 2008 *Globalization and Labor*, Rowman & Littlefield Publishers Inc. Lanham, Boulder, New York, Toronto, and Plymouth

Strange, S. 1997a *The Retreat of the State: The Diffusion of Power in the World Economy*, Cambridge University Press, Cambridge

Strange, S. 1997b 'The erosion of the state', *Current History*, 96(613): 365–369

Summers, L. 2015 'The global economy is in serious danger', *Washington Post*, 7 October. Retrieved 3 March 2016, www.washingtonpost.com/opinions/the-global-economy-is-in-serious-danger/2015/10/07/85e81666-6c5d-11e5-b31c-d80d62b53e28_story.html

Summers, L. 2016 'Voters deserve responsible nationalism, not reflex globalism', *Financial Times*, 10 July. Retrieved 17 July 2016, https://next.ft.com/content/15598db8-4456-11e6-9b66-0712b3873ae1

Sutcliffe, B. 2002 'How many capitalisms? Historical materialism in the debates about imperialism and globalization', in M. Rupert and H. Smith (eds), *Historical Materialism and Globalization*, Routledge, Taylor & Francis, London and New York: 40–58

Sutor, K. 2003 'Globalization: a long-term view', *Medicine, Conflict and Survival*, 19(2): 94–106

Sweezy, P. 1949 *The Theory of Capitalist Development*, Dennis Dobson Limited, London

Swyngedouw, E. 2010 'The communist hypothesis and revolutionary capitalisms: exploring the idea of communist geographies for the twenty-first century', in N. Castree, P. Chatterton, N. Hynen, W. Warner and M.W. Wright (eds), *The Point Is to Change It: Geographies of Hope and Survival in an Age of Crisis*, Wiley Blackwell, Chichester: 298–319

Szakonyi, D. 2007 'The rise of economic nationalism under globalization and the case of post-communist Russia', *Vestnik: The Journal of Russian and Asian Studies*, 16 May

Tabb, W.K. 2010 'Marxism, crisis theory and the crisis of the early 21st century', *Science and Society*, 74(3): 305–323

Tant, T. 1999 'Marxism as social science: celebration or nonchalance', in A. Gamble, D. Marsh and T. Tant (eds), *Marxism and Social Science*, University of Illinois Press, Urbana IL and Chicago IL: 104–125

Tanzi, V. 1998 'The demise of the nation-state?', *IMF Working Paper, WP/98/120*, International Monetary Fund. Retrieved 12 July 2016, www.imf.org/external/pubs/ft/wp/wp98120.pdf

Tarr, Z. 2011 *The Frankfurt School: The Critical Theories of Max Horkheimer and Theodor W. Adorno*, Transaction Publishers, New Brunswick and London

Thanim, T. 2011 *The Monstrous Organization*, Edward Elgar Publishing, Cheltenham PA and Northampton MA

The Economist 2014 'Capitalism and its critics: a modern Marx', *The Economist*, 3 May. Retrieved 3 November 2016, www.economist.com/news/leaders/21601512-thomas-pikettys-blockbuster-book-great-piece-scholarship-poor-guide-policy

Therborn, G. 2008 *From Marxism to Post-Marxism*, Verso, London

Therborn, G. 2012 'Class in the 21st century', *New Left Review*, 78

Thompson, E.P. 1957 'Socialist humanism an epistle to the philistines', *Marxist Internet Archive*. Retrieved 20 May 2016, www.marxists.org/archive/thompson-ep/1957/sochum.htm

Tilly, C. 1975 'Reflections on the history of European state making', in C. Tilly (ed), *The Formation of National States in Western Europe*, Princeton University Press, Princeton NJ

Tosh, J. 2010 *The Pursuit of History*, 5th edn., Routledge, London and New York

Trotsky, L. 1953 *The First Five Years of the Communist International in Two Volumes: Volume II*, Pioneer Publishers, New York

Trotsky, L.D. 1965 *The History of the Russian Revolution, Volume One*, translated by M. Eastman, Sphere Books Limited, London

Trotsky, L. 1970 *The Third International After Lenin*, Pathfinder Press, New York

Trotsky, L. 1971a *My Life: An Attempt at an Autobiography*, Penguin Books, Ltd., Harmondsworth, Middlesex

Trotsky, L. 1971b *In Defense of Marxism*, New Park Publications, London

Trotsky, L. 1972 *On Marxism and the Trade Unions: Trade Unions in the Epoch of Imperialist Decay*, New Park Publications, London

Trotsky, L. 1973 *The Bolsheviki and World Peace*, Hyperion Press Inc., Westport CT

Trotsky, L. 1974 *Collected Writings and Speeches on Britain, in Three Volumes – Volume Two*, edited by R. Chappell and A. Clinton, New Park Publication, London

Trotsky, L. 1977 *The Transitional Program for Socialist Revolution: Including the Death Agony of Capitalism and the Tasks of the Fourth International*, 2nd edn., Pathfinder Press, New York

Trotsky, L. 1986 *Problems of Everyday Life and Other Writings on Culture and Science*, Pathfinder Press, New York

Trotsky, L. 1996 'The war and the international', *Marxists' Internet Archive*. Retrieved 5 June 2015, www.marxists.org/archive/Trotsky/1914/war

Trotsky, L. 2006 'Presenting Karl Marx', in L. Trotsky (ed), *The Essential Marx*, Dover Publications Inc., Mineola NY: 1–43

Trotsky, L. 2010 *The Permanent Revolution and Results and Prospects*, Red Letter Press, Seattle WA

Tsoulfidis, L. and Paitaridis, D. 2012 'Revisiting Adam Smith's theory of the falling rate of profit', *International Journal of Social Economics*, 39(5): 304–313

Uchida, H. 2004 *Marx for the 21st Century*, Routledge, Taylor & Francis Group, London and New York

United Nations Development Program 2014 *Human Development Report 2014*. Retrieved 12 February 2016, http://hdr.undp.org/en/2014-report

Van der Pijl, K. 2002 'Historical materialism and the emancipation of labour', in M. Rupert and H. Smith (eds), *Historical Materialism and Globalization*, Routledge, London and New York: 129–146

Veltmeyer, H. 2013 'The global capitalist crisis and Latin America', in B. Berberoglu (ed), *Beyond the Global Capitalist Crisis: The World Economy in Transition*, Ashgate Publishing, Burlington VT: 103–122

Vilrokx, J. 1999 'Towards the denaturing of class relations? The political economy of the firm in global capitalism', in P. Leisink (ed), *Globalization and Labour Relations*, Edward Elgar Publishing Ltd., Cheltenham and Northampton MA: 57–77

Wainwright, J. and Kim, S.J. 2008 'Battles in Seattle Redux: transnational resistance to a neoliberal trade agreement', *Antipode*, 40(4): 513–534

Walker, D. 2015 'Towards a new gospel of wealth', Ford Foundation. Retrieved 2 November 2016, www.fordfoundation.org/ideas/equals-change-blog/posts/toward-a-new-gospel-of-wealth/

Wallerstein, I. 1986 'Marxisms as Utopias', *American Journal of Sociology*, 91 (6): 1296–1308

Waterman, P. 1993 'Social movement unionism: a new model for a new world order?', *Review (Fernand Braudel Center)*, 16(3): 245–278

Waterman, P. 1998 *Globalisation, Social Movements and the New Internationalisms*, Continuum, London

Waterman, P. 2001 *Globalization, Social Movements and the New Internationalisms*, Continuum, London and New York

Webster, E., Lambert, R. and Bezuidenhut, A. 2008 *Grounding Globalization: Labour in the Age of Insecurity*, Blackwell Publishing, Malden MA

Weisbord, A. 1937 'The conquest of power', *Marxists Internet Archive*. Retrieved 17 March 2016, www.marxists.org/archive/weisbord/conquest17.htm

Weston, J. 1986 'Introduction', in J. Weston (ed), *Red and Green: A New Politics of the Environment*, Pluto Press, London: 1–8

Wheelwright, E.L. 1953 'Trade unions and the state', *The Australian Quarterly*, 25(2): 26–36

Whitfield, S. 1996 'Historical materialism', in I. McLean (ed) *The Concise Dictionary of Politics*, Oxford University Press, Oxford: 220–221

Wiggershaus, R. 1994 *The Frankfurt School: Its History, Theories and Political Significance*, Polity Press, Cambridge

Wills, J. 2004 'Re-scaling trade union organisation: lessons from the European front line', in R. Munck (ed), *Labour and Globalisation: Results and Prospects*, Liverpool University Press, Liverpool: 85–104

Wolf, M. 2004 *Why Globalization Works*, Yale University Press, New Haven CT

Wolf, M. 2009 'Seeds of its own destruction', *Financial Times*, 8 March. Retrieved 4 March 2016, www.ft.com/intl/cms/s/0/c6c5bd36-0c0c-11de-b87d

Wolff, R. 2010 'In capitalist crisis, rediscovering Marx', *Socialism and Democracy*, 24(3): 130–146

Wood, E.M. 1997 'Back to Marxism', *Monthly Review: An Independent Socialist Magazine*, 49(2): 1–9

Wood, E.M. 1998 'Capitalist change and generational shifts', *Monthly Review: An Independent Socialist Magazine*, 50(5): 1–10

Wood, E.M. 2002 'Global capital, national states', in M. Rupert and H. Smith (eds), *Historical Materialism and Globalization*, Routledge, Taylor & Francis, London and New York: 17–39

Wood, E.M. 2004 *The Empire of Capital*, Verso, London and New York

World Bank 1995 *World Development Report: World Development Indicators*, Oxford University Press, New York

Wright, E.O. 1979 *Class, Crisis and the State*, Verso, London

WTO 2016 *Report on G20 Trade Measures (mid-October 2015 to mid-May 2016)*, WTO-OMC. Retrieved 22 July 2016, www.wto.org/english/news_e/news16_e/g20_wto_report_june16_e.pdf

Yates, C.A.B. 2003 'The revival of industrial unions in Canada: the extension and adaptation of industrial union practices to the new economy', in P. Fairbrother and C.A.B. Yates (eds), *Trade Unions in Revival: A Comparative Study*, Routledge, Taylor & Francis Group, London and New York: 221–243

Young, G. 1976 'The fundamental contradiction of capitalist production', *Philosophy and Public Affairs*, 5(2): 196–234

INDEX

abstract categories 66
Accumulation of Capital (Luxemburg) 49
activity spheres 19
Adorno, Theodor 42–3
African-American Environmentalist Association 121
alienation, Marxist conception of 6, 10, 53, 118
anti-capitalist movements 14, 97; and globalisation 114; Harvey on 146; and nationalism 104; potential directions of 110, 126, 131–2, 139; social movement and identity politics in 25, 136; and the working class 114, 149–50
anti-colonial movements 28, 45
anti-communism 75
anti-globalisation movement 97–9, 101, 123; and anti-capitalism 107; dislocation of 24; and nationalism 104, 113–14, 125–6, 129–30; social movements and identity politics in 25
Asian Economic Crisis (1990s) 75
Australia, state interventions in 80

Badiou, Alan 148–9
base-superstructure concept 6, 44–6, 65–6, 95, 137, 158, 165
Bello, Walden 24, 125, 130
Bernanke, Ben 105
Bernstein, Eduard 38–9, 43, 46, 53, 69, 119, 125, 129
Black Lives Matter 154
Blair, Tony 26
Bloch, Ernst 28, 42–3
Bolsheviks 156
Brenner, Robert 138
Bukharin, Nikolai 112
business cycles 39, 77; *see also* capitalist crisis, cycles of

Callinicos, Alex 45, 48
Capital (Marx) 20; themes in Volume 1 56; Volume II 95
capital: concentration of 22, 57, 78; interconnected uses of 95; merchant and industrial 89; organic composition of 85; reproduction of 64, 142–3, 155
capital accumulation 89–90, 94, 112
capital flows 22, 87, 90–1, 103
capitalism: breakdown of 28, 47, 69, 77, 81; class relations within 9, 82, 136, 140; contradictions of 72, 85–6, 140, 146; epochs of 20, 46–7, 72; existential threats to 73–6; future of 156; Golden Age of 28, 34, 44–7, 77; and identity politics 119–21, 128; and Marxism 6, 22, 37, 50–1, 60, 62, 135, 144; need for challenge to 70, 130–4, 136–9, 142, 150–1, 160, 162–3, 166; and populism 130; primary elements of 64; qualitative change in 12, 78, 87–109, 137, 166; reasons for survival of 1, 6, 8–9, 14, 32, 67–9, 160–1, 169–70; reproduction of 77, 140, 143, 155, 167; self-regulation and resilience of 38–9, 46, 79–80

capitalist crisis: current stage of 80–1; cycles of 76–9; features of 22–3, 57; intensification of 10–11; Marxism and 12, 19, 29–30, 37, 60, 75, 134, 139, 161–3; materialist reading of 64–8; responses to 138; and stabilisation 4, 73; use of term 21
capitalist development 11; and crisis 13–14; post-war 45; role of state in 18; unevenness of 90, 103
capitalist globalisation *see* globalisation
capitalist paradigm 70–3
China, and the US 67, 108
class: in classical Marxism 6, 9, 35, 49, 62 (*see also* working class); in Critical Theory 43; and social identity 152–5
class conflict *see* class struggle
class consciousness 49; in Marxism 43, 60, 146–8; weakening 82–4, 107, 116–17
class struggle: and class consciousness 117; in classical Marxism 27, 35–6, 49, 58, 158; Frankfurt School on 43; and globalisation 113; in post-Marxism 29; state suppression of 81–4
classical Marxism: and contemporary Marxism 13, 16, 45–6; and crisis of Marxism 27, 44; and globalisation 26, 36; and Kondratieff 39; as optimistic 34–5; return to 64, 170; and the state 17; use of term 4–5
climate change 76, 120
Cold War 25, 44, 65, 73, 75–6
colonialism 89–90
commodity capital 95
communist organisations 151
competitive capitalism 20, 46
competitiveness 85, 127
contradiction, in Marx's method 55–7, 65
Contribution to the Critique of Political Economy (Marx) 35
co-revolutionary theory 132
Crenshaw, Kimberlé 122
crisis, use of term 4
Critical Theory 42–3
culture, transformative role of 28, 45
currency trading 94
deglobalisation 24, 111, 125, 129–30
democratisation, global 99, 104, 113
determinism 65, 157
Deutscher, Isaac 5–6, 29, 159, 165
developing world: growth of capitalism in 22, 78, 91; inequality in 101–2; working class in 141
dialectics: in Marx's method 54, 56, 65; use of term 59

Eagleton, Terry 83, 157
Economic and Philosophic Manuscripts of 1844 (Marx) 118
economic growth 103, 143
economic nationalism 7, 20, 87, 99–100, 105–7, 109, 129–30, 156, 167
economism 115, 127, 157
ecophilosophy 120–1
elite theory 17
EMDCs (emerging markets and developing countries) 101
Engels, Friedrich: on class struggle 81; and classical Marxism 5–6; *Communist Manifesto* 2; and dialectics of nature 59; on false consciousness 63; on historical materialism 58, 66; and patriarchy 120; on the state 17–18, 70; on trade unions 115
European Union 100
Evolutionary Socialism (Bernstein) 38

false consciousness 18, 63, 73, 83, 131
FDI (Foreign Direct Investments) 87, 94–5
feminist politics 120
finance capital 87, 94, 96, 112
finance capitalism 22–3, 57, 78, 94
financialisation 22–3, 87, 91–2, 94, 97, 105, 108, 137
Ford Foundation 154–5
Frankfurt School 27–8, 42–3, 64, 144
free trade 88, 105–7
Freud, Sigmund 28

Germany, socialist movement in 37, 40–2, 61
GFC (Global Financial Crisis) 18, 22–3, 78, 80, 95, 156
Giddens, Anthony 26

Gindin, Sam 43
global economy, stagnation of 80
globalisation 8, 14; analyses of 15–16, 19–20; and capitalist crisis 23, 78; dialectic of 105; drivers of 26, 89–91; as essential to capitalism 92, 111, 114, 140; impact on politics of 119–20; institutions of 91, 112; intensification of 10–12, 15, 67, 70, 78, 95–7, 104, 110, 167; Marxist theory of 36, 57; and rate of profit 86; reaction and opposition to 23–7, 88, 109, 112–13, 117, 125–6 (*see also* anti-globalisation movement); as transformation of capitalism 103
Gorz, Andre 45, 47
Gramsci, Antonio 18, 48, 83, 116
grand narrative 45
Great Depression 46, 73, 75, 79
Greece 139, 146

Harvey, David 19, 64, 77, 146
hegemony, Gramsci on 18, 83
Hilferding, Rudolf 23, 49, 94
historical materialism 12, 54; applied to itself 63; and classical Marxism 6, 27, 57–60; and globalisation 11, 57, 67; and internationalism 41; Plekhanov on 62
historicism 58
History and Class Consciousness (Lukács) 41
Hobsbawm, Eric 106
Horkheimer, Max 42–3
humanism, radical 154
Hungarian Revolution: of 1919 74; of 1956 44

identity politics 14; and anti-capitalism 110–11, 118–22, 150–1, 153–4; and globalisation 24–6, 113; and Marxism 7, 29, 153, 161
ideology: in classical Marxism 6, 73; of populism 130; and social revolution 63; and survival of capitalism 69–70, 82–4, 86, 120
ILO (International Labour Office) 102
IMF (International Monetary Fund): on aftermath of GFC 79–80; growth forecasts 66–7; and imperialism 112; on inequality 101
imperialism: economic impact of 90; and globalisation 51, 112; new form of 93
industrialisation 66, 89–90, 117
inequality: capitalism as driver of 21, 111, 143–4; and globalisation 20, 24; growth of 8, 10, 14, 81, 86, 96–7, 100–2, 105; sources of 102–3
instrumentalist theory of the state 17–18
internationalism 25, 38, 41, 61, 103, 130, 151
intersectionality 122
Ionesco, Eugene 1

Kondratieff, Nikolai 39
Korsch, Karl 10, 31, 41, 44, 54, 63–4, 141
Kouvelakis, Stathis 30–1
KPD (Communist Party of Germany) 41
Kuznets, Simon 143

labour: alienation of 118; casualisation and informalisation of 102, 127, 168; Gorz's theory of 47; integration into capitalist state 82, 116; in Marxist analysis 54, 56; relationship with capital 9, 18, 40, 73, 102 (*see also* class struggle); share of income 86; social nature of 64; *see also* working class
labour power 72, 83; sale of 95
Laclau, Ernest 29–30, 53
Lapavitsas, Costas 23
leadership: crisis of 11, 14, 61, 84, 148–9, 165; Marxism as offering 49–51, 117
Lebowitz, Michael 18, 83, 133, 138, 142–3, 151, 155, 158
legitimising identity 118
Lenin, Vladimir: on class consciousness 49; on imperialism 112; and Marxism 5–6, 42, 44, 57; on revisionism 38; on spontaneity 149–50; on the state 71; on trade unions 115, 117, 139; on uneven development 90

Lukács, György: on false consciousness 63; and Frankfurt School; 28; on hegemony 82; on historical materialism 11; *History and Class Consciousness* 41; on Marxist orthodoxy 53–4
Luxemburg, Rosa 5; against Bernstein 37–9, 46, 115; and classical Marxism 6; theory of capitalist breakdown 69, 77; on workers and science 138
Lyotard, Jean-François 45

Mandel, Ernest 39
Manifesto of the Communist Party 2–4, 19, 63, 147, 151
manufacturing, and globalisation 91, 95–6, 141
Marcuse, Herbert 28, 45
Marx, Karl 1; analytical approach 8, 54–6, 131, 137, 163 (*see also* Marxist analysis); on capitalism 20, 35–6, 71–2, 85, 89, 114; on class 49, 122, 145, 152–3; and classical Marxism 5–6; *Communist Manifesto* 2; on free trade 107; on freedom 106; and inequality 102–3; materialist conception of history 35–6 (*see also* historical materialism); on petty bourgeois politics 132; as philosopher 48; and science 59; on the state 97; on trade unions 115
Marxism: 20th century developments in 40–7, 164; class and identity in 121, 135–6, 153; contemporary state of 6–8, 11–12, 31–3, 47–8, 51, 93; crisis in 10, 13, 15, 27–31, 34–5, 54, 63, 118, 141, 144–51; essence of 40, 140–1; fragmentation of 1–2, 8–10, 50, 53, 137, 161–2; interpretations of the state 17; materialist analysis of weaknesses of 60–4; and nationalism 104; philosophy and economics in 48, 59–60; political expression of 37, 147; potential areas for research in 166–9; purpose of 6, 49–50, 136–7, 142, 155–9, 164–5; and qualitative change in capitalism 108–9; reform or revolution in *see* reform/revolution debate; relevance of 3–4, 12–13, 34, 48–52, 111, 126, 138–9, 144, 150, 158–63, 165–6, 169–70; and social movement politics 130–1, 139, 163–4; Stalinisation of 12, 27–8, 54, 162 (*see also* Stalinism); theory of history 45 (*see also* historical materialism); *see also* classical Marxism
Marxist analysis 53–4; and class 47, 49; elements of 54–7; and historical materialism 11; as reactive 4; and science 59
Marxist political parties 147, 168
middle class, radicalised 132–4
money capital 95
monopoly capitalism 20, 72
Mouffe, Chantal 29–30, 53
multinational corporations *see* transnational corporations

national capital 18, 20, 112
national liberation movements 28
national unity 74, 88, 105–6, 109, 153
nationalism: and globalisation 125; opposition to 150; resurgence of 88, 108, 129, 161; as social control 106; and split in Marxism 41, 44, 54, 61–2, 74; in the working class 37–8, 97, 99, 103–4, 107, 109; *see also* economic nationalism
nation-states: as basis for politics 86, 93; and capitalism 8, 71, 74, 95–6, 105, 140; dominant 23, 156; and globalisation 19–20, 88, 93–4, 96–100, 109, 112–13, 163, 167; and social democracy 27; *see also* nationalism; the state
nature, dialectics of 59
neo-liberalism 15–16, 24, 26, 91, 129
neo-Marxism 3, 9, 27–8, 46, 53, 144
New Left: and Marxism 28, 43–5, 51, 144; social movement and identity politics 118, 124; theory and practice in 159, 165
non-class politics: in anti-globalisation movement 8, 27, 109–11, 132; identity politics as 29, 121–2, 154; and Marxism 134, 165; and post-Marxism 45–6; social movements as 124–5; and trade unions 25

Occupy movement 123, 125, 128–9, 146, 150
OECD (Organisation for Economic Cooperation and Development) 102
One Dimensional Man (Marcuse) 28
optimism: capitalist 76–7; Marxist 1, 4, 24, 34–5, 135
over-production 22, 57, 78, 85

Panitich, Leo 43
Pannekoek, Anton 156
patriarchy 120
people power 117
Piketty, Thomas 135, 143–4
Plekhanov, Georgi 5–6, 38, 62, 144
pluralism, conception of the state 17
political parties 115, 121, 147, 151, 168
Popper, Karl 43, 58
populism 7, 88, 97, 129–30, 167
post-Marxists 144; and class 29–30, 149; and identity politics 25; and neo-Marxism 53; and postmodernism 45–6
postmodernism 45
Poulantzas, Nicolas 18
power, concentrations of 92–3
primitive accumulation 20, 144
production: modes of 55, 58, 72, 83; relations of 57
productive capital 95–6, 105
productive forces: dialectical interactions between 58; globalisation of 74; growth under capitalism 80; Marx on 35–6; private ownership of 65
profit: and surplus value 95; tendency for rate to fall 22, 57, 70, 78, 81, 85–6, 89, 96, 140
profitability, drive to maintain 86, 91, 96
project identity 118
proletarianisation 90, 145, 167
proletariat, dictatorship of the 35
property relations 56
protectionism 88, 105–9, 113, 125, 128, 167; *see also* economic nationalism
protest politics 25

Rancière, Jacques 155–6
reform/revolution debate 37–9, 69, 138; and Regulationism 47; and social movements 123, 126; and trade unions 115
Regulation Theory 46–7, 142
resistance identity 118–19
revisionism 34, 38, 40, 53
revolutionary movements 44, 60, 123–4, 159
Ricardo, David 85
Russian Revolution: centenary of 7; and crisis in Marxism 9, 27, 29, 37, 40, 62, 74, 162

Sanders, Bernie 129
science, Marxism as 13, 38, 43, 54, 58–9
Seattle protests of 1999 25, 107, 113, 125, 128, 150
Second International 26, 40–1, 62
Smith, Adam 85
social democracy: integrated into state 84; and Marxism 26–7; reinvigoration of 24; working-class support for 37, 42
social discontent 14, 88, 97, 99–101, 103–5
social formations 55
social inequality *see* inequality
social movement politics 14, 110–11; and anti-capitalism 122–6, 130–1; and globalisation 24–6
social movement unionism 25, 127–8
social movements: life cycle of 124–5, 129; and Marxism 30; use of term 25
socialism: in one country 74, 162; scientific 43, 59, 64, 138; utopian 28, 42, 59
Soviet Union: end of 29, 75–6, 168; official Marxism of 31
Spain 146
SPD (Social Democratic Party of Germany) 41
spontaneity 48, 114, 117, 136, 149–50
Stalinism: end of 168; integrated into capitalist state 84; and survival of capitalism 74; and weakness of Marxism 31, 60–2, 147, 149, 161–2, 168; and Western Marxism 10, 27, 32, 44–5, 51
the state: and capitalism 1, 16–18, 69–70, 77, 80–2, 88, 103, 146, 167;

dual role of 97; institutions of control 84; *see also* nation-states
state sovereignty 17, 116
statism 15–16
student activism 29
Summers, Larry 66, 99
supra-class approaches 8, 29, 132, 153
surplus value 21, 60, 72, 83, 85, 95, 133, 137, 140

theory and practice: divorce of 5, 27–8, 159, 165; Marxism combining 3–4, 6, 31, 48–50, 64, 111
theory building 11–12, 16, 34, 162, 170
Third International 40
third way 24, 26, 43
third-world radicalism 28, 45
Thompson, E. P. 44–5
thousand Marxisms, a 2, 30, 137
Time magazine 155–6
trade unions: and capitalism 139; and globalisation 24–5, 110, 116–17; integration by state 84, 124, 127; Marxism on 115–16; and social movements *see* social movement unionism
transnational capitalism 88, 92
transnational corporations 87, 91, 94, 107–8, 117
transnational ruling class 20, 72, 78, 93, 98, 104
Trans-Pacific Partnership 108
Trotsky, Leon 1; on capitalist crisis 66; and classical Marxism 5–6; and German Social Democracy 61; on globalisation 89–90; and ideology 63; on imperialism 112; and Kondratieff 39; and Korsch 41; on political leadership 49, 132; on the state 70; on trade unions 115, 124
Trump, Donald 130

under-consumption 22, 57, 78
uneven development *see* capitalist development, unevenness of
union movement *see* trade unions
United States: 2016 presidential elections 129–30, 150; as capitalist hegemon 71, 75; diversity of working class in 128; and economic nationalism 108
universality 117
utopianism 24–5, 28, 41–3, 59, 104, 106

wages, general decrease in 91
Wallerstein, Immanuel 2, 5–6, 30, 137
Western Marxism 9–10, 144; development of 40–2, 61, 161; fore-runners of 27, 41; and philosophy 48; and Russian Revolution 40–1; shift in focus of 43–4, 51, 157, 162; theory and practice in 159, 165
Wolf, Martin 67
working class: false consciousness of 63, 116; and globalisation 24, 88, 90, 95–6, 100–1, 103, 106–9, 113–14, 167–8; growth of 22, 57, 78, 99, 102, 139, 141, 170; and identity politics 25–6, 118–19, 122, 152–4, 168–9; influence of nationalism on *see* nationalism, in the working class; integration into the state 70, 82–4, 97, 107, 110, 114–15; New Left on 28–9; political organisation of 146–8; post-Marxists on 29; racial differences within 128; and reproduction of capital 142–3; role in Marxism of 5–7, 10, 40, 47–51, 62, 118, 132–6, 139–42, 145–6, 149, 158–9, 161–5; and social movement politics 123, 127; *see also* proletariat
World Bank 91, 112
World Social Forum 113, 125
World War I: and capitalism 73–4; and nationalism 61; and split in Marxism 28, 41, 54
World War II 75
WTO (World Trade Organization): on economic nationalism 105; inception of 91; protests against 25, 107, 113, 125, 128; on world trade 80

Zimmerwald Conference 62

For Product Safety Concerns and Information please contact our EU
representative GPSR@taylorandfrancis.com
Taylor & Francis Verlag GmbH, Kaufingerstraße 24, 80331 München, Germany

www.ingramcontent.com/pod-product-compliance
Ingram Content Group UK Ltd.
Pitfield, Milton Keynes, MK11 3LW, UK
UKHW022110190926
475702UK00013B/1357
9780367731465